With Children and Youth

Studies in
**Childhood and Family**
in Canada

A broad-ranging series that publishes scholarship from various disciplines, approaches, and perspectives relevant to the concepts and relations of childhood and family in Canada. Our interests also include, but are not limited to, interdisciplinary approaches and theoretical investigations of gender, race, sexuality, geography, language, and culture within these categories of experience, historical and contemporary.

*Series Editor:*
Cynthia Comacchio
History Department
Wilfrid Laurier University

*Send proposals to:*
Lisa Quinn, Acquisitions Editor
Wilfrid Laurier University Press
75 University Avenue West
Waterloo, ON N2L 3C5
Canada
Phone: 519-884-0710 ext. 2843
Fax: 519-725-1399
Email: quinn@press.wlu.ca

# With Children and Youth

Emerging Theories and Practices
in Child and Youth Care Work

Editors: Kiaras Gharabaghi,
Hans A. Skott-Myhre, and
Mark Krueger

WILFRID LAURIER
UNIVERSITY PRESS

Wilfrid Laurier University Press acknowledges the financial support of the Government of Canada through the Canada Book Fund for our publishing activities.

Library and Archives Canada Cataloguing in Publication

With children and youth : emerging theories and practices in child and youth care work / Kiaras Gharabaghi, Hans A. Skott-Myhre, Mark Krueger, editors.

(Studies in childhood and family in Canada)
Includes bibliographical references and index.
Issued in print and electronic formats.
ISBN 978-1-55458-966-1 (pbk.).—ISBN 978-1-55458-967-8 (pdf).—
ISBN 978-1-55458-968-5 (epub)

1. Social work with children. 2. Social work with youth. I. Gharabaghi, Kiaras, 1967–, author, editor II. Skott-Myhre, Hans Arthur, author, editor III. Krueger, Mark A., author, editor IV. Series: Studies in childhood and family in Canada

HV713.W48 2014          362.7          C2014-901796-0
                                        C2014-901797-9

Cover design by David Drummond. Text design by Lime Design Inc.

This book is printed on FSC recycled paper and is certified Ecologo. It is made from 100% post-consumer fibre, processed chlorine free, and manufactured using biogas energy.

Printed in Canada

Every reasonable effort has been made to acquire permission for copyright material used in this text, and to acknowledge all such indebtedness accurately. Any errors and omissions called to the publisher's attention will be corrected in future printings.

# Contents

# Acknowledgements

**A book like this doesn't come around every day;** even we, the editors, realize that this book is unique in its selection of essays, the varying writing styles of the contributors, and the range of themes and topics addressed. Therefore, we are thankful for our publisher's enthusiasm for moving forward with this book, and would like acknowledge the work of all those involved at WLU Press.

Kiaras Gharabaghi would also like to thank Mark Krueger and Hans Skott-Myhre, as well as the contributors to this volume, for supporting and contributing to its completion. Child and youth care is a complicated field, but it is a field where there are friendships aplenty. Also, thank you to all the child and youth care workers whose daily practices and engagements with young people are the ground out which this thought and reflection are generated. Finally, thanks to all the young people, families, and communities whose struggles are always our own and whose generosity, in allowing us into their lives, is an inspiration to us all.

KIARAS, HANS, AND MARK
*November 2013*

# Introduction

KIARAS GHARABAGHI, HANS SKOTT-MYHRE, AND MARK KRUEGER

**Child and youth care (CYC) practice** is the work of people who engage with children, youth, and families. Their work occurs in community centres, schools, after-school programs, group homes, camps, shelters, prevention programs, residential centres, correctional facilities, the streets, and many other places and programs, including virtual spaces created through social media. In recent years there has been an explosion of new research, writing, thinking, questioning, and critiquing related to the work. Much of this is centred on three themes. First, child and youth care work is *relational and developmental*. It occurs in relationships among unique developing beings within and across social, political, organizational, and familial systems. Second, the work is a way of being in the world *with* youth. Workers and youth bring self to the moment and interact. Finally, *critical and postmodern* theories and practices emphasize the political, anti-oppressive, libratory, and revolutionary capacities of the work for both young people and adults working toward common ends.

Over the course of the past two decades, myriad perspectives have evolved within the broader context of youth work that rely on distinct theoretical orientations, philosophical priorities, and practice-based approaches. Scholars from Canada and the United States have contributed to a highly diversified, stimulating, and at times also fragmenting and divisive field of study and practice. This book represents an effort to provide a snapshot of the field of youth work at a moment in time, at a time when the world itself is undergoing rapid and potentially dramatic changes politically, economically, culturally, intellectually, and ecologically. In so doing, we aim to illuminate current debates and controversies while setting the stage for where this field may be headed in the coming years. Importantly, we note that we are neither making an attempt to reflect the current status of the field comprehensively, nor intending to suggest a particular or concrete direction for the field. Instead, we aim to allow the texts of the chapters to stand on their own, in the hopes that they will be read as an invitation to engage broadly or specifically. Incorporating work that seeks to build on the field's foundations as well as work that pushes the field into new and unchartered territory, and mixing theoretical approaches with practice-oriented ones, the book features both respect for the field's origins as well as the desire to move beyond the limitations of those origins into a postmodern world. As such, the chapters presented here address questions about the nature of youth work; the field's clinical, professional, and political agenda; and themes related to culture, identity, existential premise, and contextual epistemology. At the same time, the chapters seek to present clear and actionable foundations for youth work interventions and approaches that critically but constructively weigh the possibilities of theory for practice.

Scholars and practitioners have expanded on these themes with books, articles, workshops, curricula, retreats, online conversations, and a number of other sources. Modern, postmodern, critical, phenomenological, and developmental perspectives have enriched our understanding of the work in the lived experience, or as we sometimes say, "daily living environment." Much has also been written about the work as moral, accountable, and ethical praxis.

The chapters in this anthology are an attempt to advance, or perhaps more accurately, to "push" this discussion. Each of us came at the topic from a unique perspective grounded in doing and studying child and youth care work. Contributors were asked to write "as they feel," meaning that we encouraged them to be creative, to avoid trivialities, and to feel empowered to put into words their thoughts, observations, and arguments in their rawest form. As a result, the chapters collected here are different not only in content but also in form. From scholarly writing to satirical prose, we have collected text that we think reflects the eclectic nature of our field. Our hope is that these chapters will leave the reader a little dazed, surprised, and ultimately motivated to do his or her own thinking about the field. Our view is that good practice is based on bold and courageous thinking, and we are confident that the chapters in this book represent just that.

Inspiration and the idea for the book came from two retreats that addressed the future of the field. In attendance were scholars and practitioners from universities and youth organizations in Canada and the United States. Held in the mountains of northern New Mexico, the retreats were appropriately named the El Salto Discussions after one mountain, the Spanish word *salto* conveying the notion of jumping or leaping into the future. In the spirit of productive discourse, this book was written for those who would like to take the leap with us. We hope readers will question, critique, and build on what is said.

Our work, like that of many of our colleagues, is enriched by the research and thinking of members of other fields. We believe this is a sign of the field's maturity. For many years we worked to develop the identity of our field as a profession with its own knowledge base. While this was essential to our development, it also made us somewhat insular. We tended to read, speak to one another, and contribute to the literatures in our field. Now more and more we are opening ourselves to the ideas and thoughts of others. This is not to say that many members of the profession have not always been open to these influences; rather, it seems more the norm now to mix genres and to include in our studies enriching and informative sources from outside the field. Many of our most creative thinkers were way ahead of us. Like them, we have discovered there is much to be learned from arts and humanities, social sciences, other professions, and science, just as those working in these fields can learn from us.

It is perhaps important to speak to what this book is not, and also to what is not included in this book in any substantive measure. In no way should this book be taken as an exhaustive overview of the field of child and youth care. Clearly, the chapters presented here do not cover the richness of our field, or the diverse research pursuits, discussions, and political movements that are currently underway. We do not, for example, speak to the ever-evolving efforts of professionalization within our field that are notable not only for their increasing organizational forms, but also for their strong academic and conceptual features. As part of this movement, one might mention the important role of articulating competency frameworks for the field, as has indeed been done both with respect to the practice of child and youth care and in the context of accreditation movements of post-secondary child and youth care education. Many publications have been offered in this regard, including recently a special issue of the journal *Child and Youth Services*, guest edited by Fusco and Baizerman (2013), which captures this movement particularly in the U.S. context.

Also not represented in significant measure in this book are chapters that explore the field in the context of specific settings. A wealth of research and publications related to residential care, education settings, the homelessness sector, the family, and the community can easily be accessed through the academic and professional journals of our field, including the independent journals *Relational Child and Youth Care Practice*, published through Vancouver Island University in Nanaimo, B.C., as well as *International Journal of Family, Child and Youth Studies*, published online by the School of Child and Youth Care, University of Victoria, B.C.

Many sub-themes of our field are either not mentioned or mentioned only in passing. We note, for example, that themes such as restorative justice, care leavers and transitions to independence, working with Indigenous peoples, and rapidly emerging themes such as social pedagogy, turning points, life-space intervention, and evidence-based practices are only peripherally addressed in this book. This is not, in any way, meant to suggest that these themes are not important or should be seen as secondary to the themes that are discussed here. Instead, we settled on the chapters we have collected for entirely different reasons. Our process involved offering an opportunity to discuss themes and issues from an eclectic and not necessarily research perspective, and to commit to a writing style that inevitably will be subject to critique as much for what it addresses as for what it omits. As part of this process, we wanted to represent one conversation among those passionately committed to the further development of our field. This is not the only conversation, and it is one that suffers from the same factors of exclusion as all other conversations. We believe it is important to be transparent, and to note these limitations without apology. Conversations are meant to be continued, to be taken up by those who want to engage, and to be noted but sidelined by those who do not. Far too many conversations in our field have expired because they were not opened to others; this book is our attempt to create this opening.

For students in the field of child and youth care, we want to ensure that this book does not leave the impression that this is all there is to know about the field. In fact, we are happy to endorse several other recent attempts to capture aspects of the field. For the most comprehensive effort, we recommend Carol Stuart's innovative text *Foundations of Child and Youth Care* (2009), which provides arguably the most excellent overview of the field in North America. For more advanced students and also scholars and practitioners, we believe that the anthology edited by Gerrard Bellefeuille and Frances Ricks, entitled *Standing on the Precipice: Unleashing the Creative Potential of Child and Youth Care* (2008), represents a particularly thoughtful and enriching piece of literature. For those interested in postmodernism-inspired perspectives, we recommend a volume edited by Alan Pence and Jennifer White (2010) entitled *Child and Youth Care: Critical Perspectives on Pedagogy, Practice, and Policy.*

In addition to these books and edited volumes, we can also recommend special issues of journals that in our view are particularly comprehensive in advancing an understanding of our field. *Relational Child and Youth Care Practice* offered a special issue on "Child and Youth Care Approaches" in 2011, edited by Thom Garfat and Leon Fulcher. The same journal offered another special issue in 2013 entitled "Daily Life Events" (Fulcher, Garfat, & Digney, 2013), which again covers quite comprehensively this important context for our work and field. *Child and Youth Services*, aside from the aforementioned special issue on professionalization, also offered a special issue on culture that is worthwhile exploring, guest edited by J. N. Little and Hans Skott-Mhyre (2012).

Finally, for all those interested in the field of child and youth care, we draw attention to the International Child and Youth Care Network and its online journal accessible through www.cyc-net.org. There is simply no more comprehensive space in our field that offers as wide a range of contributions to enhancing understanding, communication, and networking for our field. One notable feature of this virtual community within our field is its international character. We are conscious that we limited our collection of chapters to the North American context. Of course, this represents a major limitation in understanding our field globally. We want to note, therefore, that a global understanding of our field requires moving beyond our North American boundaries, and engaging in particular geographic settings where our field has evolved sometimes differently and sometimes similarly to the way it has in

North America. Of special note here are settings such as the United Kingdom, Australia, South Africa, Germany, Ireland, and Israel, but surely many others as well.

Before we proceed to the chapters, we must make one additional comment on the terms used to describe our field. As has likely been the case for many, we struggled with the use of terms such as *youth work, youth development work, child and youth care practice, child and youth counselling, child care work,* and many others. In the end, we take the position that this book is not about deciding on a term above all others; as a result, readers will find especially the terms *youth work* and *child and youth care practice* used interchangeably unless otherwise noted. ●

**REFERENCES**

Bellefeuille, G., & Ricks, F. (Eds.). (2008). *Standing on the precipice: Inquiry into the creative potential of child and youth care practice.* Edmonton, AB: MacEwan Press.

Fulcher, L., Garfat, T., & Digney, J. (Guest Eds.). (2013). Daily life events [Special issue]. *Relational Child and Youth Care Practice, 26*(2).

Fusco, D., & Baizerman, M. (Guest Eds.). (2013). Professionalization deconstructed: Implications for the field of youth work [Special issue]. *Child & Youth Services, 34*(2).

Garfat, T., & Fulcher, L. (Guest Eds.). (2011). Applications of a child and youth care approach [Special issue]. *Relational Child and Youth Care Practice, 24*(1–2).

Little, J. N., & Skott-Myhre, H. (Guest Eds.). (2012). Troubling multiculturalism [Special issue]. *Child & Youth Services, 33*(3–4).

Pence, A., & White, J. (Eds.). (2010). *Child and youth care: Critical perspectives on pedagogy, practice, and policy.* Vancouver, BC: University of British Columbia Press.

Stuart, C. (2009). *Foundations of child and youth care.* Dubuque, IA: Kendall Hunt.

# 1

**In this opening part of the book,** four writers in the field of child and youth care go head-to-head in presenting four very different perspectives on what the field is about. The discussions range from practical, no-nonsense representations of where the field is today, to much more theoretical considerations steeped in both modernity and postmodernity.

Kiaras Gharabaghi starts by delineating the ways in which the purpose of child and youth care is manifested in the field of practice, often in ignorance of scholarship and informed commentary in the literature. His focus is on the pitfalls of thinking about this field in terms of treatment goals, unless such goals are directed at the field itself rather than at young people. Skott-Myhre provides an entirely different starting point, and focuses on the roles of often assumed necessities in the field, including structure, power, and control. He takes his analysis far beyond the everyday discussions and seeks to first blow up and then skilfully reconstruct a postmodern version of "being with children."

Doug Magnuson fires back in fine form, and provides insightful critiques of virtually all approaches to the field, taking aim at both scientism and its critics, with some particularly strong questions for the critical/postmodern movement within the field. And finally, Carol Stuart provides a more measured view of the field that carefully traces both the substantive components of child and youth care practice and the organizational elements of the field itself. Her message: "Get over yourself!" ●

# Chapter ❶

## The Purpose of Youth Work

**On the surface,** this chapter has a decidedly negative tone; it suggests that in spite of enormous learning and growth in thinking about youth work over the course of the past few decades, there continue to be some major weaknesses in how the purpose of youth work is conceptualized *in practice*. The chapter is not based on any systematic research, although it is informed by several of my research projects that included in-depth conversations with child and youth workers and those who manage services where child and youth workers are employed (Gharabaghi, 2009b, 2012b; Gharabaghi & Phelan, 2011). It is, nevertheless, a fair assumption that my biases, as author, are deeply embedded in everything that follows. The chapter is based, however, on more than just my opinion. I have worked side by side with child and youth care practitioners in Ontario and Nova Scotia for over twenty years in most settings where child and youth workers are found. I continue to work actively with teams of youth workers in residential care settings, education settings, and community-based services. In the past five years, I have visited about three hundred residential programs in Canada, the United States, Germany, Switzerland, and South Africa, and I have talked with child and youth workers in all of these places. Over the past three years or so, I have been actively working with nearly every children's mental health service provider in several regions across Ontario, and I have listened to senior managers and directors talk about the programs (and the child and youth workers) where children and youth are served. And finally, I teach child and youth care at a well-established university-level program in Toronto, where about half my students are currently employed full time in child and youth care settings, reflecting on their professional experiences during class discussions and in their assignments.

My overall experience with child and youth workers has been an enormously positive one. In circumstances where young people are facing acute crises, adversity difficult to imagine, and heartbreak that appears irreversible, I have seen what child and youth workers can do. They are the professional group I admire most, in particular given their seemingly limitless capacity to be in relationship with young people at precisely those times when all other relationships appear to have broken down. It is because I have been a lifelong supporter of child and youth care practice as a professional endeavour, and of child and youth workers as a professional group, that I offer the critique of *purpose* as outlined in what follows. In so doing, I emphasize that "practice" and "purpose" are not the same thing. "Practice" is what child and youth workers do, in the moment, face to face with a young person, in whatever setting or program context. "Purpose" relates to why they do what they do. Purpose is about what precisely it is we are trying to achieve with our everyday presence in the lives of young people. In our literature as well as in our teams of practitioners, we have many conversations about practice but relatively few conversations about purpose. Given the mandate of this book, described as "taking positions that are uncomfortable, probing, challenging, and perhaps even 'a little out there,'" I don't want to spend much time on practice, since I believe that there are already many excellent contributions in this area covering virtually every component of the child and youth care system. Instead, I want to take a position, even if unpopular or uncomfortable to some, on how seeking purpose in youth work has not exactly kept pace with the nuances and complexities of thought and theory in our field.

## Defining Purpose

THE CORE CONCEPTS, CORE THEMES, AND CORE PRACTICES of youth work have been outlined effectively and with considerable literary elegance many times, including by Krueger (1991) and more recently by Garfat and Fulcher (2011). Stuart (2009; aimed at the introductory level), as well as Bellefeuille and

Ricks (2008) and Pence and White (2010; offering a critical and postmodern perspective), recently published excellent work outlining the core concepts and themes of child and youth care practice. In addition, over the course of the past decade or so, enormous work has been completed that provides a "field guide" to child and youth care practice by defining and explaining core competencies for practitioners. Nevertheless, at some point in the deliberations about how to advance youth work as a profession, and what to do in response to the ever-increasing demands for outcomes and evidence-based practices, the purpose of youth work may have become obfuscated, particularly in practice settings. Indeed, there are many different ways of articulating such purpose today, all with quite different implications for practice. At the very least, we can identify the following general themes in the various articulations of the "purpose" of child and youth care practice on the part of practitioners as well as their employers: changing behaviour, preparing young people for independence, strengthening resilience, exploring identity, imposing containment and promoting safety, increasing performance, and advocating for social change. Each of these themes has merit on its own and in combination with the others; it is, in fact, a common mistake to simply dismiss a behavioural focus, attention to transitions, and other themes only because they are steeped in language that may not be in vogue any longer. However, each of these themes also promotes an approach to being with young people that undoes much of what youth work can be. In fact, although the language and conceptual foundations of each of these themes differ considerably, I will argue below that all of these themes fundamentally are about the valorization of treatment. *In practice,*[1] all of these themes lead to an overemphasis on the context of youth work, and an underemphasis on youth work per se.

### Seeking Behavioural Change

Many youth work practitioners in North America still define their professional purpose as the pursuit of behavioural change on the part of young people. This may not be the kind of statement that corresponds to the current themes in the scholarly and philosophical literature that surrounds youth work practice, and it may not indicate much traction of that literature among practitioners. But this should come as no surprise to anyone, since the vast majority of practitioners in North America have limited, if any, exposure to youth work literature.[2] This does not mean that their practice is poor, or substandard. Perhaps surprisingly, and just a little annoyingly, some of the youth workers I admire most are those who have never been trained formally in youth work, but whose capacity to work in relationship, to care, and to be present appears limitless. Still, it is perhaps important at this stage to put the facts about youth workers on the table. Most have limited training in the field, most still work in residential care (group homes, treatment facilities, boarding schools, custody, hospital in-patient units, shelters, etc.), and most are informed about their practice by supervisors and employers who know virtually nothing at all about youth work.[3] Those who do have pre-service education in a field related to youth work often spent much of their education studying psychopathology, developmental theory, professional issues, and legislative contexts, and working with other professionals, including youth worker roles in the case management process, documentation of behaviour, and social work principles of treatment (Little, 2011). (Ben Anderson-Nathe speaks to the tension between social work and youth work later in this volume.) Youth workers trained in the nuances of youth work theory, including relational practices, the reflective nature of practice, engagement strategies and their connection to self, and the ideas of "being with" or "becoming with" young people, are relatively rare. Even more rare are youth workers who have this training in their pre-service preparation for the work *and* maintain their focus on this training in their everyday practice, because within that practice, they are bombarded with expectations related to team loyalties, behaviour management, containment, and a normative approach to problem solving.

In this context of unpreparedness to do youth work and to be a youth worker, as well as employment contexts that hardly support the nuances of youth work, it is no surprise that for many practitioners, the purpose of their professional endeavour is that which can be observed relatively easily, measured relatively accurately, and reported on with relative confidence. It is also no surprise that many practitioners seek comfort in the easy fit between youth work and common sense when the purpose of that work is defined as creating behavioural change. What is perhaps more difficult to understand is how this focus on changing behaviour has survived so many scholarly, research-based, conceptually sound, philosophically sophisticated, and all-around compelling attacks, critiques, and dismissals by the field's scholars, writers, prominent commentators, and leading practitioners. Almost no one of any stature in the field of youth work would articulate the purpose of this work in the context of changing behaviour. And yet this is what it is; far too often, youth workers go to work, tell young people to stop doing this or that, to follow the rules, to conform to societal values, and to comply with the rules of the program, the expectations of the staff, and the commands of the treatment plan. And every day youth workers judge their work to be successful when young people demonstrate such conformity and compliance, and they admonish young people when they fail to do so. The rhythm of youth work is based on a simple, common-sense, three-variable formula:

Desirable behaviour = rewards (good behaviour) + punishment (bad behaviour)[4]

Given this formula, the purpose of the youth worker is to address any imbalances that occur. If there is too much bad behaviour, increase the punishment and reduce the rewards. If there is too much good behaviour, increase the rewards and reduce the punishments. Fundamentally, the purpose of youth work remains static; it is to seek desirable behaviours, defined in the context of conformity and compliance, and to reinforce such behaviours through the manipulation of the balance between rewards and consequences.

Thinking about the purpose of youth work in terms of behaviour change may not do justice to what scholars and learned commentators in the field want practitioners to think about as they work with youth. But this often does correspond to what employers want them to think about, and it very much corresponds to what funders are looking for. Fundamentally, all the major stakeholders in youth work, except for young people themselves, are looking for ways to make troubled young people less troublesome for the rest of us. Success in youth work thus conceived then becomes a relatively simple measure of behavioural change. A young person who is less aggressive, who is more compliant, and who reflects broad societal expectations related to positive citizenship is a young person successfully treated.

Philosophically, it is easy to challenge this way of thinking. From a pragmatic perspective, however, it is much more difficult to convince practitioners that changing young people's behaviour from what might be seen as maladjusted to something more reflective of societal norms is not particularly useful or even beneficial to the young person. The reality is this: behaviour-focused interventions work well. So long as the goal is to mitigate the immediate concerns expressed by those around the young person (such as parents, siblings [although they are rarely consulted], social workers, law enforcement personnel, teachers, principals, and others), behavioural interventions, ideally featuring a great deal of external control, work exceptionally well. Some such interventions have been fine-tuned to the degree of "scientific evidence" of their effectiveness. Today we have many different packaged interventions, some trademarked and copywritten, that have a well-researched record of effective outcomes (e.g., Stop Now And Plan [SNAP], Multi-Systemic Therapy [MST], Collaborative Problem Solving [CBS], 1,2,3 Magic, etc.). Young people subjected to these intervention strategies, when the interventions are characterized by high levels of fidelity with the packaged "program," indeed leave their programs with seemingly fewer issues, suppressed troubles, fewer criminal involvements, and greater social and academic functioning. So long as we are able to put aside the humanity of each young person a youth worker might encounter, thinking about behavioural change as the purpose of youth work makes eminent sense and is supported by very strong evidence of successful treatment outcomes that can be reinforced with ongoing psycho-pharmacological interventions.

### Preparing Young People for Independence

Many youth workers, and especially those with more experience, recognize that behavioural change cannot be the sole purpose of their practice, largely because such change is often superficial and thus not sustainable beyond the external controls imposed by the program. Young people will eventually have to stand on their own two feet, and for those youth workers, the purpose of their practice is to prepare young people to do so successfully. In fact, their perspective is backed up by considerable evidence. Throughout North America, outcome studies show that young people who grow up in foster care, group homes, or other institutional settings often regress significantly when discharged. Moreover, given their relatively poor performance in school, their prospects for employment are low, resulting in significantly higher rates of criminal involvements, homelessness, and mental health concerns as they navigate the early years of adulthood and independence (Mann-Feder, 2007; Wall, Koch, Link, & Graham, 2010).

There is considerable overlap between this way of articulating the purpose of youth work and the aforementioned purpose related to seeking behaviour change. For many youth workers, being prepared for independence really means being compliant and conforming to the expectations of society as they perceive them.[5] As a result, even youth workers who focus squarely on the preparation for independence still work hard to seek behaviour change on the part of young people, although they do so not as an end in itself, but instead as a well-intentioned way of increasing the young people's chances at a successful transition to independence. Their argument commonly is that in the "real world," antisocial or noncompliant behaviours will result in negative outcomes and exclusions from educational, economic, and housing opportunities (Gharabaghi & Phelan, 2011). A significant component of the interventions carried out by these youth workers therefore remains behaviour modification, based on the same three-variable formula that is used by their colleagues who understand their purpose to be exclusively about changing the behaviour of young people. In addition, however, youth workers focused on preparing young people for independence also work hard to teach, or to impart, independence skills to young people. Such skills include everything from budgeting to finding employment, and from nutrition to understanding where to access adult services when those are needed. These are the youth workers who have fully bought into the language of "social skills" and "life skills," terms that appear to capture the whole smorgasbord of adequate preparation for independence.

There is much to be said for this perspective on understanding the purpose of youth work. Common sense would seem to confirm the importance of being prepared to stand on one's own two feet. Given that young people involved with youth workers often lack a predictable and reliable informal support system (such as family or friends with resources), this focus on getting them ready to manage on their own seems reasonable enough, and is certainly compatible with what a great deal of research suggests; transitions, and especially the transition to independence, really do matter, and the underwhelming focus on preparing young people for these transitions is a problem (although perhaps a greater problem is the lack of funding to support young people in the process of transitioning and in the early stages of their independence). In fact, the rise of semi-independence programs, transition programs, and more specific skill-building programs confirms that preparation for independence is widely recognized as a major task for the helping systems. On the other hand, this perspective also has several built-in contradictions, or at least tensions. For one thing, many of the youth workers seeking to prepare young people for independence have themselves not quite reached that stage of life. In addition, the sterile view of the "real world" as one where compliance and conformity are universal values is likely based more on politically entrenched norms than on the everyday experience in the "real world." Many of the most useful skills of living day to day are sadly dismissed within this framework, including skills related to manipulation, risk-taking, experimenting, and resolving conflicts in realistic (rather than textbook) fashion. Perhaps most importantly, feedback from young people themselves suggests that skills and resources are only part of what is needed during transitions; relationships, a sense of belonging, and mitigating the loneliness that comes with leaving care are arguably just as important. Preparation for independence is therefore at best an incomplete way of understanding the purpose of youth work; it leaves the needs of young people post-transition without response.

### Strengthening Resilience

In the past decade or so the resilience movement across North America and elsewhere has really taken off and contributed to a re-articulation of the purpose not only of youth work but indeed of many of the helping professions (Ungar, 2002, 2004). The conceptual foundation of resilience is relatively simple: some people facing considerable adversity in their lives nevertheless manage to achieve rewarding lives with economic success and personal fulfillment. The factors that contribute to their overcoming of adversity are thus recognized as resilience factors. From the perspective of youth work, the implications are easily recognized. If one can replicate resilience factors in the lives of troubled young people, their outcomes should improve. This logic has given rise to significant research efforts that have sought to identify "assets" that might contribute to strengthening resilience. Often such assets are listed in two streams, internal and external assets. The former refer to those factors that a young person carries with him or her throughout life, such as self-esteem, prosocial values, good work ethic, and confidence. External assets are those that affect young people in their everyday lives, such as supportive family relationships, positive peer groups, an active involvement in religious organizations, and success in school (Scales, Benson, Leffert, & Blyth, 2000).

For some youth workers, and also for some of their employers, this framework of strengthening resilience has usurped their behavioural focus and even their commitment to preparing young people for independence. Recognizing that the adversity faced by young people cannot be entirely wiped out by professionals, they reason that a focus on strengthening young people's ability to manage such adversity is a more meaningful way of doing youth work than trying to pretend such adversity can be entirely eliminated. These youth workers are informed in their everyday practice by the need to build assets for the young people, and thus they focus on helping young people feel better about themselves, on assisting them with their connections to family, on supporting positive peer relationships, and on teaching positive and pro-social values.

There is no question that this way of articulating the purpose of youth work carries considerable meaning and also is at least on paper empowering to the youth, as well as sensitive to their unique circumstances. Translating a resilience framework into practice, however, turns out to be exceptionally challenging, in part because the institutional contexts of doing youth work almost never support this approach fully. At the rhetorical level, there has been considerable support for this approach, and professionals and scholars alike from many different disciplines have endorsed the idea of strengthening resilience as the core of the intervention. In reality, however, none of this has resulted in the necessary adjustments of the context in which youth workers do their work. Most young people living in residential care, for example, still have as their exclusive peer group the other young people living in their group homes or treatment centres. Family work still is largely limited to more formalized counselling sessions and office-based interventions, notwithstanding an increasing literature on child and youth care approaches to family work (Garfat, 2004; Garfat & Charles, 2010) and also the proliferation of (small) family support projects. And prosocial values, defined as compliance and conformity with the values embedded in the organization where young people receive service, still is the absolute priority and the measuring stick for growth and treatment progress (Gharabaghi, 2009a).

As it turns out, in practice at least, strengthening resilience is not at all about the young people per se, but instead, is about imposing on young people a very particular way of being in this world. Not coincidentally, this particular way of being in this world is very much shaped by the societal norms and expectations of the day, much like it is for those youth workers who define their purpose as changing the behaviour of young people. Thus, while the language of resilience may suggest something more compelling than strictly behavioural approaches to youth work, in practice the difference is often hard to identify.

### Exploring Identity

Self-proclaimed progressive youth workers have raised their voices in recent years, and have, at least at the level of scholarly writing and informed commentary, expanded the conversation about the purpose of youth work considerably. Although a focus on identity in youth work practice is not new, articulating the very purpose of the practice as exploring identity is indeed a novel approach to youth work. Much of this relatively new movement in the youth work field is the result of a questioning of many of the assumptions of modernism and the often empiricist treatment literature in the helping professions generally. Youth work scholars have turned to critical theory and postmodernism as a way of engaging the field in discussions about what youth work is really about (Pence & White, 2010; Skott-Myhre, 2008). From their perspective, traditional approaches focused on behavioural intervention, on concrete interventions in order to prepare youth for independence, or even on resilience factors are inherently reflections of political (and often economic) forces and dynamics that provide little hope for young people to find a sense of belonging and self in society. Youth workers committed to this perspective tend to prioritize the exploration of identity over any kind of functional or measurable interventions, and rather than focusing on outcomes, they are preoccupied with mitigating the inevitable power structures and impositions in the helping process, at both the interpersonal and the systems levels. Indeed, as the chapter by Pacini-Ketchabaw (this volume) indicates, the very notion of identity is replete with power dynamics, and thus it is necessary to free our language and thinking from oppressive categories such as gender identities, developmental identities (including the distinction between youth and adult), and even relationship identities such as interpersonal versus human–nonhuman relationships (also Little, 2011).

Articulating the exploration of identity as the purpose of youth work has been a powerful way of critiquing the more instrumental approaches to articulating the purpose of youth work, but beyond that critique it has not been especially useful in visualizing youth work on a day-to-day basis. While scholars and commentators have given the field much to think about, the transfer of that thinking into youth work practice has been slow, perhaps invisible. Nevertheless, for a very small number of youth workers, this way of articulating their professional purpose may have helped to loosen the grip of their own compliance and conformity to organizational or employer expectations and rules, thus opening up some new possibilities in specific worker–youth interactions.

## Imposing Containment and Promoting Safety

For many youth workers, especially in the contexts of residential treatment and youth justice facilities, as well as hospital-based crisis units, the core purpose of the work is to contain "at-risk youth" and to promote safety in their lives, primarily in the form of avoiding their access to any situations to which they may respond in an unsafe manner. This view of youth work continues to be widespread and have at least implicit support from caregivers, most notably from child protection/welfare authorities. This is also an approach that very easily finds connections with other professional disciplines, especially psychiatry, which uses primarily chemical interventions for the purpose of containment.

One of the reasons for the ongoing popularity of this approach to articulating the purpose of youth work is the widely held view (a rather convenient view) that in the absence of significant incidents (such as physical aggression, running away, or self-harming), treatment must be working well. For youth workers, this framework gives rise to language such as "good shifts," "strong worker," "consistency," and "leadership." All of these terms are references to the success of individual workers in avoiding issues, containing behaviours, and "shutting down" escalating young people (Gharabaghi & Phelan, 2011).

Youth work within this framework has almost nothing to do with relationships, caring, or engagement, and instead is strictly focused on the consistent, reliable, and predictable enforcement of rules and regulations, as well as the constant monitoring (sometimes using cameras) of young people's activities. The measure of success is based on the lack of incidents, the lack of anything to report, and the extent to which young people approach total compliance to workers' commands. While none of this corresponds to anything even remotely similar to the principles of youth work one might find in the scholarly literature, this approach nevertheless maintains strong currency because of its "out of sight, out of mind" appeal to child welfare workers and other professionals. So long as nothing is happening, there is no need to really engage the case (a.k.a., the young person).

Of course, even within this framework we cannot adopt an entirely dismissive stance. In reality, there are young people who reach crisis to such acute levels that at least for a moment in time, containment is indeed the most useful contribution we can make. As a practice, therefore, containment and safety are often critical factors of good youth work; but as a purpose, these are very limiting concepts that likely achieve nothing beyond their momentary presence.

### Improving Performance

Yet another way that some youth workers articulate their professional purpose is to focus on the performance of young people in various settings, including the group home, schools, the family, and the community. Similarly to those focused on changing behaviour, the performance-focused youth workers seek to motivate and sometimes compel young people to perform according to the expectations in the program (most commonly the group home), and to perform according to universal standards in schools. This approach is different from the behaviour change approach only inasmuch as it is less focused on the young person and more focused on the degree to which the young person satisfies the needs of the program, school, family, or community. The measure of successful youth work in this context is achieving higher privilege levels in the group home, fewer suspensions in school, less conflict in the family, and less trouble in the community. Typical interactions in this framework for youth work include power struggles over the completion of chores, consequences for behavioural issues at school, threats to withdraw home visits in the context of family work, and the imposition of restrictions in terms of access to the community.

Performance-based approaches to youth work do have their own logic. If young people can meet the expectations of various settings, they will be better placed to avoid negativity and distractions as they march toward adulthood, and they will be better placed to manage adulthood issues if they have performed well in school. As such, even this approach to articulating the purpose of youth work is not entirely without merit, but it is an approach that easily deteriorates into labelling (when performance issues are chronic) and deficit-based practices. It is also an approach that relies almost entirely on external controls and pressures, and therefore suffers from a lack of sustainability in terms of any of the hoped-for gains made by the young person.

### Advocating for System Change

Some, albeit very few, youth workers see themselves less as social service workers and more as political activists whose role it is to change the way systems respond to the needs of troubled young people. These youth workers are often frustrated by the gap between what they have learned about anti-oppressive practices and the importance of youth empowerment on the one hand, and the restrictive policies and sometimes oppressive treatment approaches encountered in service settings on the other hand. Quite rightly, these youth workers argue that the odds are against troubled youth to get their lives in order, not because they lack capacity or behave in antisocial ways, but instead because they are constantly subjected to discriminatory practices, to judgment and dismissal, and to exclusions. These youth workers articulate their professional purpose as one of advocating for system change, which is very much connected to upholding the rights of children as stipulated under the United Nations Convention on the Rights of the Child.

Youth workers who see themselves as system change agents are often much better at the rhetoric of children's rights and the political discourse of anti-oppression than at spending time with young people and practising what they preach. Indeed, they often overlook the simple reality that one's political convictions related to social justice are not automatically accompanied by socially just youth work practices. Although radical in their rhetoric, these youth workers are often less available to young people as they are preoccupied with political struggles at the organizational, the systemic, and the policy levels. Their measure of success is not so much what happens to particular young people as their successful imposition of the radical, anti-oppressive, social justice voice in the conservative contexts of case conference meetings, organizational forums, government consultations, and scholarly conferences and meetings. Terrible things that may happen to the young people in the meantime simply confirm their need to speak out whenever the chance arises.

Again, it is important to point out that there are many youth workers who combine political activism and effective practice seamlessly. They are able to integrate their everyday work with young people into a persuasive argument for system change, and in some cases even involve and empower young people to fight for such change themselves. There is much that is positive about this way of practising youth work, but articulating political activism as the purpose of youth work risks abandoning young people for a more glamorous role in the human services.

### The Valorization of Treatment in Youth Work

Although youth workers articulate their professional purpose quite differently, there is a common theme in all the articulations of purpose cited above. This is the valorization of treatment as the guiding concept of what youth work is all about. Treatment has a long history in Western societies' ways of responding to those who do not appear to conform to the norm in terms of their conduct, their thinking processes, or their ability to conform to performance expectations in various settings. Foucault has provided a particularly insightful history of the concept of treatment, albeit one that is specifically focused on issues of mental health and psychiatric disorder. In compelling fashion, Foucault demonstrates that one cannot understand treatment as a concept outside of the power dynamics within social relations (Foucault, 2008).

Treatment has great currency in many professional disciplines, oftentimes in rather obvious and explicit ways. Psychiatry, as the self-proclaimed champion of treatment, is explicitly focused on responding to "abnormality" by whatever means necessary. The very essence of contemporary psychiatry is to match a series of symptoms to a diagnosis, and then to prescribe a treatment regimen that is almost always a combination of psychosocial intervention along with the use of pharmacological supports (in reality, chemical interventions are what the treatment plan rests on most of the time). Nurses, family doctors, psychologists, professional counsellors, and often social workers are committed to the idea of treatment as the most meaningful way of responding to troubled young people. Expressed simply, treatment is the assumption that with a given intervention, a hoped-for outcome can be achieved. As such, treatment always seeks to create change in the conduct of young people, and such change is always prescribed to be a particular kind of change (Pazaratz, 2009).

Youth workers often have limited training in treatment (as mentioned, they often have limited training even in youth work), often speak the language of treatment only very poorly, are frequently frustrated with the directions proposed by treatment plans, and complain loudly about their perceived second-class role in multidisciplinary treatment teams (Salhani & Charles, 2007). And yet they are as committed to the idea of treatment as all the other professionals, and their articulations about their everyday practice often reflect the deeply embedded desire to look like, sound like, and be recognized like a treatment specialist. All the articulations of the professional purpose of youth work cited above are fundamentally about imposing change on young people. In and of itself, this is not problematic, and one can hardly argue with the necessity of change given the often dire circumstances of young people's lives. The real question is not about the merits of change, but instead it is about the method by which change can be achieved, and the roles of those contributing to that change (notably the role of the young persons themselves). Treatment, in the final analysis, is a method for change, not change itself. It is a particular way of moving young people through their developmental process that prescribes not only the final outcomes, but also the timing of when specific stages must be achieved, how these must be achieved, and what is to be done when they are not achieved. Treatment, as a method, relies on the agency of the treatment provider for moving the young person along the continuum of change, and limits the agency of the young person through an emphasis on conformity and compliance.

It is important to note that neither conformity nor compliance is an inherently negative process; conversely, neither nonconformity nor noncompliance is an inherently positive process. The challenge is to find a role for resistance in the process of change, and to allow young people agency in exploring how resistance may contribute to their change process (Skott-Myhre, 2005, 2006). Whether youth workers are seeking to change behaviour or are preparing young people for independence, whether they are building resilience or containing young people in the name of safety, these articulations of the purpose of youth work are designed to limit resistance to change and to move as expeditiously as possible toward the predetermined desirable outcome. In this way, the logic of treatment has penetrated to the very core of youth work and is constantly reinforced by the structures and processes of intervention strategies, treatment programs, and employment expectations.

At the level of everyday practice, the pre-eminence of treatment logic has many implications, including the following:

- A quasi-religious belief in the virtue of consistency; in spite of its multidisciplinary nature, treatment is inherently one-directional, whereby all efforts on the part of the treatment team members, including youth workers, are required to contribute to the treatment plan and its aimed-for outcomes.

- A reliance on sequential process; treatment plans are based on treatment goals, and proceed sequentially from one goal to the next. Stable (and positive) behaviour, for example, is often seen as a prerequisite to moving forward with family work, academic efforts, and opportunities to access resources in the community.

- A strong behaviour focus; since the evaluation of treatment progress relies on validated measures, youth workers are trained to focus on the observation and documentation of behaviour, which can then inform case conference sessions seeking to evaluate treatment progress.

- Enforcement of routines; much of the everyday actions of youth workers are designed to herd young people through a set of routines that are universally imposed on all the young people present in a particular program. Such routines are typically focused on a set of very few performance expectations related to morning routines (brushing teeth, having breakfast, getting ready for school), school routines (focused on attendance and making it through the day without major incidents), therapeutic program routines (such as therapeutic groups or recreational activities), chores, and bedtime routines.

- Translation of daily observations into treatment language; every day, youth workers seek to detect patterns in the conduct of young people that can then be aligned with clinical language. For example, a young person who refuses to participate in program routines may be labelled "oppositional." A young person who resists relationships with staff may be labelled "attachment-disordered." Youth workers who excel in the use of clinical language are often seen as particularly competent and thoughtful by other members of the treatment team.

These characteristics of contemporary youth work in practice are the result of several mutually reinforcing dynamics within the helping professions generally. On the one hand, the value of the helping professions is largely determined by those professions' ability to set themselves apart from the more "trivial" processes of parenting, providing care, and nurturing young people, which are typically seen as processes that unfold outside of the professional world. In addition, the valorization of treatment relies heavily on the construction of *difference* as a clinical problem of considerable magnitude. Helping professionals have a vested interest in rendering the uniqueness of young people in service settings as complex as possible, since professional intervention would appear unnecessary if those differences were seen as strengths rather than major risk factors. Moreover, the complexities of young people's circumstances justify disappointing treatment outcomes; what can one expect, after all, when young people are this damaged?

The rise of evidence-based practices in youth care settings, and especially in explicitly treatment-oriented settings, is symptomatic of the language games played by the helping professions and their political allies. Typically, evidence-based practices are seen as a major leap forward compared to the more intuitive and often experimental nature of interventions and program designs of years gone past. Rendering treatment as a scientific process elevates the status of service providers and the professionals involved in the treatment process. An alternative perspective on the rise of evidence-based practices might take a much more cynical view and point out that the main impact of the drive to install evidence-based practices has been the exclusion of young people who may not contribute to the validation of the evidence (Gharabaghi, 2012a).

It is, of course, easy to point to all the systemic and political issues in the helping systems as a way of rationalizing the current state of youth work. In fact, however, youth workers themselves are contributing to the ever-deepening commitment to clinical practice and treatment logic in youth services across North America through their unwillingness to defend the principles of youth work that gave rise to their profession in the first place *in opposition* to clinical practices and treatment logic (see Fewster, this volume). While the ambition to be recognized as valuable contributors and knowledge-based professionals within the broader helping systems is understandable, leaving behind young people in order to advance one's career is not entirely ethical.

Youth work has its origins in the resistance to treatment per se; much of what we understand to be unique about youth work is the focus on everyday moments, the relational connections with young people, and the understanding that our work with young people is always moderated by the peculiarities of the self (Fewster, 1990; Garfat & Fulcher, 2011). The power of youth work is in its desire to transcend power dynamics by simply not caring about outcomes. This is indeed a unique foundation for a professional activity. Much of what we have learned through our increasing focus on postmodernity is that power cannot be abandoned or eliminated, that it is ever-present, and that it has an incredible capacity to transform itself to suit the current circumstances (Skott-Myhre, 2006, 2008). Still, even with these seemingly intractable characteristics of power, youth work aims to challenge power dynamics at their source: the concern over what happens next. Power, after all, requires this concern. In its most totalitarian form, power rests on vested interests in terms of what happens next. In its more benign form, power rests on general interests, values, ideologies, and preferences in terms of what happens next. Youth work is concerned less with what happens next, and much more so with what is happening right now; "it is immediate and focuses on the moment as it is occurring" (Garfat & Fulcher, 2011, p. 8). Specifically, youth work provides the rare and therefore precious opportunity for youth worker and young person to experience the moment, to reflect on the moment, to engage the moment, and to do all of this together, in relationship (Fulcher, 2004; Gharabaghi, 2012a; Ward, 1998).

## Moving Forward in the Past

WHILE IT MAY SEEM REDUNDANT to move forward in the past, and perhaps just a little mundane and excessively traditionalist, I think we must do so in order to correct a major thinking error our field has committed some time ago. Fundamentally, this is an error related to articulating our purpose as a discipline, a profession, and an everyday practice. I think we have done well to identify the importance of seeking behaviour change, preparing for independence, building resilience, ensuring safety and imposing containment, and advocating for system change. We have, however, used these frameworks for the wrong targets. Instead of cementing these articulations of purpose with respect to what we do to (or sometimes with) children and youth, we should redirect these efforts at ourselves. It is us, the scholars, practitioners, and leaders in the field of youth work, who are in need of treatment. We need to change our behaviour by abandoning our nuanced ways of rationalizing our narcissism on the backs of young people; we need to prepare for our independence as a professional field by learning to decouple (but not separate or exclude) from the "higher" professions focused on clinical work. We need to build our resilience so that we might move from complaining about adversity to overcoming it in ways commensurate with our field's core concepts. And we need to learn about how to do this in safe ways, how to challenge the systems that create barriers for unrestricted youth work, and how to build an identity that celebrates differences, resistance, rebellion, and noncompliance. And yet we also need to learn about containment, inasmuch as many of our colleagues' enthusiasm for the re-engineering of young people needs to be contained and sometimes abolished.

I am unsure about whether it is possible to articulate a purpose of youth work that captures all the complexities and nuances of being with young people. I am, however, very sure that the many child and youth care practitioners in the field right now are engaged in mostly excellent practice, but it is a practice that is limited by what are limiting views of purpose. With this chapter, it has not been my intention to be critical of practitioners, and certainly not to be critical of academics and learned commentators in the field. To the contrary, I remain impressed by the wealth and quality of thinking and practice to which our field has given rise. I do, however, wonder what opportunities for different kinds of practices are missed, solely because we have not yet had enough of a conversation about the purpose of youth work rather than the practice in youth work.

I believe that the purpose of youth work, ultimately, is to find ways of becoming present in the lives of young people, to become a character in the stories they tell about themselves, and to connect to all the other characters in those stories so that young people can live their lives within the context of multiple relationships, experiences, and meanings. It seems to me that there is good evidence to support this view: every one of us has a story to tell, and for every one of us it is our story, and it is a story without predetermined plot lines, characters, or endings. ●

NOTES

1   It is important to note the emphasis on "in practice" here; much of the scholarly literature provides more nuanced analysis and argumentation in which an emphasis on transitions, for example, is never articulated in isolation of other core aspects of being with young people. The problem I am getting at here relates to some of the challenges of translating good thinking into good practice.

2   Here I must emphasize that the lack of knowledge about child and youth care literature cannot be blamed solely on practitioners; it has been a challenge in many employment sectors for practitioners to be given access to appropriate training and professional development material that reflects their specific professional role and discipline.

3   This is not to suggest that supervisors or employers trained in other disciplines necessarily know nothing about youth work; there are many social work–trained individuals, psychologists, and others who not only understand youth work well, but are themselves brilliant practitioners.

4   This formula is the basis of point and level systems and token economies popular in residential care settings and increasingly also used in education settings. Powerful critiques of this formula and its resultant applications can be found especially in the work of Karen VanderVen. See, for example, Tomkins-Rosenblatt & VanderVen, 2005.

5 In Ontario, young people in care receive support beyond their time in care only if they continue to follow a path that corresponds to standard expectations of society at large, such as going to school or participating in employment-readiness programs, even though such expectations are often not placed on young people reaching adulthood while living with their families.

## REFERENCES

Bellefeuille, G., & Ricks, F. (Eds.). (2008). *Standing on the precipice: Inquiry into the creative potential of child and youth care practice*. Edmonton, AB: MacEwan Press.

Fewster, G. (1990). *Being in child care: A journey into self*. New York, NY: Haworth.

Foucault, M. (2008). *Psychiatric power: Lectures at the College de France, 1973–1974* (G. Burchell, Trans). New York, NY: Picador.

Fulcher, L. (2004). Programmes and praxis: A review of taken-for-granted knowledge. *Scottish Journal of Residential Child Care, 3*(2), 33–34.

Garfat, T. (Ed.) (2003). *A Child and Youth Care Approach to Working with Families*. New York, NY: Haworth Press.

Garfat, T., & Charles, G. (2010). *A guide to developing effective child and youth care practice with families*. Cape Town, South Africa: Pretext.

Garfat, T., & Fulcher, L. (2011). Characteristics of a child and youth care approach. *Relational Child & Youth Care Practice, 24*(1/2), 7–19.

Gharabaghi, K. (2009a, July). The potential (ultra-)conservatism of resilience theory. *CYC On-Line, 1125*. Retrieved from http://www.cyc-net.org/cyc-online/cyconline-july2009-gharabaghi.html

Gharabaghi, K. (2009b). Private service, public rights: The private children's residential group care sector in Ontario, Canada. *Residential Treatment for Children & Youth, 26*(3), 161–180.

Gharabaghi, K., & Phelan, J. (2011). Beyond control. *Residential Treatment for Children & Youth, 28*(1), 75–90.

Gharabaghi, K. (2012a). *Being with edgy youth*. New York, NY: Nova.

Gharabaghi, K. (2012b). Translating evidence into practice: Supporting the school performance of young people living in residential group care in Ontario. *Children & Youth Services Review, 34*, 1130–1134.

Krueger, M. (1991). Central themes in child and youth care. *Journal of Child and Youth Care, 5*(1), 22–41.

Little, J. N. (2011). Articulating a child and youth care philosophy: Beyond binary constructs. In A. Pence & J. White (Eds.), *Child and youth care: Critical perspectives on pedagogy, practice, and policy* (pp. 3–18). Vancouver, BC: University of British Columbia Press.

Mann-Feder, V. (Ed.). (2007). *Transition or eviction: Youth exiting care for independent living.* San Francisco, CA: Jossey-Bass/Wiley.

Pazaratz, D. (2009). *Residential treatment of adolescents: Integrative principles and practices.* London, England: Routledge.

Pence, A., & White, J. (Eds.). (2010). *Child and youth care: Critical perspectives on pedagogy, practice and policy.* Vancouver, BC: University of British Columbia Press.

Salhani, D., & Charles, G. (2007). The dynamics of an inter-professional team: The interplay of child and youth care with other professions within a residential treatment milieu. *Relational Child and Youth Care Practice, 20*(4), 12–21.

Scales, P., Benson, P., Leffert, N., & Blyth, D. (2000). Contribution of developmental assets to the prediction of thriving among adolescents. *Applied Developmental Science, 4*(1), 27–46.

Skott-Myhre, H. (2005). Captured by capital: Youth work and the loss of revolutionary potential. *Child & Youth Care Forum, 34*(4), 141–157.

Skott-Myhre, H. (2006). Radical youth work: Becoming visible. *Child & Youth Care Forum, 35*(3), 219–229.

Skott-Myhre, H. (2008). *Youth and sub-culture: Creating new spaces for radical youth work.* Toronto, ON: University of Toronto Press.

Stuart, C. (2009). *Foundations of child and youth care.* Dubuque, IA: Kendall Hunt.

Tomkins-Rosenblatt, P., & VanderVen, K. (2005). Perspectives on point and level system in residential care: A responsive dialogue. *Residential Treatment for Children & Youth, 22*(3), 1–18.

Ungar, M. (2002). *Playing at being bad: The hidden resilience of troubled teens.* Lawrencetown Beach, NS: Pottersfield Press.

Ungar, M. (2004). *Nurturing hidden resilience in troubled youth.* Toronto, ON: University of Toronto Press.

Wall, J., Koch, S., Link, J., & Graham, C. (2010). Lessons learned from 14 years of outcomes: The need for collaboration, utilization and projection. *Child Welfare, 89*(2), 251–267.

Ward, A. (1998). A model for practice: The therapeutic community. In A. Ward & L. McMahon (Eds.), *Intuition is not enough: Matching learning with practice in therapeutic child care* (pp. 70–91). London, England: Routledge.

# Chapter ❷

## Becoming the Common

HANS A. SKOTT-MYHRE

**I worked for many years** in runaway and homeless youth shelters. One of the events that occurred routinely in every shelter in which I worked was the discharge of young people onto the streets. This could happen for a variety of reasons, from administrative restraints on length of stay to assaults on staff. Indeed, a wide range of events could lead to a young person's losing the relative safety and security of the shelter. I saw young people discharged to the streets for fighting, smoking, drug use, sexual activity, insulting the staff, refusing to participate in programming, or encouraging other young people to challenge the staff's authority. In each of these instances, the discussion around discharge focused on whether or not the events justifying discharge had occurred and were sufficiently grievous to warrant the consequences. Occasionally, there was a discussion around contingency planning for alternative safe shelter for the young person, but more frequently the conversation centred on the importance of consequences for the young person and safety for the staff and the institution. The thinking was that the young person had created an unsafe environment by his or her behaviour and needed to be expelled in order to re-establish the parameters of safety for the remaining young people and staff.

Initially, as a front-line worker and later as an administrator, I found myself troubled by both the event and the logic. The conceptual frameworks surrounding consequence and reward systems in residential care have been critiqued effectively (Fewster, 2011; Gharabaghi, 2010; Phalen, 2006, 2010; VanderVen, 1999) and I won't repeat those arguments here. Instead, I would like to engage the event of summary discharge to the street from an ethological perspective. In this context, I use the term *ethology* to refer to the study of an organism's capacities—what any given thing can do. I want to stretch the term a bit to encompass not just the capacity of any given organism, but also the capacity of that organism as a set of relations.

In engaging the field of CYC in this way, I am hoping to pursue the aim of this edited collection in using critical and postmodern theory to conceive of our work as fundamentally political. I will be opening lines of inquiry here that emphasize a tradition of young people and adults working toward common ends. The ethological perspective is one that acknowledges the importance of reading our field as a set of capacities in a given historical moment. This chapter will propose CYC practices and institutions as sites of revolutionary possibility in a time of social and cultural upheaval.

In doing this, I am drawing on two conceptual frameworks. First, I draw on the thinking of the philosopher Spinoza (2000), who proposes that no body can express its capacities without interaction with other bodies. By "bodies," Spinoza is referring to anything that has form, from simple bodies such as subatomic particles to complex assemblages like humans, to enormously complex systems such as stars and galaxies. Each of these "bodies," Spinoza suggests, has an idiosyncratic and unique set of capacities that only that body can express. For Spinoza, these expressions are the becoming aspects of God, or what he calls "substance." They are the way in which substance comes to know itself and produce itself. For Spinoza, then, the singularly most important event that can occur is the expression of a body's given capacities, as this act is that of God coming to know itself in its infinite manifestations.

Spinoza goes further to suggest that capacity is elicited only through necessity. There is no volitional expression by force of will. Necessity is the product of discovering what is required in interactions with other bodies. It is only in the encounter with the other that one can discover what one's capacities are or might be.

Based on this, Spinoza proposes an ethics premised on the capacity to express and to act. In such an ethics, all that is good enhances capacity and all that is evil constrains capacity. From an ethological perspective, this implies that the study of any given organism's capacity can only be done in the context of its encounters with its environment and the other bodies in that environment. It is impossible to extract a body and its capacities from the contingent encounters that elicit or constrain its capacity to act. Since action is dependent on the collision with other bodies, any elimination or constraint of another body reduces the capacity of all bodies in the immediate environment. Within this philosophical framework, the discharge of a young person from a program reduces the overall capacities of all the others—the staff and young people left behind.

This leads me to my second pair of conceptual ethological frameworks, eco-psychology and Indigenous paradigms of relational ecology. According to Dave Segal (2011), eco-psychology is a response to the "lack of recognition [of] the inextricable connection between human health and the state of the natural world" (p. 1). Again, this echoes the centrality of body–environment relation. In the context of eco-psychology, the concern is with the ways in which the human body has been separated conceptually from its environment. This separation, it is argued, allows for dangerous and pathological modes of thinking that allow us to believe that the capacities of our body (referred to as health in this context) can be managed without reference to the overall "health" of the broader ecosystem.

Similarly, Indigenous scholars such as Wilson (2003) and Kovach (2009) argue that knowing must be premised in a deep understanding of life as an interconnected web of relations. No one can be separated from this set of relations and no action can be seen as a singular series of cause and effects. All actions affect all relations. Current Western frameworks of individual accountability and the valorization of humans as separate from and superior to other forms of life are seen as ecologically suicidal and dangerous to all life (Goldtooth, 2012). We might pause, briefly here, to ask how much of our programming that leads to discharge is premised on individual accountability and a sense of moral or ethical superiority.

Of particular interest in relation to the ethological perspective I am proposing here is the idea in eco-psychology that "individualized and skin encapsulated notions of the self are replaced with notions of an ecological self, where nature is viewed as an extension of oneself and the cultivation of one's ecological identity becomes a central feature" (Segal, 2011, p. 1). Following systems theory, Segal (2011) uses the example of a bear being conceptualized as "only 5% fur, teeth, and claws, and 95% salmon streams, old growth forests, and alpine meadows" (p. 1). It is important to note that this perspective and paradigm echoes understandings also deeply rooted in Indigenous culture and knowledge (Kovach, 2009; Wilson, 2003).

This notion of an ecological self that is not bounded by the conceptual frameworks of being an individual, nor encapsulated by our skin, opens a way of thinking about capacity that is not limited to what any bounded body can do. Instead, as Spinoza implies, the capacity of any given body is an assemblage of all bodies that come together in any given moment, in any given place. From an ethological perspective, this means that an organism's capacity is not limited to its own force. Instead, its capacity must be read as a dynamic and ever-shifting contingent set of relations with all elements of its environment.

From this perspective, the logic that led to the expulsion of a youth from the emergency shelter is what Spinoza (2000) would call inadequate. Inadequate, not so much because it was wrong or false (it may well be true that events occurred or rules were violated), but because the conceptual framework surrounding the event does not account adequately for its own set of causes. For Spinoza, that set of causes has to include the broadest and most complete understanding of the web of relations involved and account for the impact of the act ethically in either enhancing the capacities of the bodies involved or restraining those capacities. The decision is inadequate in that it is limited in both definition of the problem and its context. To make this point in a slightly different vernacular, let me offer three stories.

## Franco Basaglia and the Asylum

FRANCO BASAGLIA was an Italian psychiatrist responsible for the deinstitutionalization of the entire Italian system of aslyums in the latter half of the twentieth century. Often associated with the anti-psychiatry movement, Basaglia was deeply influenced by Marxist and phenomenological lines of thought. As a Marxist he was keenly focused on the ways in which the mental health system of asylums served the capitalist class by recasting the misery of poverty and disenfranchisement as madness and mental illness (Lovell & Scheper-Hughes, 1987).

The vast over-representation of the poor within the asylum demonstrated for him a failure and contradiction in the capitalist organization of society. The fact that these institutions were brutal, dehumanizing, and profoundly antidemocratic was driven, in his view, by the logic of domination in the broader society. In the asylum, he saw a replication and intensification of the class relations of hierarchy and control found in the broader society. However, in the asylum, such relations were not mediated by the fiscal mechanisms of capitalist control such as consumerism and the promise of fiscal reward. Instead, Basaglia (1987) argued that the asylum demonstrated the unmediated contradictions and antagonisms of capitalist society: contradiction, in that it was an institution committed to healing that was actually brutally iatrogenic; antagonism, in that the class relations of control and domination of the poor and working class were fully replicated in the hierarchies of the institution. Indeed, he called the staff "technicians," pretending to "be workers which [they] are not ... [whose] profession often involves [them] as hidden accomplices" (p. 149) to the regimes of dominations.

He called for staff to "[reject] one's role and authority dialectically through a critique of science as ideology, or a tool for manipulating consent" and to come to understand "the direct relationship between the dominant group, the functionary (both the intellectual or the theoretician who produce the ideology and the technician who translates it into practice), and the dominant group's use for that ideology" (p. 149).

In rejecting the conceptual frameworks of domination, or what he called "ideology," Basaglia opened the asylum to radically democratic practices. He instituted open meetings in which staff and patients participated with community members (artists, students, factory workers, family) on an equal footing, to determine how to run the institution and determine its relation to the broader community.

In terms of the ethological perspective we have been tracing, such reorganization of the governance of the institution opens the possibility of greater and less-constrained encounters between bodies. This, in turn, from a Spinozist perspective offers the enhancement of capacity for each body involved. The flattening of hierarchy also opens the door to a more adequate knowledge of the causes of the ways in which the institution or community fails in relation to one of its members.

In the opening to the community, Basaglia unlocked all the wards and allowed patients of the asylum full access to the community. Community members could enter the asylum and patients could enter the community. Of course, this was not without risk. Basaglia tells the story of how during the early stages of opening the asylum, a patient went into the community and killed himself. The discussion that followed this tragedy (held with patients, community members, and staff), however, did not focus on how the patient's pathology led to his death or how the policy of open access was a dangerous failure. Instead, the patients, staff, and community members wrestled with how to organize themselves in such a way as to provide a better network of support for each other in order to mitigate future tragedies. From an ethological perspective, the focus did not turn toward the failure of the individual patient, but rather to the development of the community's common capacity for caring for one another in the future. In relation to the issue of discharging youth, we might ponder how we might approach such a decision differently if we didn't focus on the failed relations of the individual, but instead on our collective responsibility for mutual care.

## Kaleidoscope and Unconditional Care

ANOTHER STORY that might help to illustrate the question of capacity and adequate knowledge is that of Karl Dennis. Karl Dennis was for many years the director of a program in Chicago called Kaleidoscope. In that role, he was one of the founders of what has come to be known as the wraparound services approach to social services. His work is notable for its unflagging belief in human capacity and commitment to "doing what is necessary." Like Basaglia, "he didn't think about children's problems strictly in terms of bad parenting or bad genes. He believed societal factors—sexism, racism, poverty, violence in the communities—also played a part in what went wrong" (Marlan, 1999, para. 23).

A number of years ago I was on a panel with Karl and heard him tell the following story.[1] One morning a staff member called him to tell him to wear jeans to work. When he asked why, he was told that someone had burned the office down. As it turned out, the arsonist was a young man in their program who had been through sixteen different placements since entering care at a young age. Karl's reaction to the news was twofold. First, he reflected that his angry feelings and sense of violation and loss about the arson must mirror in a close way the feelings of the arsonist. The young man's actions, Karl thought, were "no more hostile or criminal than what adults had done to him for years by failing to provide him with a stable home" (Marlan, 1999, para. 41). Second, he wished that he could engage the young man in assisting him in cleaning up the mess and working with him. He was not interested in terminating the young man's relationship with Kaleidoscope; rather, he wanted to offer something this young man had never experienced—that being what Dennis calls "unconditional care."

Unconditional care in this context echoes Basaglia's call for the refusal of the conceptual frameworks of domination that would create us as technicians of practical knowledge, rather than a community of idiosyncratic capacities, none of which can be excluded without a loss to all the rest. Karl Dennis's unconditional care, in this sense, is not a moral or even compassionate caring for the other. It is, instead, a collectively valorizing assertion of our capacities together. Dennis recognized that we all are complicit in the chain of events that led to the burning of his office. The termination of that chain cannot be found in further separation and alienation, but only in joint and common struggle against the logic and conditions that forged the chain in the first place.

## Accountability of Us the Elders

A FINAL STORY is one I once heard about an Aboriginal community. The story takes place not too long ago and involves a group of young people from the community who had gone into an all-white town on a weekend. It seems that the youth had gotten into some confrontations with townspeople that led to some fights and property damage. The police were contacted by the townspeople and headed out to arrest the youth who had caused the disturbance. As they approached, they were met by a group of elders from the community who blocked their way. The police explained that they were there to arrest the young people who had been involved with the trouble in town and detailed the alleged infractions of the law. The elders listened patiently and then said that if anyone was to be arrested it would have to be the elders. The police thought perhaps the elders had misunderstood and so they reiterated that these young

people needed to be held responsible for their actions and face the consequences for their behaviour. The elders then explained that the young men
would be accountable to the clan and community, but that the youths were not
the ones responsible for their actions. Instead, the responsibility rested with
the community who had raised them. From their perspective, there was no
individual member of the community who held responsibility for their own
actions. All actions were the actions of the collective group. Since they were
the oldest members of that group and had raised everyone else, if anyone had
to be held to the white man's individually based legal system, it should be the
elders themselves. Perplexed, the police withdrew to try to figure out what to
do with this cultural impasse.

What is of interest for us here, in terms of ethology, is the echo of our eco-
psychological definition of self. However, here we must turn to the Indigenous
paradigm of deep relational ecology (Kovach, 2009; Wilson, 2003). In this
story the self is collective, acts are collective, and accountability is collective.
There is no ability to punish by exclusion or alienation. *We* speak, *we* act, *we*
are accountable. In this, there is also a generational sense of collective becoming, in which the elders see themselves as becoming through the acts of the
young people. Rather than separating, diagnosing, isolating, or incarcerating
those who act in troubling ways, this way of knowing envelopes, owns, and
integrates troubling acts as information about who we are becoming, what
needs our attention and care. As Wilson (2001) points out, Indigenous constructions of knowledge are rooted in

> the fundamental belief that knowledge is relational. Knowledge is
> shared with all creation. It is not just interpersonal relationships ... it
> is a relationship with all of creation. It is with the cosmos; it is with the
> animals, with the plants, with the earth that we share this knowledge.
> It goes beyond the idea of individual knowledge to the concept of re-
> lational knowledge ... you are answerable to all your relations. (p. 92)

This is a way of knowing far more in keeping with Spinoza's adequate knowledge in that it takes a more comprehensive account of the complex array of
causes involved in the young people's behaviour.

## Discovering the Common in CYC

THESE THREE EXAMPLES open a vista of possibilities for a rethinking of child and youth care as an ethological enterprise centred on the generative possibilities of the collective capacities to be found in the institutions where CYC takes place. Such capacities are rooted in the encounters that take place in such institutions and their extended networks in schools, outdoor programing, and street work. What the stories above suggest is a radical reconfiguration of our programs that engages what Hardt and Negri (2009) call "the common." The common is a political concept that has been around for centuries in European thought. Hardt and Negri have suggested recently that it is even more relevant within the context of the emerging world of globalization. They define the common as

> First of all the common wealth of the material world—the air, the water, the fruits of the soil, and all nature's bounty ... also and more significantly those results of social production that are necessary for social interaction and further production, such as knowledges, languages, codes, information, affects and so forth. This notion of the common does not position humanity separate from nature, as either its exploiter or its custodian, but focuses rather on the practices of interaction, care and cohabitation in a common world, promoting the beneficial and limiting the detrimental forms of the common. (p. viii)

The common, for our purposes, is centred on what has been called the "relational aspects" of our field, or what Hardt and Negri refer to as the "results of social production." These are the ways in which we express our capacity for generating meaning and producing information about ourselves and the world in which we live. It is also, increasingly, the overtly generative mode of production under the regimes of global capital. Indeed, Hardt and Negri argue that social production has become increasingly commodified as immaterial labour in the expanding realm of digital commerce such as e-learning, social networking, social skills training in the workplace, and the communications industry. Hardt and Negri refer to this expansion of social production as affective labour and note that it is a significant development in the scope of capitalism's range of exploitation and appropriation.

Under industrial capitalism, the focus of exploitation and discipline was largely on the body's capacity to produce within the factory. While there was some attention paid to developing modes of social control in the arenas of management and the manipulation of consumer desire through marketing and advertising, these efforts were largely directed at producing what Foucault (1979) calls "docile bodies." These bodies were defined by their function as instruments of capitalist production and governance. They were docile in the sense that they were passively available to be used within the machinery of industry.

Of course, as Foucault (1979) points out, the project to produce docile bodies was never fully realized. This was because the force of any given body's capacity always exceeds the force of any system attempting to contain it. This is what Foucault means when he proposes that any effort at domination will be met instantly with an act of resistance. Negri (2003) clarifies this further, in ethological terms, by suggesting that resistance precedes domination. Which leads us back to Spinoza and then on to Marx.

Resistance precedes domination because systems of domination are always secondary to systems of production. Without an initial expression of creative capacity, there would be nothing to dominate. Put simply, what any given system of domination seeks to control is the force of life itself as manifested in any given historical period.

Analogically, we might think of this in terms of the construction of a dam on a river. The concept of the dam would be impossible without an initial recognition of the force of the river. The force of the river, however, is not limited to the location of the dam, but rather is composed of an extensive and complex ecosystem. The force of the river's ecosystem might well include small tributaries, streams, other rivers, evaporation from oceans and lakes, rainfall in upper elevations, glaciers, and snow packs. However, consonant with our eco-psychological definition of a bear, the force of the river also includes salmon runs, bears that feed on the salmon, people who rely on the salmon for food, and other ecosystems that interconnect in extremely complicated ways with the point on the river where the dam will be constructed. As a result, the attempt to harness or dominate the force of the river will always meet with a whole range of ecosystemic complications and excesses that will challenge and quite possibly, over time, undo the integrity of the dam's ability to dominate the flow of the river.

In terms of an ethological investigation of CYC practices of exclusion or inclusion such as our discharge of young people from programs, the river might be read as the force of living production on the part of adults and young people in any given program. That is to say that what makes up the energy and creativity of any given program is the acts and thoughts of all the people within that program. All the encounters, private moments, secret actions, thoughts, and desires of the young people and adults in a program constitute a flow of constantly shifting force that shapes and drives what we conceive of as child and youth care work. The dam would be any system that would attempt to control or dominate that production in order to exploit or appropriate it. The ecosystem is all of the force of life itself in all its productions, animate and inanimate. Returning to the concept of the common above, capitalism as a mode of industrial production attempted to dominate our bodies through labour. However, it became clear over time that the physically labouring body could not be dealt with separately from its modes of social production. Resistance, in the form of unions, political groups, revolts, and revolutions, was fomented in the necessary act of bringing bodies into proximity with one another in the cities and factories essential to capitalism's growth. As Hardt and Negri (2009) point out, it was in the forge of social interaction that the creative capacities of innovation developed that built all the infrastructure and machinery of industry.

As Marx points out, capitalists did not create the world we live in. The world was created by those who actually produce and who struggle to overcome the obstacles to their freedom to express their capacities fully. Capitalists are merely the latest in a series of groups who attempt to rule over and control the productive work of others to their own ends. Such groups have historically failed as empires have fallen and ruling classes have been overthrown. What is important for us to note here is that all efforts at domination are founded in the exploitation and corruption of the common production of life itself. In our current historical period, that common is increasingly composed of our social capacities to create knowledge, language, codes, information, and affects. This kind of common is precisely what takes place in all CYC institutions and practices. If CYC is a relational field, then it is, by our definitions above, a site of the common under global capitalism. It is a both a laboratory and a factory that experiments with and produces new forms of social relations and subjectivities.

If the sites for CYC, such as residential programs, group homes, emergency shelters, schools, and streets, constitute a form of the common, then they hold the capacity for developing subjective and social forms of revolt and resistance. The innate capacities of the assembled bodies of youth and adults form a machinery of creative force that exists, by definition, as a monstrous space of deviance. Foucault (1986), in his essay "Of Other Spaces," defines a kind of space he calls "heterotopias," "of deviation: those in which individuals whose behavior is deviant in relation to the required mean or norm are placed" (p. 24). His argument about heterotopias is complex, but suffice to say that a heterotopia is a space that exists not as an ideal outside of society as a utopia, but rather as an existing social outside that is inside society, such as a psychiatric hospital, a prison, or a CYC facility. While Foucault outlines several features of such spaces, of note here is his characterization of a heterotopia as "most often linked to slices in time—which is to say that they open onto what might be termed, for the sake of symmetry, heterochronies. The heterotopia begins to function at full capacity when men arrive at a sort of absolute break with their traditional time" (p. 25).

If CYC spaces are both heterotopias and production sites of the common, then they hold the capacity for social antagonism as harbingers of new social forms heterochronic to their own time. They operate at full capacity, when they signal a crisis through a rupture with the norms and means of their own time. To use Nietzsche's term, they are untimely and function as a hinge to the future. In Marxist terms, CYC sites as heterotopias develop as a response, not to individual or familial problems, but to crises in society provoked by transitions between modes of production. Hardt and Negri (2000), following Marx, argue that the way we produce the world (through farming, industry, or global media technology) both produces and is produced by forms of subjectivity unique to a given historical period. As we move from industrial capitalism to the new order of global technology, we simultaneously begin to shift who we are. We literally become what Deleuze and Guattari (1994) refer to as "a becoming people." In the transition, our very subjectivity that has been formed around the old mode of production and all the dominant modes of control and discipline associated with that mode are thrown into crisis. This, of course, produces deviant subjects and the necessity for the old order to attempt to control and contain emerging perverse and rebellious subjects. Hence the need for heterotopic spaces that contain subjects that function on the edge of a break with their own time.

This view of CYC institutions is quite different from the traditional way we see them. From this perspective, all CYC practice is located at the edge of ongoing insurrection, resistance, rebellion, and refusal, both on the part of young people and the staff. Given this, it is not surprising that all such institutions function either in crisis or at the edge of crisis at all times. From an eco-psychological point of view, the heterotopic institution cannot be understood in any singular way outside the broader social context. CYC institutions reflect the crisis of rule in the face of insurrectionary new forms of social subjectivity. Their very existence signals the failure of the form of dominant rule to control and contain its subjects.

Indeed, one might argue that the heterotopic space of the CYC institution is ideally suited to the production of the common and its revolutionary democratic aspirations. In a similar vein, one might then argue that the system of rule imposed by the dominant forces of conventional society within such institutions is a perversion of the common. Such a perversion takes the creative force constituted by bodies of deviance, rebellion, and refusal and turns it against itself into resentment, apathy, conformity, and self-destruction. This what Hardt and Negri (2009) refer to as the corruption of the common.

Hardt and Negri (2009) argue that for the new form of economy signalled by the turn toward global social production to emerge fully, there must be certain conditions. First, they suggest that social creativity cannot emerge under conditions of obedience or contractual obligation. They argue that "the legitimation of authority … always and inevitably dampens or even blocks the production of the common through subjectivity" (p. 308). Instead, they call for freedom developed through education that trains all of us "how to work with language, codes, ideas and affects … to work with others." They also call for a new subject who is not an individual. They state that "an individual can never produce the common, no more than an individual can generate a new idea without relying on the foundations of common ideas and intellectual communication with others" (p. 303). Finally, they call for forms of equality premised in a valorization of difference. They suggest that the creative force of the common is significantly restricted "when differences configure hierarchies" (p. 304).

Returning to our ethological analysis, the question becomes what does a CYC institution do? According to our analysis thus far, it constitutes a significant site of social struggle between new and old modes of social production, subjectivity and appropriation, domination and creativity, and rebellion and compliance, as well as refusal and obedience. As the common, it is a site of social production where new modes of social interaction, as well as knowledges, languages, codes, and information, are produced in an ongoing contestation. As we have noted, Hardt and Negri posit the common as the new mode of production for the emerging world of global technology. In this sense we have suggested that CYC institutions hold the possibility of being laboratories for new forms of social and political production. However, in their current configuration as sites of behaviour management and social control, they constitute what Hardt and Negri refer to as a corruption of the common. The question becomes, is there an uncorrupted form of the common that CYC institutions might investigate?

Hardt and Negri (2009) offer a brief but evocative section on the relationship of insurrection and the institution. They note that the project of developing democratic social forms composed of autonomous subjects capable of communication, cooperation, and creativity is in some ways inimical to the development and sustenance of institutions. They also suggest, however, that without institutions to sustain revolutionary change, it will ultimately succumb to some form of dominant rule. The trick is to develop institutions of a different sort. This, then, is the task I would propose for CYC institutions in the closing section of this chapter.

What is this different kind of institution? First, it is not an institution premised on a social contract in which one forfeits the right to rebellion and conflict in exchange for social stability. Instead, there is an acceptance of conflict as "internal to and the constant foundation of society" (p. 355). In terms of CYC, this would mean that we would open ourselves to conflict, resistance, and rebellion as healthy indicators of those things that need to change. Like Basaglia, we would see the institution as composed of all of us together in struggle with accountability across all components of the institution. Like the elders, we would not hold any one person responsible for a disruption or a conflict, but instead would see any conflict as an indicator of our collective need to creatively respond. To do this, we would need to engage in a politics of difference premised not in hierarchy, but rather in equality mediated by function. Instead of negotiating rules or contracts for certain behaviour with sanctions and punishments such as discharge, we would negotiate terms of creative struggle and conflict open to the necessity of constant revision.

This institutional openness to conflict and struggle would require a different mode of decision making. Hardt and Negri suggest what they call "a myriad of micropolitical paths." By this we might imagine CYC practice as collective decision making that occurs throughout the day at multiple sites throughout the institution. Decisions are premised contingently on the conditions present in any given interaction as it occurs, rather than on preset institutional values or rules. Common practices are arrived at and composed through conflict. Such practices are not delivered from an administrative top-down structure but are made up through the concretion of myriad and multiple creative exchanges always open to transformation as conditions change.

While this may sound radical at first, it actually reflects what our field has valorized as the relational practice of the encounter and the magic of the milieu (Burns, McDermott, & Hartley, 2006). In perverted and corrupted form, these practices have been driven by the needs of dominant institutions where relationships are bargained for privileges or acceptance and the milieu becomes a sophisticated form of groupthink and psychological bullying. Under the form of the common, these practices are released into autonomous and voluntary encounters in which singular subjectivities struggle to express their capacities.

In such a model, the institution is shaped by the bodies that compose it. Such an approach stands in opposition to the more conventional model of CYC, where both the staff and the youth are shaped to the ends of the institution. This means that the institution forms what Hardt and Negri call a constituent rather than a constituted power. Instead of a form of rule that is composed of preset structures and rights of dominion, CYC institutions would have norms and obligations established by those living and working there. Such institutional structures and practices would be open to a process of constant evolution that would focus on two primary elements of governance: (1) the refusal of any party to dominate or control the institution, and

(2) the practices necessary for successfully mediating destructive conflicts. In my own experience, the two are not unrelated.

Finally, Hardt and Negri follow Lenin in acknowledging that "human nature as it is now is not capable of democracy. In their habits, routines, mentalities and in the million capillary practices of everyday life, people are wedded to hierarchy, identity, segregation and in general corrupt forms of the common" (p. 362).

This is certainly true of most of the young people and staff that I have encountered in my own work. And it is certainly true of myself on any given day or any given situation. So how do we get from where we believe ourselves to be, to where we actually are as heterotopic harbingers of the common to come? Part of the answer is to be found in Foucault's implied rejection of the utopic. Rather than seek the perfect ideal from what we have sketched above, we need to begin a practice of searching for those small indicators of possibility indicated in every interaction we have. The family therapist Steve de Shazer (1985) built his whole therapeutic practice on the idea that people already know how to solve their problems and in fact are already acting in ways that, if continued, would solve their problems. However, most of us are so sure of our deficits and problems that we dismiss our successes because they are too partial or incomplete. The founder of narrative therapy, Michael White (1990), similarly advised people to seek the unique outcomes in their lives. These would generate successful outcomes that they have traditionally ignored or overlooked. In the case of CYC institutions, I would suggest that we might well investigate the capacities already expressed by young people and staff when they exceed the institutional parameters of discipline and act instead with love. By "love" in this instance I mean the commitment to struggle with another so that each may express his or her capacity to the fullest.

Hardt and Negri (2009) state that "misery is the condition of being separated from what one can do, from one can become" (p. 380). To the degree that our institutions separate anyone within them from what they can do or become, they are machines that produce misery. The alternative is to create institutions that promulgate joy. Joy is the affect of bodies together creating and innovating while collectively governing themselves. I would call on each of us to imagine a CYC practice premised in joy and love. In such a practice it would become an impossibility to discharge vulnerable young people onto the streets, because we would know that the fight we are having with them is the fight we are having with ourselves and that the key to bringing a new world to come rests in the willingness to continue to struggle together as one. ●

1 Apologies to Karl if I am misremembering any aspect of this story. I have found partial accounts in interviews, but not the full story as I remember it.

REFERENCES

Basaglia, F. (1987). Peace time crimes: Technicians of practical knowledge. In A. Lovell & N. Scheper-Hughes (Eds.), *Psychiatry inside out: Selected writings of Franco Basglia* (pp. 143–160). New York, NY: Columbia University Press.

Burns, M., McDermott, D., & Hartley, A. (2006). *Healing spaces: the therapeutic milieu in child and youth work*. Kingston, ON: Child Care Press.

Deleuze, G., & Guattari, F. (1994). *What is philosophy?* London, England: Verso.

de Shazer, S. (1985). *Keys to solution in brief therapy*. New York, NY: W. W. Norton & Company.

Fewster, G. (2011). Commandment 8: Gradually replace rigid rules with personal boundaries. *CYC-Online, 154*. Retrieved from http://www.cyc-net.org/cyc-online/cyconline.html

Foucault, M. (1979). *Discipline and punish: The birth of the prison*. New York, NY: Vintage.

Foucault, M. (1986). Of other spaces. *Diacritics, 16*, 22–27.

Gharabaghi, K. (2010). Three profoundly stupid ideas. *CYC-Online, 138*. Retrieved from http://www.cyc-net.org/cyc-online/cyconline.html

Goldtooth, T. (2012, January 26). Occupy talks: Indigenous perspectives on the Occupy Movement. Retrieved from http://www.youtube.com/watch?v=zFWnD5UhbhY

Hardt, M., & Negri, A. (2000). *Empire*. Cambridge, MA: Harvard University Press.

Hardt, M., & Negri, A. (2009). *Commonwealth*. Cambridge, MA: Harvard University Press.

Kovach, M. 2009. *Indigenous methodologies: Characteristics, conversations, and contexts*. Toronto, ON: University of Toronto Press.

Lovell, A., & Scheper-Hughes, N. 1987. *Psychiatry inside out: Selected writings of Franco Basglia*. New York, NY: Columbia University Press.

Marlan, T. (1999, September 16). Intensive care. *Reader*. Retrieved from http://www.chicagoreader.com/chicago/intensive-care/Content?oid=900223

Negri, A. (2003). *Negri on Negri*. New York, NY: Routledge.

Phalen, J. (2006). Controlling or managing behavior: A crucial decision. *CYC-Online, 86*. Retrieved from http://www.cyc-net.org/cyc-online/cyconline.html

Phalen, J. (2010). Some non-sensical CYC approaches; please avoid. *CYC-Online, 136*. Retrieved from http://www.cyc-net.org/cyc-online/cyconline.html

Segal, D. (2011). The promise of ecopsychology: Addressing the psychological and spiritual pain associated with the industrial growth society. Retrieved from http://postgrowth.org/the-promise-of-ecopsychology/

Spinoza, B. (2000). *The ethics*. New York, NY: Penguin.

VanderVen, K. (1999). The case against point systems and grading in behavior programs. *CYC-Online, 3*. Retrieved from http://www.cyc-net.org/cyc-online/cyconline.html

White, M., & Epston. D. (1990). *Narrative means to therapeutic ends*. New York, NY: W. W. Norton & Company.

Wilson, S. (2001). Self-as-relationship in Indigenous research. *Canadian Journal of Native Education, 25*(2), 91–92.

Wilson, S. (2003). Progressing towards an Indigenous research paradigm in Canada and Australia. *Canadian Journal of Native Education, 27*(2), 161–178.

# Chapter 3

## Stop Breaking People into Bits
### A Plea for a Peopled Youth Work

DOUG MAGNUSON

**In 1948 Grace Longwell Coyle said** that group work intends the "expansion and development of our powers, the essential satisfactions of companionship, at times the deeper pleasures available in a creative and democratic group experience, and for some at least the means to participate in the vital constructive struggle for a better life for all" (p. 25), aiming at participation in the "deeper meaning" of life. For many, including Coyle, these conceptions of group work (and leisure) were an improvement over older ideals of person that "cut people into bits" (p. 28), for example, the faculty psychology of the nineteenth century, the educational psychology of Thorndike, and the behaviourism of Skinner.

There is now, again, some reason to worry about the academic inclination to "cut people into bits." Those in higher education who teach and do research about youth work in the United States and child and youth care in Canada are facing pressures and temptations from within and without to "disappear the self," the contemporary version of cutting people into bits. This pressure comes from two directions. One is from the point of view of critical theory, corresponding to Foucault's announcement of the death of man, Derrida's deconstruction of the subject, and Barthes's proclaiming the requiem for the author. The other direction is from science—specifically, scientism—where the person is too easily lost in a blizzard of neurons, synapses, assets, and behaviours. These tendencies come from fetishizing theory and particular epistemological views. The consequence can be to lose the child in the theory and to leave behind the grit and grime of the work with children.

In response to criticism from similar points of view, Gary Alan Fine (2003) wrote a gracious essay in which he defended his own ethnographic research and, at the same time, made room for the contribution of other researchers whose underpinnings are different from his own. I am borrowing portions of his argument here to offer a defence of a certain kind of writing and a certain kind of history of the field, perhaps somewhat less graciously than Fine.

Fine argued that ethnographic research may be modelled on two dimensions, one having to do with the presence or absence of theory and the other with the presence or absence of data. Three out of the four cells of this two-by-two table are types of ethnography: postulated, personal, and peopled. "Postulated" writing aims for theoretical development. Examples are used to illustrate the theory, but there is not a consistent attempt to support the theory with data and study of practices. I have written several things characteristic of this approach, and there is a substantial amount of literature in this frame from critical theorists, post-structuralists, post-feminists, and the like.

In comparison, "personal" writing includes "substantial local data" and an absence of theory; in Fine's terms, writers in this vein are interested in "the personal relationship between observer and observed that vouches for the legitimacy of the ... endeavor" (Fine, 2003, p. 46). This style of writing has a long history in our field, and it is especially seen in publications that serve practice fields and certain types of narrative research.

The third option, "peopled writing," includes both "substantial data and substantial theoretical development. The ultimate goal of this writing is to see people in action or, perhaps more precisely, to see people in interaction" (Fine, 2003, p. 46). It has become fashionable in higher education to dismiss peopled and personal writing as, on the one hand, unscientific, or, on the other, as "uninterested in theory." Yet peopled writing needs a defence, because those who are interested in it and those who write in this form are increasingly dismissed, breezily, by some scientists and some critical theorists alike. And there is a history of the field that is ignored, to our loss.

## Holistic Practices, Whole Persons

AS COYLE SUGGESTED, the purpose of voluntary education, recreation, association, and affiliation through leisure was to enhance democratic participation, and the ideal of democracy pervaded almost every context of work with youth. In 1940 the theme of the White House Conference on Children and Youth was "Children in a Democracy." Democratic practice principles were promoted in education by Kilpatrick (e.g., *Group Education for a Democracy*, 1940) and Dewey (e.g., *Democracy and Education*, 1916), and these ideas were taken to the streets in settlement houses by Jane Addams (1893), in summer camps by Hedley Dimock (Dimock & Hendry, 1929) and Lois Blumenthal (1937), in applied social psychology by Kurt Lewin (Lewin, Lippitt, & White, 1939) and Gordon Allport (1945), and in psychiatry by Fritz Redl (1966). What all of these disparate fields shared was an interest in voluntary participation, freedom, and social attitudes as crucial to learning, and what tied many of these together in voluntary, informal education was group work. For example, Lewin, Lippitt, and White (1939) did an experiment on the effects of democratic, authoritarian, and laissez-faire leadership in Boy Scouting, and Lewin devoted years to studying groups as a context for social change.

A method associated with leisure and voluntary education was providing opportunities for self-directed, autonomous play—for its own sake and for developmental and educational possibilities—which cut across everything from Addams's settlement houses for the improvement of immigrants' lives, to the study of adult leisure avocations, to Redl's somewhat later writing about working in psychiatric institutions, whose organization he said he modelled after summer camps. Some of the most elemental and yet brilliant phenomenology of play was done in the early twentieth century.

While one could assume different approaches to leisure experience, for example, voluntary association, education, psychology, social work, sociology, and recreation, the idea of a person was not, at least in this tradition, carved into individual attributes, personalities, ideologies, and professional territories. Neighbourhood houses were still integrative and not homes for specialists. Professional recreation had yet to become synonymous with sports management. Social work had not devolved into academic specialties, and educational options were becoming more flexible with the advance of continuing education, experiential education, lab schools, institutes, and adult education.

## The Quest for a Meaningful Life and Youth Work Practice

YOUTH WORK WRITING IN, roughly, the first sixty to seventy years of the twentieth century includes characteristic, integrative themes of being "peopled." First, across programs and settings, writers insisted that a meaningful, useful life is crucial to growth, learning, and healing, even when working with youth who have specific needs and problems. Konopka (1954) said, for example, that the purpose of group care is no different from that of other kinds of work: "The final purpose of any work with people, whether they are healthy or sick, young or old, is to help them use as many of their capabilities as possible so that they are themselves happy and can contribute to society as a whole" (p. 15). And "the ... purpose ... of all education or treatment in our culture is related to our democratic way of life, that is, to have people who can constructively participate in the building of better human relationships" (p. 16).

Second, there was an emphasis on everyday life and the pedagogy of everyday life across settings. In group care, Redl (1966) talked about the "clinical exploitation of daily life events" in residential treatment and cited both Anna Freud and Konopka in support of the importance of the organization of everyday life in enhancing development. In summer camping, Dimock and Hendry (1929) said, "Learning and living are identical ... growth is in proportion to purposeful participation ... experience is valuable to the degree that it is social or shared" (p. 41), and he used the phrase "curriculum of living." Much later, in very different contexts, de Oleivera (2000), in a study of street workers in Brazil, and Dennison (1969), in a description of an alternative school, pick up on the same ideas: "We conceived ourselves as an environment for growth, and accepted the relationships between the children and ourselves as being the very heart of the school" (Dennison, 1969, p. 4). De Oleivera described what street workers do as, following Freire, the "pedagogy of presence" and "guaranteeing space for the critical participation of the child" (2000, p. 81). Popular education in Latin America is in part a movement to mobilize citizens in everyday life and to integrate domains otherwise separated, such as politics and education (Beck & Purcell, 2010).

In an early work on community organizing, Ross (1955) described the work of a medical doctor, in the process illustrating these pedagogical group work principles:

Kark does not direct, impose, or lead his staff in the traditional sense. There are frequent staff meetings in which village practices are discussed and in which Kark questions many of the assumption and value judgments of staff members. This, as suggested, is difficult for some staff persons—all their lives they have been taught what was "right" and what was "wrong." They see many "wrong" practices in the village and feel that their duty is to correct them. This is their job as they conceive it. To have a director who not only does not support their efforts at reform but questions their authority for judging "right" and "wrong" makes for a difficult period of adjustment. But Kark's philosophy with staff is approximately the same as with the villagers. Roughly it might be summarized thus: "As a rule of thumb, one should never attack the fundamental types of beliefs directly. If erroneous and incompatible with reality, the fundamental beliefs will themselves dissolve in the course of time, but nothing gives them life like a direct attack upon them. (p. 31)

Again, this is an example of a group work principle that cuts across practices.

Third, the writing is accessible to all who may be interested across disciplines, professions, and, perhaps most importantly, volunteer, professional, and academic endeavours. In a more recent work with the same spirit, Paley (1990) says, "Play is Truth and Life," and in her telling of the tales about "The Boy Who Would Be a Helicopter," she animates the epigram.

Fourth, peopled writing cautions us against fads. Peopled writing refuses to reduce practice to slogans and people to automatons; early in the twentieth century, youth workers resisted behaviourism's influence. In the 1980s, 1990s, and today, this resistance was needed but missing, as program fad and principle rolled through youth services, diverting attention from sound programs to the cult of the presumed new that would sprinkle magic dust on our problems: outdoor adventure, service learning, experiential learning, community development, positive youth development, trauma and loss counselling, wraparound services—everyone has their own list.

Another example of caution is surprising. In the 1960s Tom Cottle (1967), in some ways at heart a romantic, wrote persuasively, with common sense, about the necessity of adults to be authority figures rather than friends. This

was an excellent counter story to the 1960s and the misuse of the more ethereal
of Rogerian maxims (Rogers, 1951). More recently, Whittaker (Whittaker &
Maluccio, 2002), a co-author of *The Other 23 Hours* (Trieschman, Whittaker,
& Brendtro, 1969), with a long history in social work and youth services and
in academia, summarized a history of fads in child welfare and suggested that
perhaps it was time to stop looking for magical cures. When writing about
practice is peopled, it is more difficult to look for simplistic solutions.

Fifth, there was, associated with this work, an explosion of literature
in sociology from which youth work drew, including studies of populations
of interest such as street youth and gangs (e.g., Shaw, 1930, *The Jack-Roller*,
and Thrasher, 1927, *The Gang*) and neighbourhoods (e.g., Hollingshead, 1949,
*Elmstown's Youth*). These too were peopled and drew the attention of youth
workers toward understanding persons in context. Later work by academics
associated with youth work, such as *Cottage Six* (Polsky, 1962), drew on this
tradition, and today some of the best work is done outside of North America,
such as Wästerfors (2011), linking sociological theory about "going concerns"
to the daily life concerns of boys in a group home. This work aims to use theory to understand everyday life rather than everyday life to illustrate a theory.

## Becoming Respectable
### A Tale in Two Acts

ONE BRANCH OF YOUTH WORK IN NORTH AMERICA might be divided,
somewhat simplistically, into two eras. One originates in the Progressive Era,
with the emergence of settlement houses, voluntary youth organizations, organized outdoor programs, the playground movement, group work, orphanages,
public health campaigns, and political activism—such as garbage strikes—for
the improvement of quality of life. The work was often informal and driven by
idealism and an interest in the well-being of the poor and the vulnerable. It
was blue-collar work theorized by members of the white-collar classes, many
of whom had a prescient vision of the value of play and the importance of
healthy communities in the lives of children. These activists had a keen eye
and ear for informal education possibilities embedded in everyday life.

One indicator of the tenor of the interests is book titles. The Association
Press was one of several that aimed for an audience of theorists and practitio-

ners: *Spiritual Values in Camping* (Bowman, 1954), *The Community* (Lindeman, 1921), *Studies in Group Behavior* (Coyle, 1937), *Experience and Nature* (Dewey, 1926), *The Consequences of Social Action for the Group Work Agency* (Hall, 1936), *Lay Participation in Improving Environment* (Hendry, 1936), *Education and the Social Crisis* (Kilpatrick, 1932), *The Interests of Young Men* (Sonquist, 1931), *Roughing It with Boys* (Hinckley, 1913), *The Community: An Introduction to the Study of Community Leadership and Organization* (Lindeman, 1921), *A Philosophy of Play* (Gulick, 1920), *Boy Life and Self-Government* (Fiske, 1921), *Social Education: An Interpretation of the Principles and Methods Developed by the Inquiry during the Years 1923–1933* (Lindeman, 1933), *Leisure—A National Issue: Planning for the Leisure of a Democratic People* (Lindeman, 1939), "The Psychology of Participation" (Allport, 1945).

Over the course of the first three-quarters of the twentieth century, the informal gave way to the formal as programs in social work and recreation were established in higher education and educational qualifications were promoted as standards for being allowed to run residential programs, manage municipal parks and recreation, administer welfare benefits, design playgrounds, and direct summer camps. The work was still often blue collar, and those who performed the day-to-day, face-to-face contact were still likely to be less well educated and less well paid, but those who supervised them were more likely to have professional degrees. And what was originally a mass of progressive-era social action diverged into separate streams of professionalism in higher education, including social work, recreation and parks, and nonprofit management.

In the 1960s and 1970s, in an effort to become more professional, social work left group work and direct practice behind, and in the process it loosened its connection to its blue-collar roots in face-to-face care and advocacy. Many social work programs have no group work courses and no opportunity to learn how to do street outreach; run shelter programs; manage peer counselling programs; learn to use recreation for developmental, therapeutic, or educational goals; learn play theory; manage a community social service; design residential group care; do programming; or do public health education. Nor are these seen as their responsibility.

This was an opportunity, for those who stayed with direct practice, and a justification for promoting training and education programs in higher education and in the field. At the University of Victoria, where I work, the program in child and youth care began in the 1970s to fill the gap in direct practice, and the same was true in other locations. Many large child welfare institutions started their own training and evaluation institutes, and there were new and renewed efforts to organize practitioners into associations. This work has continued over the last three to four decades, although the success of these efforts has varied widely by geography and jurisdiction.

Decades later, higher education programs in youth work and CYC may face a similar fate as social work forty years ago. There is the possibility that faculty will be less interested in the work as a practice, especially the "care work" part of the practice. In the effort to be "theoretical" and/or scientific, academic, and contemporary, we are increasingly drawn to theories, discourses, and research methods that appear to be unrelated to or uninterested in practice, and, on occasion, academics are dismissive of the interest of practitioners.

I am not concerned about the use of theory to understand practice. I am concerned about the lure of theory as a pursuit in itself and the lure of specific theoretical interests and research methodologies to pull us into self-referential dialogues. For example, the disappearance of the self from academic writing has consequences. It is now possible to write and publish an eight-thousand-word paper, ostensibly about youth work, with very few references to real people, in context, and so the complex practices that, say, make up the daily life of a street worker and her clients disappear. Writing moves from talking about diverse people and their lives to talking about the importance of diversity, from thinking to talking about the importance of thinking, from ethnography to interview, from interview to text and from text to discourse, from practice to critique, from advocacy to opposition, from youth work to counselling, from craft to professional distance, and, most characteristically, from blue collar to white collar. It is the lack of interest in the blue-collar nature of the work that intrigues me most about academic social work and youth work. The long-term consequences remain to be seen, but the precedent of social work is worth contemplating.

## The Pressures of Upward Mobility and the Slipperiness of the Self

HIGHER EDUCATION PROGRAMS IN NORTH AMERICA have aspirations of upward mobility that even the recent recession has failed to dampen. Diploma institutions want to be degree institutions, degree institutions want to be research institutions, and research institutions sneer at the teaching institutions and conspire to improve their rankings against other research institutions. Such aspirations change requirements for faculty hires, making it less likely that faculty will have practical work experience or familiarity with professional associations and practices. They influence how faculty spend their time and where they desire to publish, and they certainly change how faculty write, as well as their audience.

One of the side effects is that many faculty write and do research from theoretical positions and using methods that distance them from practitioners. This challenge can be managed; more worrisome is the increasing tyranny of language games that signify superiority and that are used to keep others at a distance. Our students learn it from us: recently I heard one of our students saying to another that they needed to keep in mind that the practitioners with whom they were working did not have the advantage of knowing about all the "postmodern perspectives they learned in school." It was patronizing and snide, and they did not give much thought as to whether the practitioner understood something they did not.

Scientism has its own diversions: the appeal to exotica such as neuroscience, the worship of numbers, the substitution of research expertise for practice expertise, the dismissal of experience in favour of moneyed research projects, and the like. Writers in many research avenues often make claims about epistemology that their own positions cannot justify, and both scientism and post-structuralism/postmodernism assume verification principles for the legitimacy of ideas and research that have yet to be proven necessary in practice. It is an odd thing to make truth claims while denying others the right to make truth claims, and both make claims about epistemology that require a vantage point that is denied by their own theories. Post-structuralism and critical theory elevate research methods into a metaphysic and a stylized fetish insisting, evangelically, that any idea must be legitimated by conforming to one's own pet epistemology. Yet when one reads this work, the research methods used are neither exotic nor meaningfully different than many straightforward methods.

There also is a simple-minded scientism at loose in the world that insists that we know nothing without, say, double-blind experiments, statistical controls, and a simple-minded raw empiricism. Oddly, both perspectives unite in their view of the history of ideas: each has a creation story about the origin of truth. Post-structuralists will deny truth claims, themselves excepted. Scientism accepts truth claims, but only under narrow circumstances. You can see this at the beginning of papers when the epistemological stance or criterion through which data are filtered names criteria that, not surprisingly, turn out to rationalize their own findings, allow them to dismiss findings based on other traditions, and eliminate the need to pay attention to any verification principles at all. One wonders why data are needed, because the first few paragraphs often are enough to know what the findings will be.

In such research it is difficult to develop a sense of who the subjects are. As Fine (2003) says about one such article, "We barely meet these women" (p. 56), complaining that everything about their lives that is important to understanding their interaction and to informing a larger understanding is left out.

A last lament about these ideological issues is that all sides claim a history that only makes sense if you do not read anything outside of these narrow language games. Too often we require researchers and writers to practise and assume a kind of solipsism, like some of our students who insist they are A students, all evidence to the contrary, and maintain the belief by avoiding any idea or task that requires them to do something difficult. In all these aspirations is a desire to leave embodied immanence behind and to aspire, like O. B. Hardison (1989), to a kind of post-religious godhead where the messiness of "accomplishing a self" can be left behind.

And yet there are many examples, in the history of youth work writing, of transcendence within immanence, to borrow a phrase from Schrag (1997). The practitioner *par excellence* of peopled youth work and writing, Jane Addams, was a harsh critic of unbridled capitalism, and she sacrificed the adulation of the public by courageously opposing the participation of the United States in World War I. Surprisingly, Elshtain (2002) says Addams rejected Marxism and socialism because of the "stated presumption that somehow only Marx, or those who subscribed to his doctrine, really understood those 'laws of motion' that govern capitalist society and the bourgeois social order. They alone, then, had access to the truth. She also pokes fun at the utopian fantasies associated with Marxism and socialism" (p. 4). Redl ridiculed scientism even while advocating for more rigour.

Something of the same resistance to the excesses of both positivism and post-structuralism is needed here, and the source of this resistance may be an empirical and empiricist sense of the harm done by untested ideas forced onto people and into people without listening. "Human nature being 'incalculable,' in Jane Addams's account, there can be no single interpretive entry point into the human condition" (Elshtain, 2002, p. xxxiii). By "incalculable," Addams did not mean the "empty" self of post-structuralism or scientism. She had anticipated Bakhtin's (1981) idea of "unfinalizability," an emerging self that transcends but does not leave immanence.

Similarly, Redl (1966) said, in reference to the very specific context of psychiatric treatment, "May I be allowed to add at least the demand that we become more specific about this point and stop confusing our own recreational taste buds, philosophical convictions, and habits of social interaction with objective assessments of what is or is not useful in the treatment of a given patient at a given time?" (p. 73). Whether Redl was aware of philosophical undercurrents is unclear, but the harm done by ideological enthusiasms was obvious to him.

Addams's resistance to the excesses of capitalism and socialist utopianism was grounded in decades of experience, the peopled youth work's primary claim of expertise. Again borrowing from Fine (2003), these interpretations are both theoretical and built on extensive experience and observation. They extend and build on theory and maintain an analytic distance between writer, subject, and idea. They claim what Fine calls a "wobbly authority." Addams illustrates this wobbly authority in a brilliant essay, "The Subtle Problems of Charity," in which in the midst of a brilliant analysis of the complexity of home visiting, she says, "The [charity] visitor is continually surprised to find that the safest platitudes may be challenged" (1893, p. 67).

But instead of carving out a territory and erecting barricades where only those who speak their language may enter, they grounded theory in practices that did not reduce persons to discourses or digits and, in the parlance of later theorists, opened up praxis to those who can practise "lived-body" without requiring subjugation to a language game. Again in modern terms, human beings, even while situated, transcend discourse, and access to meaningfulness is promised to both gods and simpletons. More radically, to borrow a phrase from Christianity, "the last shall be first and the first last." Access to heaven is promised not to those of us who master the language game of the upper classes—our language games—but to those who learn to serve.

In 1950 and 1959 the theme of the White House conferences was personality development, and, in 1970, at what turned out to be the last conference, the focus was on individuality and identity (Child Welfare League of America, n.d.). The trend was increasing specialization and more psychologizing. We were well on our way to again "breaking people into bits." Still, restoring persons to the work and the study of the work was done once, and it can be done again. ●

REFERENCES

Addams, J. (1893). The subjective necessity for social settlements. In H. C. Adams (Ed.), *Philanthropy and social progress, seven essays by Miss Jane Addams, Robert A. Woods, Father J. O. S. Huntington, Professor Franklin H. Giddings and Bernard Bosanquet. Delivered before the School of Applied Ethics at Plymouth, Mass., during the Session of 1892.* New York, NY: Thomas Y. Crowell.

Allport, G. W. (1945). The psychology of participation. *Psychological Review, 53*(3), 117–132.

Bakhtin, M. M. (1981). *The dialogic imagination.* Austin, TX: University of Texas Press.

Beck, D., & Purcell, R. (2010). *Popular education practice for youth and community development work.* Exeter, England: Learning Matters.

Blumenthal, L. (1937). *Group work in camping.* New York, NY: Association Press.

Bowman, C. M. (1954). *Spiritual values in camping.* New York, NY: Association Press.

Child Welfare League of America. (n.d.). *The history of White House Conferences on Children and Youth.* Arlington, VA: Author.

Cottle, T. (1967). *Time's children: Impressions of youth.* Toronto, ON: Little, Brown & Co.

Coyle, G. L. (1937). *Studies in group behavior.* New York, NY: Association Press.

Coyle, G. L. (1948). *Group work with American youth: A guide to the practice of leadership.* New York, NY: Harper & Brothers.

Dennison, G. (1969). *The lives of children: The story of the First Street School.* New York, NY: Addison-Wesley.

de Oleivera, W. (2000). *Working with children on the streets of Brazil: Politics and practice.* New York, NY: Haworth Press.

Dewey, J. (1916). *Democracy and education.* New York, NY: Macmillan.

Dewey, J. (1926). *Experience and nature.* New York, NY: Open Court Foundation.

Dimock, H. S., & Hendry, C. E. (1929). *Camping and character.* New York, NY: Association Press.

Elshtain, J. B. (2002). *The Jane Addams reader.* New York, NY: Basic Books.

Fine, G. A. (2003). Towards a peopled ethnography: Developing theory from group life. *Ethnography, 4*(1), 43–60.

Fiske, G. W. (1921). *Boy life and self-government.* New York, NY: Association Press.

Freire, P. (1996). *Pedagogy of the oppressed.* New York, NY: Penguin Education.

Gulick, L. (1920). *A philosophy of play.* New York, NY: Association Press.

Hall, H. (1936). The consequences of Social Action for the Group Work Agency. *Proceedings of the National Conference of Social Work.* Chicago, IL: University of Chicago Press.

Hardison, O. B. (1989). Disappearing through the skylight. New York, NY: Penguin Books.

Hendry, C. E. (1936). Lay participation in improving environment. In *The community approach to delinquency prevention.* New York, NY: National Probation Association.

Hinckley, G. W. (1913). *Roughing it with boys: Actual experience of boys at summer and winter camps.* New York, NY: Association Press.

Hollingshead, A. B. (1949). *Elmtown's youth: The private lives of American adolescents and the forces influencing them.* New York, NY: Science Editions.

Kilpatrick, W. H. (1932). *Education and the social crisis.* New York, NY: Liveright.

Kilpatrick, W. H. (1940). *Group education for a democracy.* New York, NY: Association Press.

Konopka, G. (1954). *Group work in the institution.* New York, NY: Association Press.

Lewin, K., Lippitt, R., & White, R. K. (1939). Patterns of aggressive behavior in experimentally created social climates. *Journal of Social Psychology, 10,* 271–301.

Lindeman, E. C. (1921). *The community: An introduction to the study of community leadership and organization.* New York, NY: Association Press.

Lindeman, E. C. (1933). *Social education: An interpretation of the principles and methods developed by the inquiry during the years 1923–1933.* New York, NY: New Republic.

Lindeman, E. (1939). *Leisure—a national issue; planning for the leisure of a democratic people.* New York, NY: Association Press.

Paley, V. G. (1990). *The boy who would be a helicopter.* Cambridge, MA: Harvard University Press.

Polsky, H. W. (1962). *Cottage six: The social system of delinquent boys in residential treatment.* New York, NY: Russell Sage Foundation.

Redl, F. (1966). *When we deal with children.* New York, NY: Free Press.

Rogers, C. (1951). *Client-centered therapy.* Cambridge, MA: Riverside Press.

Ross, M. G. (1955). *Community organization: Theory and principles.* New York, NY: Harper & Brothers.

Schrag, C. (1997). *The self after postmodernity.* Princeton, NJ: Yale University Press.

Shaw, C. R. (1930/1966). *The jack-roller: A delinquent boy's own story.* Chicago, IL: University of Chicago Press.

Sonquist, D. E. (1931). *The interests of young men.* New York, NY: Association Press.

Thrasher, F. (1927). *The gang.* Chicago, IL: University of Chicago Press.

Trieschman, A. E., Whiitaker, J. K., & Brendtro, L. K. (1969). *The other 23 hours.* Piscataway, NJ: Transaction.

Wästerfors, D. (2011). Disputes and going concerns in an institution for "troublesome" boys. *Journal of Contemporary Ethnography, 40*(1), 39–70.

Whittaker, J. K., & Maluccio, A. N. (2002). Rethinking child placement. *Social Service Review, 76*(1), 108–134.

# Chapter ❹

# Developing the Profession
# from Adolescence into Adulthood
## *Generativity versus Stagnation*

CAROL STUART

**This chapter explores the past, the present, and the future** of professional child and youth care using a developmental metaphor. I start from an unusual social location in the writing of the chapter, in that I begin with an excerpt from paper that I wrote, presented, and never published ten years ago. The title is a reference to the tasks of young adulthood as they are described by the developmental theorist Erik Erikson (1950/1993). He describes the second stage of adulthood as one where the individual focuses on establishing and guiding the next generation. As I first wrote this paper, members of our profession were concerned about stagnation in the field and the reliance on ideas and knowledge from outside of the discipline. There was uncertainty about how to generate our own knowledge, and how to ensure practitioners continued to advance with new methods. Mature practitioners were worried about how to ensure that new practitioners advanced in their learning.

> Our field is fragmented. Front-line workers in the business (educated as child and youth practitioners) can work in the same organization for twenty years and not be required to obtain additional professional development unless they choose to join their professional association and thus be certified and required to do professional development....

Our theoretical and conceptual approach(s) to practice are poorly articulated. We know what the skills are to be expected of child and youth care practitioners. We draw on theoretical knowledge from child development, behavioural change theory, psychopathology, and ecological systems theory but there are skills that go beyond the application of these theories in the milieu that have a conceptual basis to them that we need to define.... We need to define and "test" our theoretical approaches. (Stuart, 2001)

The paper implies that "we" need to grow up, to get beyond excuses for not generating our own ideas.

Rather than being an idealistic adolescent profession that complains and challenges those in authority without the skills to plan or to create a significant effect, we need to get busy and make those plans. Rather than being the "stay at home parent" allowing the needs of the developmentally "younger" children who require more support to consume our time and "waiting until they are older" to devote more time to "ourselves," we must recognize that only by getting out of the "house" now will all children and youth receive the kind of care necessary to thrive. (Stuart, 2001)

Ten years on, these concerns and admonitions seem less relevant. There has been a significant increase in the writings generated from within the field. Nationally and internationally, many new books and texts are coming forward articulating ideas and concepts from within the field in new ways. It is no longer possible to "know" everyone or to identify who or what is "within" the boundaries of the discipline. These are sure signs of growing up—we have left the safe confines of our neighbourhood and are exploring the world beyond. The profession as a collective, though, still needs to attend to the creation of a new generation of professionals in the social context of a changing definition of professionalism and new attitudes evident in the younger generations.

Self-identifying as a child and youth care practitioner, I started working in the field as the "professionalization" movement was beginning; education programs were starting, certification and training were being developed, governments with more liberal philosophies were funding organizations to provide quality care and treatment for children and youth. In Canada, post-secondary programs in child and youth care were beginning to proliferate, and other (new) professions such as social work were advocating for and becoming regulated through legislation.

My use of the developmental metaphor to understand the evolution of the child and youth care profession is purposeful. We work with young people throughout a period of intense growth and development, and therefore the metaphor and the extent of change are familiar both theoretically and experientially. I can apply this theoretical and experiential understanding to the collective development of our profession. Developmental change is the norm in life and time; we are constantly learning and evolving. Development occurs as a result of internal and external influences on both individuals and collectives of individuals, in this case the collective of child and youth care practitioners striving toward being a profession. By considering the developmental trajectory of the profession as a whole and the social context in which it currently exists *and* where it has grown up, perhaps we can formalize the status of the profession using a model that is unique to our own developmental path.

Theorists and researchers have struggled to understand and to predict an individual person's developmental path along a specific line of development. In turn, they have been critiqued for suggesting that development is deficient or abnormal when it does not follow the predicted path and for suggesting that a universal path of development exists across peoples and cultures. The social and cultural contexts affect the predictable path of development—if indeed there is a predictable path. These contexts are also critical for understanding group development, which is influenced by the lines of development of individual members as well as the group's own collective and synergistic developmental growth and change. It is the development of the group—the profession of child and youth care—that I attempt to analyze here, in order to understand how we might collectively influence our professional future. The analysis requires that I consider the group itself, the individuals within the group, and the social context in which we exist. Changing our existing developmental path requires an understanding of the existing structures and potential future structures, as well as an understanding of the collective and individual will to influence those structures. In other words, we need to consider the structural influences on the development of the child and youth care profession, as well as understand the characteristics of the practitioners within the collective and our capacity for agency or influence on our own path of development.

Suttle's (2011) analysis of the professionalism of lawyers in today's society argues that internal changes in the collective of young professionals, such as shifts in values, beliefs, and morals, have disrupted the development of professionalism among individual lawyers. He argues that professionalism is one "line of development," which individuals follow at varying rates. Since the members of the collective create the structures of professionalism, this analysis suggests that the development of the profession also reacts to the internal changes impinging on individuals. For example, if young people today do not exhibit the same commitment to service of the profession and are more egocentrically focused than young people in the past, then child and youth care as a young profession could struggle to achieve the traditional markers of professionalism because its members do not have a commitment to the profession.

In this chapter I summarize, from my own mid-life perspective, the struggles we have had, the things we have learned, our current issues, and what we need to do to continue the progression toward an individuated profession, if indeed that should still be the goal. The task of adolescence, as described by developmental theorists, is defining a unique identity, or becoming an individual, separate but related to family.[1] Becoming an individuated profession, according to traditional definitions, would imply that we are clearly recognized by the public, regulated separately from other professions, and uniquely entitled to certain types of work based on our education and competence. In short, we have a unique and recognizable identity and are valued for our contribution by society.

Development of the profession needs to be set in an ecological context that defines the conditions for growth and development. In the context of Canadian and North American culture, where individuation is the goal, child and youth care has worked toward defining its identity, differentiating the profession from others, and establishing our purpose. As we have focused on these tasks of adolescence and young adulthood, we have identified other professions as role models and tried to imitate them. At the same time, we have rejected their structure and models as inappropriate for our own collective. Perhaps this is because we create within our work "contained spaces of deviance" (Skott-Myhre, this volume) and we simply can't figure out how to use our own agency to revolutionize the available professional structures to fit our own view of professionalism. What can we learn from the struggles of other professions and embed in our approach to create a unique model of professionalization that carries forward the social creativity and makes use of the struggle, and taps our agency, rather than bowing to models embedded in power and regulated decision making?

To answer this question, I examine three struggles we have carried forward from our professional childhood and I then consider what we need to know and understand about today's environment for professionalism. I examine how the definition of a profession has changed; I look at how the individual contributions to the collective have shifted as new generations of young people enter the profession; and I then examine the current social and cultural context for our development as a profession, with a particular emphasis on North America and the distinct differences between Canadian and American structures that influenced our development. Finally, I attempt to consider what we need in today's context to continue our development as a mature professional group.

## Quandaries from Our Professional Childhood

FROM OUR PROFESSIONAL ADOLESCENCE, we are left with three quandaries as we move into our professional adulthood. These are unsettled issues that we need to leave without resolution in order to move forward with our development as a profession in today's social context and tomorrow's world. Right now it is important that we carry on in spite of or because of these quandaries.

The first quandary is our professional identity: Who are we? What is the scope of practice? How does the world know us? How do we recruit new young professionals to an identifiable cause? The second quandary is the creation of theory within the field. We began as a multidisciplinary profession, drawing on the theory of other disciplines. What are our own thoughts, ideas, and theories about how the world operates for young people and families? The third quandary is legitimacy. At what point do we feel that we have real competency and contributions to make? How have we disseminated our contributions and communicated them within our own collective and to other professions?

## Professional Identity

The identity of the field and the profession has been a struggle. In the introduction of this book the following definition is offered:

> Child and youth care work is the work of people who work with children, youth, and families. Their work occurs in community centres, schools, after-school programs, group homes, camps, shelters, prevention programs, residential centres, correctional facilities, the streets, and many other places and programs. . . . [Recent work] is centred on three themes. . . . First, child and youth care work is *relational and developmental*.... Second, the work is a way of being in the world *with* youth. . . . Finally *critical and postmodern* theories and practices emphasize ... young people and adults working toward common ends.

We always begin with the definition, indicating that we continue to seek clarity and "truth" about what we do and to define the boundaries around our identity and our membership. Professional associations in Canada and the United States capture on their Websites the key characteristics and scope of practice for child and youth care.[2] Textbooks and special focus journals spend whole chapters or articles on the key characteristics or themes that distinguish the field (Fusco, 2012; Garfat & Fulcher, 2011; Gharabaghi, 2010; Stuart, 2013). Sercombe (2010) argues that the codes of ethics in North America, Europe, and Australia developed as part of an identity struggle and, as such, represent a set of principles that govern practice.

It is said that young people today stay at home longer and spend more time contemplating what they do, how they do it, and how to enjoy life while doing it. The time we have taken to collectively contemplate our identity leaves us well connected and consistently open to multiple definitions. We need to leave this quandary behind and embrace a level of comfort with this open-ended lack of specificity. As an "adult" profession, we have an identity, we can self-define, and we no longer need to pursue struggles with defining who we are. Sercombe, for example, states simply that "youth work is a professional relationship in which the young person is engaged as the primary client in their social context" (2010, p. 27). This definition incorporates paid and unpaid work, and multiple locations, and it describes the nature of the relationship as professional, making a collective understanding of "professional" an essential aspect. Overall, the profession continues to be perplexed about capturing its identity. I will pick up this exploration of "professional" in the next section on the changing definitions of professionalism because the context for defining a child and youth care identity/profession must be understood in the broader context of how the definition of professionalism is changing.

## The Creation of Theory and Knowledge

The profession emerged out of "living with children" in residential care, in educational/therapeutic communities, and in orphanages in North America. Young adults lived with young people who were unable to live with their families and provided twenty-four-hour care. The theory that guided child and youth care practice was drawn from the expertise of the educators, administrators, psychologists, physicians, and psychiatrists who initiated these communities of care. Our beginnings as a multidisciplinary profession meant theory was borrowed from other disciplines to develop the training and formal education that began to emerge for front-line practitioners in the 1970s. Newly educated graduates learned that they needed to know this theory and that this new knowledge should guide their practice. However, existing front-line practitioners resisted theory and continue to do so, preferring to work with intuitive knowledge and experiential learning (Ward & McMahon, 1998).

From psychology, with a focus on the individual, we drew on developmental theory to help practitioners understand how to guide growth and development; developmental psychopathology was applied to understand the emergence of disorders of the mind and deviations from the normal path of development; social psychology began to help guide the understanding of group interactions and the impact of group living on individual development.

Criticism of theory, based on the front-line experience, began to modify and adjust theory in application. Psychopathology, for example, was resisted by our adolescent selves, leading to the conceptualization of a strengths-based perspective (Ferguson, Pence, & Denholm, 1993). Developmental theory has been criticized for cultural relevance and its claims to universal application (Pacini-Ketchabaw, 2008).

From educational psychology we drew on learning theory and began to understand the influence of reinforcement and punishment on the learning of new behaviour (Bandura, 1986, 1997); the various modes of learning (Kolb, 1984) tied to theories of multiple intelligence (Gardner, 2011). From sociology we drew on systems theory to understand the influences of the collective and interactions between individuals as they contribute to the collective culture of a group and groups within groups. We also drew on ecological theory (Bronfenbrenner, 1979) to understand the influence of culture and the development of culture and social norms.

On the front lines, developing our own theory was tough in the midst of being "with children." Theory was actively rejected or intuitively adjusted to fit the daily life experiences of the young people who were being cared for. Active rejection of the ideas and theories of the elite and powerful is classically adolescent (if you subscribe to developmental theory) or characteristic of engaging with the oppressed; and youth are often constructed as an oppressed collective (Sercombe, 2010; Skott-Myhre, this volume). No matter what the reason, active rejection of theory led to a "stuck" place in the creation of our professional group because we were following the writings of sociologists who studied the creation of professional collectives and who identified theory and the generation of new knowledge as characteristic of a profession. Our strong links to practice and the experiential nature of the profession rejected such essential structures.

Recent writings have reconceptualized and extended the field-based applications of concepts into theory. Life-space intervention (Gharabaghi & Stuart, 2013) describes the theory of life-space and integrates it with the sociological concepts of structure and agency to guide practitioners in thinking about and working with the life experiences of young people, a modern version of how to "live with" children while not actually residing with them twenty-four hours a day. The use of daily life events is backed up by the philosophies of Fritz Redl, Henry Maier, and others (Garfat, 2002). Skott-Myhre (2008; this volume) discusses radical youth work and the application of love as an agent of political change in the practice of youth work.

With the formal development of educational programs for child and youth care and the strong links between education and practice that have evolved within those programs, publications have emerged with a unique and distinctly child- and youth-care base. Embracing the diversity of perspectives and strengthening the links among this knowledge, theory, and existing field-based knowledge and theory must be addressed and carried forward into our professional adulthood.

## Legitimacy: The Creation of a Base

The creation of theory and the dissemination of new theory and new approaches to intervention have created a base of knowledge grounded in practice, which can guide the development of new practitioners in the pre-service education programs that have proliferated in Canada and in the post-generalist programs that have developed for training and certification in the United States. The traditional markers of a base of professional knowledge, such as peer-reviewed conferences, academic articles, journals, and books, are changing within the field. There has been a significant increase in these traditional markers over the last ten years (since I first addressed this issue in my unpublished paper). In addition, the new markers of a professional knowledge base, such as podcasts, Web-based articles and reports, professional networks (Facebook groups, CYC-Net, the learning zone, AEIJ, Residential Care Network), have proliferated. Still, at the front line there is a cry for legitimacy that blocks the profession from being adult. I recently received a communication from a long-time practitioner in Nova Scotia, inquiring about when "child and youth care will be a profession." The trigger for the inquiry was the elimination of twenty-two hospital-based child and youth care positions and the comment of a manager that the positions would be replaced with "professionals." This communication described a situation that replicated one that occurred one year previously in an Ontario hospital. The question of when we will become a profession proposes that our legitimacy exists externally to ourselves. Current approaches to defining the "professions," explored in the next section, imply that once practitioners stop questioning their own legitimacy we can develop our profession. As a profession, we must find a way to help individual practitioners leave this struggle for legitimacy behind and accept that, based on more current approaches to defining what constitutes a profession, we already are one.

These quandaries, the struggles of being an adolescent trying to distinguish ourselves as unique, must be left behind individually and collectively in order for the profession to grow into adulthood. Knowing who we are (identity); thinking conceptually and theoretically (to understand the bigger picture); and developing a broad, networked understanding of self as we relate to others (group identity and induction into the social norms of adulthood in the broader world) are the tasks of adolescence. Our profession (as demonstrated above) is beyond adolescence. We have arrived in adulthood. I also have to wonder why we have been so focused on accomplishing these tasks in order to define ourselves as adults. The culture of professionalism has changed, and what it means to be a profession has changed. Sercombe (2010) rejects the markers of professionalism and argues simply that "a profession fundamentally describes a kind of relationship, rather than a status" (p. 15) or a set of characteristics.

The nature of the younger generation has changed, and as young people enter the workforce, the social environment in which professions operate is also changing rapidly; technology, workplace values, social entrepreneurship, legislation, government regulation, globalization, and interprofessional ways of working are essential contributors to the context in which we must envision ourselves as a profession. These influences are explored in the next sections.

## Understanding the Rules of Adulthood
### Changing Definitions of a Profession

THERE ARE RULES IN ADULTHOOD. Every young person knows this, and most adults long for the time when they were younger and rules did not seem so important. Rules provide the structure necessary for organized society but also represent the collective values and beliefs about what is right and necessary. Young adults must understand the basis of the standards of a profession: rules, values, and beliefs.

At the same time, the paradigm of professionalism is changing. Recent writings in the older professions, such as medicine and law, as well as discussions in newer professions, such as social work, psychology, and nursing, question the traditional definitions of professionalism for both individuals and collectives. I draw on some of these writings to help us understand the tasks and definitions of being a mature collective profession in today's society.

According to Bryan (2011), basic professionalism is an occupation that is well defined in scope with specific financial compensation for a specific service. The ethical approach is rights- and duty-based, with power being relatively equal and a level of caring that is beneficent. Service to the client also meets the care providers' own needs, such as financial security or self-esteem. The care provider is a "decent Samaritan" (Bryan, 2011, p. 468). Accordingly, child and youth care is a *basic* profession. Practitioners are typically employed by government-funded service providers and at times struggle to meet even these basic characteristics of professionalism. The profession has repeatedly worked to define its scope and develop ethical codes.

Bryan argues that the medical profession has fallen away from its status as a higher-level profession. Higher-level professions transcend the care providers' own self-interests and are often ill-defined and broad in scope. He notes that service is often "above and beyond the call of duty," with a clear obligation to the client beyond the basic rights and duty framework. The care provider holds significant power, leading to a moral obligation to honour the client's trust. Compassion and sacrifice are involved in making the professional a good Samaritan, and there may be risks to the care provider's well-being. While individually we may all be able to think of examples of professionals who meet these criteria, collectively the profession does not go above and beyond the call of duty, take risks, or make sacrifices to care for young people as Sercombe (2010) argues that we should. Indeed, Bryan questions whether this higher level of professionalism is relevant given today's generation. He suggests we might be aspiring to the wrong model.

How sociologists have conceptualized professionalism has changed from the list of traits or characteristics of the 1950s, to the concept of service and status of the 1970s, to structural qualities (Sciulli, 2005, as cited by Adams, 2010), such as

- The provision of expert services to "dependent clients."
- The interests of community and clients at the centre.
- The requirement for advanced education and collegial organization.
- The provision of expert services consistent with a particular standard of truth and competence.

> In common parlance, the term "profession" typically refers to paid employment or any occupation; its sociological usage to refer to a special kind of occupation with status and privileges appears increasingly divorced from social reality. . . . Education, training, and a service orientation no longer appear to distinguish professions from other occupations. . . . The end result is a growing belief that professions are in decline, and that the concept itself may not be as relevant a category for sociological analysis as it was in the past. (Adams, 2010, p. 50)

Adams's research focuses on status and the mechanisms by which professions accrue status, which is both self-defined (i.e., when the profession forms an association and declares itself to have a particular status) and legally defined (i.e., when the state regulates a particular professional group). In this her work is similar to Sercombe's (2010) analysis that these structures are put in place when a profession already exists; they do not make a profession. "Youth work is a profession 'in itself' ... whether or not it is a profession 'for itself'" (Sercombe, 2010, p. 14). Adams argues that exploring the structures by which professions acquire status and examining the structures of their relationships with the state, the public, and other workers will facilitate the ability to identify professions, to focus on issues related to status and power, and to examine the important social role that professional groups play in society. She is, in essence, arguing that status and group formation and the social role that professional status and professional groups play will operationalize and identify a profession (i.e., status *is* the goal).

By and large, child and youth care practice is still attempting to achieve these outer structures without recognizing that there have been changes to how professions are defined, which may mean that we are already there. As Sercombe (2010) suggests, a profession is defined by a relationship (a professional relationship), and the characteristics or traits of a profession are the structures that protect the integrity of that professional circle. Sercombe (2010) argues that a higher-level professionalism is what we need in youth work in order to meet the requirements of ethical practice. His analysis of the codes of ethics in North America, Europe, and Australia indicates that they developed as part of an identity struggle and that, as such, they represent a set of principles to govern our practice. These principles, however, are not tied to any mechanisms to regulate or enforce them. We are not given the autonomy by employers to regulate or to sanction workers, and the socialization into the values and beliefs of the profession rests largely with the employer and with ad hoc professional groups that do not fully engage all members of the profession (professional associations). In other words, the formal structures are absent to guarantee professional accountability.

While we have pursued legislation, education, and training, as well as professional collectives to represent ourselves, we haven't made much progress under these rules and we have argued among ourselves about whether we should play by these rules. Indeed, the very concept of a profession, as studied by sociologists, may no longer have meaning. We should be alert to this struggle as it may hold the vision of a new paradigm and the new generation of practitioners may hold the keys to unlocking the process.

## Generational Change

In addition to the changing paradigms of a profession, young people entering child and youth care have generational characteristics that affect their understanding of being a professional and what a profession is. Turnover in the profession is ongoing, and the collective of mature professionals that acknowledges the rules of professional adulthood and is willing to play within them develops slowly. Our tendency toward active, moral engagement with young people in their struggles against the structure and authority that oppresses them (Sercombe, 2010) has also limited the profession's collective understanding of the rules for being a profession.

Change is a constant, so to move forward in creating the necessary structures for a profession, leadership within the profession must consider how to integrate and understand the younger generations of practitioners. The rules of adulthood vary as the generations change and their values shift. The collective adulthood for a profession is responsible for blending the generations and incorporating new practitioners with different values. Our leadership is attempting to socialize into the profession of child and youth care generations X, Y, and Z, who think differently about self, work, and obligation to a higher moral calling. Collective changes in the individual expressions of subsequent generations have been captured in both the naming of the generations and the descriptions that help the previous generations to understand their behaviour.

The higher calling of professionalism was established by the "veterans" (born before 1946), described by Bryan (2011) as those who value stability, loyalty, duty, and law and order. The baby boomers (1946–1964), today's leadership in the profession, while retaining these values about stability and duty place more importance on status and reward (Bryan, 2011). Their interest as a generation is in creating structure to establish the profession. Structures such as educational programs, journals, certification, and regulation, which would provide the profession with status, are the priorities. These efforts have been unevenly successful. Educational programs in Canada are the most significant accomplishment. Professional associations exist with declining membership, and efforts at certification and regulation are also met with some resistance. The reasons for this collective lack of success at establishing the structures for professionalism will be examined in the next section, where I consider the macro environment in which our development as a profession has been occurring. The interior struggle within the profession is with the values and characteristics of Generations X and Y (the millennials) as they enter the profession. Generation Z (the digital natives) holds great potential, not for creating structure but instead for initiating change through agency and innovation.

Generation X (1965–1979) are "resourceful, individualistic, self-reliant, and skeptical of authority" (Bryan, 2011, p. 466), and therefore they are not interested in authoritarian structures that regulate their behaviour. They change work frequently and plan their lives for balance and relaxation. They are not prepared to sacrifice for the greater good and therefore are not going to be socialized into an advanced professional model that values a moral calling as suggested by Bryan (2011) and Sercombe (2010).

Generation Y (1980–1994) are savvy with technology, value moral responsibility to care for others, and are sensitive to diversity (Bryan, 2011). They apply this moral responsibility to themselves, though, with an expectation of regular hours and the presumption that employers will tolerate their individualism. Like Generation X, they are not likely to be socialized into the higher level of professionalism because while accepting of diversity and called to a higher moral responsibility, they are also not prepared to sacrifice.

Generation Z (1995+), on the other hand, has some of the characteristics of the pioneers of our field, such as social entrepreneurism and giving back, and they have grown up wired in with Facebook, Google, and Twitter as the norm for communication and information. They have great potential to collaborate around the world and are already connected globally with a strong sense of the need to give back in thanks for their privileged positions in North America.

The leadership in the profession must work with the values of the various generations and incorporate the values of new practitioners into a new approach to the structure of what it means to us to be a profession. Structure must be balanced with agency, but it may be an appropriate time for us to conceptualize professionalism primarily in terms of agency, rather than primarily in terms of structure as the traditional sociological models have done.

## Micro to Macro
### The Changing Social Context for Development

THUS FAR WE HAVE CONSIDERED the development of the concept and the structures that are used to define professionalism and the characteristics of the multiple generations that have pursued professional status as a group. My use of the developmental metaphor was purposeful in that the profession as a whole has followed some of the developmental principles of "growing up." I've examined above the generational differences and the collective developmental tasks of the profession as it enters adulthood. Development is always set in a social context, which, along with individual personality, contributes to the unique paths that people take through developmental trajectories. What of the social context in which the profession now finds itself developing? Adulthood is a time to develop a broader awareness of the surrounding social conditions. As the collective profession enters adulthood, an understanding of our social context and the influence it has is essential.

While social work, education, psychology, nursing, and a variety of other health and human service professions have achieved professional regulation and status through legislation, moving beyond the designation of an occupation, child and youth care has not. By examining the culture or socioeconomic environment and how that influenced our development, we may

position ourselves well to understand what we need to do now to emerge as a
professional force in the current social climate.

Let's consider some of the macro influences in North America. The profession of child and youth care is characterized by significant variation just
within North America. We have experienced a very different evolution in
Canada and the United States. Canada's culture and political environment
have encouraged the creation of formal disciplines and educational programs
in child and youth care. There are child and youth care programs at public
post-secondary institutions in every province. Post-secondary education is
heavily subsidized by government and tuition has been low; this has allowed
programs to develop and be supported in the educational institutions, from
community college diploma right through to Ph.D. Graduates emerge with
less debt, and thus they are able to "afford" a job that does not pay as well but
provides personal satisfaction through professional relationships. In the last
ten years, however, many graduates have gone on to graduate studies, often
citing enhanced salary opportunities as a motivating factor. The Generation Y
desire to have good benefits, reasonable work hours, and so forth, has led to a
more educated workforce.

Although the United States, on the other hand, has somewhat afford-
able state colleges, in the large private universities tuition is high. Educational
programs must be profitable or at least pay for themselves, since government
does not subsidize post-secondary education to the same extent as in Canada.
Children are not a commodity that generates personal profit; graduates cannot obtain high-paying jobs and therefore cannot afford the education or to
become alumni who support their educational institution. Front-line workers
are "good people" who value professional relationships but cannot necessarily afford the requisite education. Thus, child and youth care is not found in
post-secondary education as a specific program, but rather is nested in older
disciplines such as education, psychology, and social work.

In the United States, program funding for residential programs, youth
development programs, and after-school care arises from large fundraising
efforts and/or federal grants that target new programs to support countrywide
social policy initiatives, such as early educational support for impoverished
neighbourhoods through after-school care or the development of key assets
that will support the resiliency of young people. Fundraising and competi-

tive federal grants have been part of the structure of children's service provision for many years. This approach to service delivery is in contrast to that in Canada, where relatively full provincial government funding has been the norm until recent austerity efforts have increased the importance of fundraising that taps those with status and wealth to support the less fortunate. Swings in the availability of funding are affected by the economy, political power, and world events.

The growth of the Internet and the expansion of available technologies have opened the membership of the profession and enabled people to communicate with one another through CYC-Net (www.cyc-net.org) and other social networking sites. "Globalization," or the understanding that we are all in this struggle together, is facilitated through this technology. Additionally, technology provides the means to connect the members of the profession, while highlighting some of the global differences in the roles child and youth care practitioners play and many inequities in the advancement of individual interests as well as the profession.

As a profession that works with the anger and resistance of young people, we must balance our engagement in the struggle of each generation of youth with our own struggle as a young profession, taking time to reflect on our collective professional needs and how to collectively assert our professional identity. How do we collectively and morally commit to serve vulnerable young people? This is the definition of being an advanced profession. Returning to the dilemma posed by front-line practitioners—when will we become a profession?—the question implies that we are stuck at the basic level of professionalism, as an occupation. How do we work to convey our moral commitment to service with young people and our definition of the profession to those with power who do not understand the commitment and the broader scope and therefore act to eliminate jobs? We must support our front-line professionals to self-advocate and educate those in power about the nature of the profession.

The social context as we enter our professional adulthood is one where conservative ideals are increasing and publicly funded services, including post-secondary education and services for young people and families, are decreasing in a climate of increased accountability. In Canada, child and youth care appears well positioned, with strong educational programs; however, the profession lacks formal recognition through regulation, leaving practitioners vulnerable to cutbacks in funding. The unique scope of child and youth care practice and its essential service nature has not been established. The moral commitment to vulnerable young people is not sufficient. The social context seems to indicate that as a profession emerging into adulthood, we must work to establish a base of power—legislated power, which defines the profession as unique and necessary. The use of power to achieve this end, though, is in opposition to the inclination of child and youth care to engage in the youth resistance movement against those who hold power. We need to develop a model that incorporates accountability, without legislation and regulation. The model needs to be transparent and in evidence for employers to protect the new generations.

## What a Mature Profession Needs in Today's Environment

IN THE BEGINNING, I POSED THE QUESTION, What can we draw from the struggles of other professions and embed in our approach to create a unique model of professionalization that carries forward the social creativity and makes use of the struggle, and taps our agency, rather than bowing to models embedded in power and regulated decision making? An analysis of the social context in which our profession is emerging into adulthood indicates that power and regulated decision making may be necessary to advance the profession.

In the foregoing discussion I have tried to demonstrate what we *think* we have within our professional forums:

- Young people who are angry and oppressed in rebellion against the oppressors and who are also described as technologically savvy, socially committed, morally outraged, and both locally and globally connected. These young people are both served by the profession and are entering the profession as educated practitioners in Canada.

- A world where there is conflict, limited economic opportunity, and limited recognition for those who recognize only themselves.

- Several generations in a profession that is maturing into this environment, where the older generation has struggled to both resist and create the traditional structures for being a profession and the newer generations have simply "gone to work."

- A profession that is expanding its scope of practice and definition, with resultant uneven values, insufficient discussion, and limited mechanisms for socialization of new people into the profession.

What we actually have is the following:

- An evolving professional identity in the midst of new generations that spend more time contemplating what they do and how they do it, are open and welcoming of new perspectives, and are digitally well connected around the globe.

- Emerging theoretical perspectives that reflect practice ideals as educated practitioners have moved into knowledge generation.

- Ongoing questions of legitimacy, perpetuated by those in power, indicating that we must find a way to help individual practitioners leave this struggle for legitimacy behind and accept their professional status.

- Evolving professional models that encourage us to think of a profession as something that is defined by a relationship and to view the characteristics or traits of a profession as the structures that protect the integrity of the professional circle.

These subtle differences imply that the leadership in the profession must incorporate the values of new practitioners into a new approach to what it means to us to be a profession. The time may be right for us to conceptualize professionalism primarily in terms of agency, rather than primarily in terms of structure, as the traditional sociological models have done. The structures of professionalism cannot be enhanced in the current social context where fiscal cutbacks and accountability are the focus of regulation. Instead, we need to view professionalism as a resistance movement that brings to the forefront of society the impact of cuts on the lives of young people and families. The adult version of the child and youth care profession needs to leave behind questions of identity, embrace their diversity, and engage with advocacy techniques to illustrate the potential outcomes of the current approaches to human service cuts. Radical youth work could become a mainstream professional movement to demonstrate the impact on lives of decisions made today. The globalization of child and youth care provides the mechanism to gather information from other social contexts that have experienced the outcomes of failure to provide services to young people and families in need and allows us to demonstrate what could happen should efforts to reduce service not be reversed. This is a different approach to being a profession, one that "fits" with the history and approach of the field.

The new foci in academic institutions are on interprofessional education and interdisciplinary approaches. These are familiar to us, because as a profession we spent our early lives drawing on interprofessional and interdisciplinary expertise. These are now essential skills for which we are well positioned. Our ongoing discussions about commonality and identity illustrate our diversity. If we can be comfortable with continuing this discussion within the profession and accepting the conflict about who we are as a characteristic or the profession, we will enter a postmodern world where identity is diversity and differences are acceptable. Rather than forcing the profession into a narrow scope of practice, we need to embrace our differences and knit together the variety into a network of strength and global advocacy for young people and families, as well as our own professional approach to the work.

Adulthood universally involves taking agency and creating the structures to protect and nurture young people. This is our work—professional relationships with young people in their social context. As a profession we have been agents of change; we have created educational programs, certification programs, and formed associations; and we have arrived as a profession.

Now we must simply work with the new generation of professionals as they enter the world of work and revolutionize our profession. They are connected and accepting of diverse ways of being, and child and youth care *is* a profession. To return to the question of when will we be a profession—we are. We need to invite the new members of the profession to use their inter-connectedness to benefit both the profession and our clients, creating a new model of professionalism that is based less in regulated power and more in the interconnected power of resisting the oppression of the current structures. This interconnection creates a model of professionalism that is "with young people" and focused on our moral commitment to enhance their lives. ●

NOTES

1   I want to acknowledge that the work of Erik Erikson, and many other developmental theorists, is strongly criticized for its Eurocentric focus and its assumption that indi-viduals in all cultures follow the same developmental path. Therefore, the reader might question my use of the developmental metaphor and the tasks of adolescence. This critique would be legitimate, and if applied to the chapter, could provide some insight into directions that the profession overall might want to take.

2   See the following sites: Council of Canadian Child and Youth Care Associations (Canada), www.cyccanada.ca/; the Association for Child and Youth Care Practice (United States), www.acycp.org/.

REFERENCES

Adams, T. L. (2010). Profession: A useful concept for sociological analysis? *Canadian Review of Sociology, 47*(1), 49–70. doi:10.1111/j.1755-618X.2010.01222.x

Bandura, A. (1986). *Social foundations of thought and action: A social cognitive theory.* Englewood Cliffs, NJ: Prentice-Hall.

Bandura, A. (1997). *Self-efficacy: The exercise of control.* New York, NY: W. H. Freeman.

Bronfenbrenner, U. (1979). *The ecology of human development.* Cambridge, MA: Harvard University Press.

Bryan, C. S. (2011, October). Medical professionalism meets Generation X. *Texas Heart Institute Journal, 38*(5), 465–470. Retrieved from http://www.ncbi.nlm.nih.gov/pmc/articles/PMC3231553/

Erikson, E. H. (1993). *Childhood and society.* New York, NY: W. W. Norton & Company. (Original work published 1950)

Ferguson, R., Pence, A., & Denholm, C. (Eds.). (1993). *Professional child and youth care.* Vancouver, BC: UBC Press.

Fusco, D. (2012). *Advancing youth work: Current trends, critical questions.* New York, NY: Routledge.

Gardner, H. (2011). *Frames of mind: The theory of multiple intelligences.* New York, NY: Basic Books.

Garfat, T. (2002). The use of everyday events in child and youth work. *CYC-Online, 39.* Retrieved from http://www.cyc-net.org/cyc-online/cycol-0402-garfat.html

Garfat, T., & Fulcher, L. (2011). Characteristics of a child and youth care approach. *Relational Child and Youth Care Practice, 24*(1–2), 7–19.

Gharabaghi, K. (2010). *Professional issues in child and youth care practice.* London, England: Routledge.

Gharabaghi, K., & Stuart, C. (2013). *Right here, right now: Exploring life-space interventions for children and youth.* Toronto, ON: Pearson.

Kolb, D. (1984). *Experiential learning: Experience as the source of learning and development.* Englewood Cliffs, NJ: Prentice-Hall.

Pacini-Ketchabaw, V. (2008). Perspectives on child and adolescent development: Challenges and possibilities for teaching. *Relational Child and Youth Care Practice, 21*(3), 39–42.

Sercombe, H. (2010). *Youth work ethics.* London, England: Sage.

Skott-Myhre, H. A. (2008). *Youth and subculture: Creating new spaces for radical youth work.* Toronto, ON: University of Toronto Press.

Stuart, C. (2001). *Developing the profession from adolescence into adulthood: Generativity versus stagnation.* Unpublished manuscript.

Stuart, C. (2013). *Foundations of child and youth care* (2nd ed.). Dubuque, IA: Kendall Hunt.

Suttle, B. A. (2011). Reframing "professionalism": An integral view of lawyering's lofty ideas. *Emory Law Journal, 61*(1), 161–208. Retrieved from http://www.law.emory.edu/fileadmin/journals/elj/61/61.1/Suttle.pdf

Ward, A., & McMahon, L. (1998) Helping and the personal response: Intuition is not enough. In A. Ward & L. McMahon (Eds.), *Intuition is not enough: Matching learning with practice in therapeutic child care* (pp. 28–39). London, England: Routledge.

# 2

**Part 2** of *With Children* focuses on an exploration of core concepts of child and youth care from perspectives that range from practice oriented to profoundly theoretical. In Chapter 5, Jack Phelan reminds us of the more fundamental elements of good practice, characterized by a commitment to relational approaches and the use of a developmental lens. Phelan critically explores the presence of power and control within everyday practice across settings where children and youth are being cared for outside of their families, and he provides practical translations of highly complex ideas and thoughts. Veronica Pacini-Ketchabaw pushes the envelope in her analysis of relationships, a concept so central to child and youth care practice and theory that invoking it has become almost banal. Unless, of course, one is prepared to take another look at relationships in ways that we rarely do: Pacini-Ketchabaw focuses on human–nonhuman relationships and challenges us to think differently.

Janet Newbury takes us on a journey through the global political economy to bring us back to a place where we can conceive of children's services and youth programs without the rhetoric of funding pressures and resource shortages. She not only tackles the operational barriers to developing meaningful services, but also takes on the very core of the global political economy and its built-in biases toward rationalized and largely economically driven discourse on being with children. Finally, Ben Anderson-Nathe tells of the challenges of speaking the language of child and youth care practice in a post-secondary education context founded on other disciplines and resistant to different ways of talking about practice. ●

# Chapter ⑤

# Thinking through a Relational and Developmental Lens

JACK PHELAN

**CYC literature in the twenty-first century** has rethought some fundamental aspects of the helping transaction, particularly when we describe the relationship goals and developmental frameworks that practitioners use in the life-space work that attempts to help abused and neglected youth and their families. This chapter will explore some of the implications of this revised view of CYC practice.

## Relational and Developmental, No Problem

EFFECTIVE CYC PRACTICE is both relational and developmental. The common-sense way of putting these ideas into practice is to recruit someone who loves children and youth, or at least is appealing and wants to be liked. Also, the individual should have a good set of values about what are normal and proper behaviour and attitudes for youth.

One of the more obvious ways to understand relational skill is having an attractive personality, so that the CYC worker can develop many relationships with others. Early CYC literature (Brendtro, Trieschman, & Whittaker, 1969, p. 57) discussed the need for CYC workers to be desirable role models for youth as a method of creating behaviour change. Some CYC practitioners had a goal of developing the most relationships with youth as a benchmark of how effective they were. Being seen as the most popular counsellor or getting post-cards or phone calls after youth returned to the community, for example, were proof of having good relationships. This conception of relational has been challenged by many recent thinkers, and rightly so. For the past fifteen years, CYC literature has focused on more complex understandings of the relational work required, which I will describe more fully in this chapter.

Developmental ideas have also shifted from an earlier model, which used developmental information to measure just how far from "normal" the youth had strayed. Educational programs trained CYC students to compare normal developmental behaviours and attitudes with the different ways that youth who have suffered abuse and neglect act. This conception of development focused on problems and deficiencies, with a goal of moving the youth toward the correct way to function, based on age and a socially appropriate behavioural model. The CYC practitioner took the position of being the expert who knew what the youth needed to look like when he or she was "fixed" (Davison, 1995, p. 229).

Unfortunately, creating behavioural change based on imitation and using developmental benchmarks to set goals for growth have not resulted in successful outcomes for most of the youth we serve.

Recent CYC literature describes the normal and logical thinking that occurs for these youth and their families because of their developmental dynamics. The challenge for effective practitioners is to appreciate the life position of the youth and to join him or her at that place. The role of coach, behaviour modifier, and promoter of normal is no longer an effective model.

Mature CYC practitioners use developmental frameworks to see the world from the logic of the youth, and relational skills to create connections that attempt to bridge the gap between the adult's perspective and the youth's beliefs about how to live successfully.

Using developmental perspectives to understand youth rather than diagnose problems has been a more recent way of using these frameworks to do effective life-space work. Relational approaches that emphasize respect for the beliefs of the other, rather than being a role model or expert on life, are now proposed.

## Safety and Control

SAFETY AND MANAGEMENT OF BEHAVIOUR are major goals in most CYC agency mandates. Many youth and families who come to us for help are behaving badly, often endangering themselves or others. Many of these young people will not voluntarily stop behaving badly without some external control, and this is often the initial approach needed. Safety is a fundamental part of the helping process for both sides. Yet the use of external control to create safety also creates an imbalance in the helping transaction, which is not useful. Therefore, the paradox of building a safe space by taking control so that helping can occur needs some analysis. How can safety be established and maintained without poisoning the helping relationship?

Destructive behaviour is not useful, and it can be dangerous for lots of reasons. So preventing dangerous and destructive activities is an important part of providing help. How we think about safety may provide us with some guidance.

Safety does not create change or learning—it merely provides the space or opportunity to unpack the tools or medicine needed to be helpful. Safety reduces fear and anxiety, allowing people to focus more fully on what they really need. Promoting a safe environment does not require a theory of change; in fact, a program or philosophy based solely on safety is really a theoretical no man's land that ignores change or growth in favour of stability and control.

Recent CYC literature has re-examined the focus on behaviour and external control, since a truly developmental and relational approach often conflicts with these methods (Holden, 2009; Phelan, 2008).

## Life Space

LIFE-SPACE WORK is not like office-based counselling; the helping process is more physical, intimate, and mundane (Smith, 2009, p. 123). The boundary dynamics are challenging because they do not occur in an artificial environment, separate from daily events. The issues and tasks are more physically practical, such as getting out of bed or going to school or work. The helping transaction can involve attending a court hearing together or visiting the food bank. Nurturing and physical caring, laughing or crying together, or just sharing space (hanging out) can be meaningful interactions. The term *client* does not resonate in effective life-space work, because it puts up an artificial barrier between people that creates an arm's-length view of the other person and denies the mutuality inherent in how CYC practice occurs. Many models of helping have been developed to be used in an office setting, which is a neutral place but not a natural place. The unpredictable dynamics and lack of environmental control present in the life-space challenges the helper in unique ways.

We are bombarded in our own literature with statements that CYC practice is relationally based, and that our main tool is the relationship we establish with the youth and/or family. Yet our understanding of this relationship work is poorly articulated, both within and outside of our professional circles. Mature practitioners absolutely appreciate the paradox of working relationally with people who have been marginalized and punished mainly because of their fundamental inability and unwillingness to be in relationship with others. In fact, mature practitioners know that the biggest professional hurdle to overcome is connecting, because it means leaving behind one's own safe coordinates, which balance and support living successfully, and choosing to join people in dangerous, frightening, and lonely places.

The closest vocational parallel is people who do rescue work, finding stranded or marooned travellers in dangerous places. The youth and families we serve often act the way they do because of *where they are, not who they are*. When people are in survival mode, they become very reactive and self-protective, without any need for social rules and mores. Our youth and families need someone who can join them in these dark places, not just offer advice from afar. The real skill in describing our work is to articulate the first step out of danger, not the eventual safe destination.

An additional complication, based on attachment dynamics and mistrust beliefs, is that there is a reluctance to signal the need for a rescuer, because being vulnerable inevitably leads to being victimized. Picture a youth who has fallen into a deep hole, yet is unwilling to cry out to passersby for help because he believes that they will laugh at him and perhaps throw things down at him for sport.

So what is needed is a professional who can physically and emotionally join with the other person's reality, remain safe and confident in spite of the danger, and display the tools and skills to move toward a better place. Life-space work at this level of connection is what effective CYC practice is all about.

Mature practitioners cannot imagine doing CYC work anywhere else than in real life-space situations. They do not picture the life space as an unpredictable, anxious place, or as a chess game where one is always planning future moves, but as a rich, complex energy field where they are fully engaged. When faced with challenges, they look inside, not outside, for solutions. Creating connections with others is totally reliant on how *you* are, not how the other person is. Opportunities for engaging are everywhere and do not need to be preplanned. Structures, routines, rules, and events are background, and emotional energy is foreground. The act of caring and building connections creates the healing and growth required for successful living, and the mature practitioner has this focus at all times (Gharabaghi & Stuart, 2013).

Some practical examples may be useful.

- A community youth worker gradually builds stronger connections between each youth and herself, among the local group of youths, and between each youth and the community, in order to establish logical reasons to act responsibly and with social empathy. Behaviour control is unimportant, except when behaviour threatens to undermine connections. So, she becomes safe and predictable, helps youth to trust one another more, and offers opportunities to contribute to the community. Typical anti-authority behaviour is challenged only when it blocks building connections. When things are going badly, she asks herself how she could be doing things differently and does not look to blame.

- Family support workers see angry, mistrustful families as trying to keep themselves safe, protecting themselves from change for good reasons. The daily chaos is a way to avoid bigger fears of loss and danger. Success will emerge when the worker gets better at joining and supporting existing relationships to be healthier, often through nurturing adults, bringing physical relief and resources, and living alongside the family without judgments or advice. Effective family support workers affect family dynamics without creating dependence on their presence.

- In residential treatment settings, the mature practitioner will slowly shift from a safe, predictable rule and routine person to a caring, individual adult, by making a favourite snack, sharing a special interest, or knowing when to back off. Soon she becomes a more substantial adult presence and can create good choices through relationship energy. After this, the real treatment work begins, and the youth sees the worker as a person who is starting to understand him and yet still likes him. As the youth expresses the pain underneath, the worker does not back away.

The actual things that mature practitioners do in daily interactions look quite simple. Bringing a loaf of bread and a colouring book on a family visit does not seem too complicated, yet the nurturing message, both from welcome food and the pleasure of mom and worker playing together by colouring, builds an experience of caring that the mother will eventually be able to transfer to her mothering energy. The timing, content, and delivery of this simple/complex learning are quite sophisticated.

Supporting an egocentric and fearful youth to both be open to nurturing and to become nurturing may involve gardening and caring for plants, or asking her to teach you a skill. The eventual activity looks simple, but the judgment about when and how to create the learning is complex.

Supporting youth to be angry, not teaching anger management techniques, can be messy and yet very productive. Unfortunately, most of our youth have excellent reasons to be angry, and the pain underneath often can be reached only after legitimizing their emotional experiences (Anglin, 2003, p. 109) Unskilled workers should not attempt this. Yet the life space offers tremendous opportunities to explore these predictable dynamics.

Mature practitioners use punishment infrequently, although it is occasionally the right response. Behaviour control is rarely the focus for mature CYC practitioners, unless safety is acutely at risk. Relationship work, when done well, increases connection and social empathy, opens youth to examining choices and egocentric logic, and develops self-control. Skilful CYC practitioners not only do relational work very well, they also resist anything that undermines this focus. Mature practitioners are often frustrated by supervisors who expect them to focus on cleanliness and good order rather than good treatment. Recent CYC literature on the life space has expanded this concept even further with the inclusion of the Internet and cyberspace as life-space realities (Gharabaghi & Stuart, 2013, p.7).

## Lunch Ideas

THE MOST USEFUL IDEAS are those that can be simply stated, are easily visualized, and lead to more complex thinking. CYC work is practised in the life space of both the practitioner and the people he or she is supporting, which is a place of straightforward, simple realities. Mark Krueger (2010) calls this "lunch ideas."

CYC practice, when it is done well, is both developmental and relational. That is, it requires an understanding of the ability and social maturity of the other person and it also requires a safe mutuality between both people, usually developed slowly through a process of trust building and caring on the part of the CYC practitioner.

It is very hard to learn how to think developmentally, because it requires you to stop assuming that others think the same way that you do. Complex descriptions such as "meaning making" (Garfat, 1998, p. 21) are built on the basic task of thinking developmentally. An example may help; every child between two and five years old thinks like a sociopath, being unable to care for anyone but themselves, yet we do not label them as such—we see it as a developmental stage that will change as they mature. When we are confronted by a teenager who is stuck in the developmental processes of a three-year-old, it is not easy to think developmentally and support her to move forward into four- and five-year-old thinking; instead, we often see pathology.

When the two-year-old shouts "No!" to every request, we are mildly challenged, but we see it as a developmental stage that is not going to be helped by fining him a dollar every time he does this; yet we often deal with profanity (an immature teen's way of saying no) in this way.

The basic difference between people who need life-space interventions, an intense method of treatment, and people who can be helped by once-a-week therapeutic conversations is developmental. The less socially aware and mature you are, the more developmental support you need and the more useful life-space work will be.

Simply put, people who are developmentally stuck at lower stages are more egocentric and unsafe in the world. We have no problem thinking about young children this way, but it requires skill and training to think about teens and adults this way. So where does relational practice fit into this?

Skilled CYC practitioners know that there is no opportunity for change and growth without building a safe relationship first. Yet this relationship alone does not create real change, even when sometimes it creates imitative behaviour, which was described forty years ago as a form of role modelling. Using relational approaches to focus on behavioural change is not really helpful, unless a developmental shift is also occurring.

Creating a safe relationship with someone supports that person to begin to see beyond him- or herself—to become less egocentric and more able to explore the world of other people safely. As a safe relationship develops, the CYC practitioner is able to discuss how he or she thinks and feels when the youth behaves different ways, and the youth is learning to take other people into consideration, to become more socially aware. This builds a social logic into the youth's critical thinking, which is less egocentric. This can happen only after the youth is able to be vulnerable (safely) in the relationship. As the youth begins to acquire a socially aware logic about how to behave, the youth starts to consider what impact he or she is having on others, which is what five- to eight-year-olds typically are becoming more aware of.

Recent CYC literature on relationship building emphasizes the creation of an "in-between space" that brings the helper out of his or her usual personality and opens up a common-ground place called "the interpersonal in-between," which is a safe meeting area where both the adult and the youth can join together (Garfat, 2008). This is not asking the youth to think like you do, or a place of role modelling, but instead a risky yet useful joining of both people's world views without judgment.

This is the foundation for connecting with youth who are living in a very desperate place by using a developmental framework, and this foundation creates developmental growth through the use of relational learning. Simple yet complex ideas.

## Thinking about Helping

HOW YOU THINK ABOUT what you are doing determines how it is done. Helping another person is both a simple and a very complex task. How I think about the task will be a critical factor, yet sometimes I attempt to help without thinking about what is happening.

When you want help and I want to help and we agree about what needs to be done, then things are easier (you have a cut finger and I have a Band-Aid). Sometimes the person needing help does not know how to ask or what help is needed, so she looks for an expert who knows more than she does. Sometimes the helper sees the need for change even though it is not understood by the other. Sometimes the person needing help knows what he needs, but the helper does not concur. Sometimes the awareness of both people about the helping process is in conflict, or the commitment to the necessary transactions is unequal.

Power and control are major dynamics for both sides in the helping transaction. Self- image and fear of vulnerability create powerful emotions, with safety and trust constantly needed by all involved. Competence is a big issue—the helper wants to come across as skilful, and the other person wants to be respected as capable also. Helpers see the need to be willingly invited to create influence, while the other person is trying to be vulnerable and powerful at the same time. The helping dance is a delicate balance for both partners. When either person believes that he or she must always be in control of the helping relationship, then that person is thinking badly. The willingness to let the other dancer lead occasionally has to happen (Krueger, 2004, p. 15).

Unfortunately, there is a power imbalance in our helping interactions. The adult helper needs to continually monitor his or her use of power.

## Power Is Naturally Fearful

THIS HEADING comes from an article I recently read on the Spanish Inquisition and its cruelties (Gopnik, 2012). One sentence stands out for me: "The values of tolerance are one of the most difficult lessons to impart, not because people are naturally cruel, but because power is naturally fearful" (p. 70). To have power over someone else and to have the capability to keep oneself safe enough to resist being fearful seems to be necessary in order to be tolerant (open to the value of another point of view). CYC practitioners are powerful people in the lives of the youth and families we serve, and self-awareness about our powerfulness is essential.

Relationships, especially helping relationships, are complex interactions, fraught with potential for disagreements. When you add the naturally occurring conflictual dynamics of adults and teenagers, there is a high need for tolerance and open-minded humility. Building bridges and connection are much more useful than trying to impose beliefs and controls.

Power and control are major dynamics in the connections we create with others, and safety and trust are constantly on the mind of both people in the helping process. Helpers see the need to be willingly invited to create influence, while the other person is trying to be vulnerable and powerful at the same time. The need for control often dominates the thinking of both sides. Both people often think that they know better (think more accurately) about what is needed, which is actually not a problem, because they are both right in their own way. In fact, the process of creating an open discussion exploring the "rightness" of each point of view will be the most helpful approach.

It is the beliefs and thoughts about power and control that block the helping process, not who knows better about what is needed (whose truth is correct). Relational CYC practitioners believe that the youth is the expert on himself, and if there is a real connection, it is based on a respect for the logical choices that have been made in the past, even though they were not the most socially useful. It is hoped that the adult can enrich and expand the youth's perspective, by creating a bridge that allows both views of the world to be honestly examined. The ability to create an open dialogue that compares the best fit for each person's set of facts and logic to the situation at hand is what is needed.

Power is naturally fearful, to return to our theme, and the ability to control our fear is a key helping skill. Fear is focused on self, not the other, with fight or flight being the normal response. When there is a power imbalance in a relationship, which is typical of CYC interactions, then fear and reactive responses are natural. The helper, feeling unsafe, will focus on his own needs and use the power imbalance to impose control, while the youth, feeling unsafe, will react to the power imbalance with a fight-or-flight response.

Mature CYC practitioners can manage the natural fear that having power (and responsibility for control) creates through personal confidence in professional competence that comes with increasing experience. Tolerance, humility, and the ability to bridge differences do not exist in fearful situations, so skilled CYC helpers can manage both their own and the other person's natural fearfulness.

Being an effective helper will require a rigorous and regular examination of the dynamics of power, fearfulness, and personal safety. Being in control of yourself does not really require you to be in control of the other person or the rightness of the opinions considered.

## Knowing More

BOTH PEOPLE OFTEN THINK that they know better (think more accurately) about what is needed, which is actually not a problem, because they are both right in their own way. The humility and respect displayed by the helper, sometimes labelled a "one-down" stance, is not just a technique but a fundamental belief system about people that is essential, especially in life-space work. Each of us is the expert on our own lives, and effective helpers support people to discover the answers from inside the self. So it is beliefs and thoughts about power and control in relationships that block the helping process, not who knows better about what is needed (whose truth is correct).

Recent CYC literature discusses postmodern views as useful for our practice, which emphasize that there is not just one way to arrive at truth, and question whether it is even helpful to focus on truth, since truth is quite relative (Skott-Myhre & Skott-Myhre, 2011, p. 43). The formulation of what is assumed to be true is often merely the logic and world view of the group that happens to be more powerful.

## Logic

EXPERIENCE IN JOINING WITH PEOPLE where they live and breathe creates an expanded awareness in the CYC practitioner. Abused and neglected youth do not share the logical perspective of a safer, more connected person. The expanded awareness that develops in a truly developmentally trained CYC practitioner creates a respect for other ways of viewing events in the life space, which helps him to relax his logical paradigm. In effect, he starts to see the complexity in the thought that "my logic is the only way to be logical, except for your logic."

When my wife and I have differing opinions, which happens sometimes, I try to show her that she is not being logical. This argument never seems to work, even though it makes perfect sense to me. In fact, she often responds that I am not being logical, then describes her "truth," which is not logical at all to me. I also believe I have a few suggestions that would improve her as a person, which she also rejects, often with several of her own suggestions about how I might improve. This, of course, does not seem logical or useful to me. Perhaps my experience resonates with some readers who may also be challenged by their partner's logic. We all have our own beliefs about the world around us, which creates our logic and reasoning.

I will describe the concept of humility, which is the ability to stay curious and unthreatened when confronted with attitudes and beliefs that contradict your own cherished ideas about life truths. The skill needed is to build bridges between my logic and yours, not to convince you that my logic is better.

Youths who have suffered abuse and neglect usually have a logic about life truths that challenges most of our *socially appropriate* norms and rules. In fact, when I have tried to use my logic about relationships, social rules, and even what is fair and just, their response has been quite frustrating. The more I appeal to common sense (my logic), the more annoying and obstreperous the other person seems to become. Often I can get other CYC people on my team to agree with me about my logic, but even the weight of our collective logic fails to be convincing to these youths.

I find that logical consequences, so cherished by me and the rest of the team, often do not fit the logic of the youth, and the frustration evident in the youths' responses mirrors my frustration at their lack of understanding (i.e., my logical perspective) of what is happening. I also regularly describe in reports, treatment contracts, and daily logs the logical suggestions that I have created for how they can improve as persons, which I can make them sign, but they do not seem to "own" them (see above description of my wife).

Rather than trying to get the youth to be more logical, I started to realize that they were very logical already, and that I needed to create bridges between our differing logic about how the world works. This is not an easy task in any relationship, but it is especially difficult when our beliefs are potentially so divergent. Fortunately, one of us is actually getting paid to be more understanding, so the task, while difficult, is possible. Humility is the first step.

## Humility

CYC PRACTITIONERS are aware of the laundry list of skills and abilities that have been compiled over the years by employers, academics, and professional bodies in an attempt to quantify the qualities of an effective CYC professional. The telephone-book-sized documents make the typical saint look quite average by comparison.

At the risk of adding to the unmanageable, I would like to discuss humility as a key ingredient.

My favourite postmodernist couple, Hans and Kathy Skott-Myhre (2010, p. 8; 2011, p. 44), often reject the use of developmental approaches in our work because it contains a built-in assumption of superior knowledge in the helper. This belief destroys any genuine relational possibilities in the helping process because of the unequal power in the relationship. I admit it took me a while to absorb this idea in a useful way, but I now see it as a helpful perspective. This is where humility becomes important.

Humility is the ability to stay curious and unthreatened when confronted with attitudes and beliefs that contradict your own cherished ideas about life truths. Respect for the other person is an essential piece, but the courage to not react defensively is also important.

Culturally different people challenge our humility, as do people with different political and religious views. The usual response to people whose beliefs differ from ours is to tolerate their right to that opinion because we are not responsible for what they believe. However, this is not true when our own children are involved. Parents often try to shape and create values and beliefs in their own children that mirror theirs.

CYC practitioners are in powerful and parental roles much of the time in their work. Sometimes the need to be controlling is a requirement foisted upon them by employers or funders; other times it is a personal need. Unfortunately, the youth and families sent to us for help need us to be humble and respectful of the differences between us rather than powerful and controlling. So far in their lives, everyone who has been challenged by the different, often asocial and illegal behaviours they display has tried to coerce them to change. Telling these youth and families to act differently has not been helpful, even when the teller has great power and influence.

The same person who would not tell someone of a different culture, religion, or political persuasion to be more like them often does exactly that when working with vulnerable people who think and act differently. Just because we have the power to control people is not a good reason to do it.

Safety is an important issue when working with youth and families, and I am not advocating standing by passively when people are creating dangerous situations. However, safety does not create change—it only creates safety. If your goal is to support change, then you must do much more than just control the situation for safety.

Humility leads to curiosity about differences. Our approaches should build bridges between our differences instead of avoiding or trying to eliminate differences altogether. Our helping assumptions and intentions need to be regularly examined and challenged in team meetings so that we do not try to manage our anxiety about what is challenging about the other person's beliefs by forcing our framework onto them (Gharabaghi & Phelan, 2011).

Many youth and families in our care have no hope that the future will be better than the past, so they live in the moment, which creates lots of difficulties. When we tell, yell at, counsel, and modify them through our power position, it does not create bridges between our differences. It may be very challenging to respect a person who lives in the moment, trusts no one, and values little that does not personally benefit him or her immediately.

Humility, the ability to stay curious and unthreatened when confronted with attitudes and beliefs that contradict your own cherished ideas about life truths, is a quality that consistently will keep you focused on the real goal of helping, which is to create bridges and new understanding for both you and the other person. This may not sound like a particularly difficult task, so let me provide a concrete example.

## Logical Lying

Well-functioning youth do not tell lies. Also, a youth who respects a particular adult would not lie to him. People do not lie when they will be easily caught in the deceit because they want to protect their reputation. The logic in all these statements is fairly obvious.

The familiar Johari window metaphor is useful here. We are most lacking awareness when we enter the quadrant of our self, which is the area labelled "what you don't know and you are not aware that you don't know it." Mark Krueger (2004, p. 8) has described effective CYC practice as being able to dance well with the youth or families—in other words, to match their rhythm and energy as we attempt to engage with them. I believe that many CYC practitioners and agencies believe that they are good "dancers" because they have never seen anyone dance better, but in fact they are not dancing well at all.

I want to pose a regularly occurring interaction between a CYC practitioner and a youth as an example of this state of benign ignorance. It occurs because behavioural events are more powerful than developmental awareness when the practitioner is not supported to understand how to do relationally based, developmental CYC practice. Unfortunately, there is enormous support for a behavioural view because a great many people doing CYC work do not know that they are making major mistakes in how they interpret and respond to the people they are supposedly trying to help.

Picture this interaction: a youth comes home after school, and the CYC practitioner greets him and asks about his day at school. The youth states that he attended all his classes and things were okay. Both the youth and the worker are aware that the school reports any absences every day before 5 p.m. The CYC practitioner gets a call from the school stating that this youth was absent for the entire day. Discussions later on, both with the youth and with the other workers, will be focused on this "lying behaviour" and perhaps adding adjectives like "pathological" or "bald-faced." The case plan for this youth will include lying as a major issue to be modified or eliminated, using behavioural reinforcements (punishment), as well as guilt inducement. The illogical thinking of the youth (he knew I would find out the truth in another hour) would be further evidence of how troubled and untrustworthy the youth is. This interaction would cause the CYC workers to be more suspicious of this youth's ability to be helped.

Awareness of moral development theory would create a very different result. Abused and neglected youths have a much more self-protective logic about right and wrong; they do not evaluate good and bad behaviour by how it affects others, only how it affects themselves. So a behaviour is good if it keeps them safe from harm, and a behaviour is bad if it creates punishment. When the youth was questioned about school, he was doing a good thing to say that he attended all day. It would have been *morally wrong* for him to freely admit to being absent, since that would have resulted in him being punished. The fact that the school was going to call later is irrelevant in his decision, and he truly believes in the moral correctness of his behaviour. Punishment and guilt are useless responses, since they only further convince the youth that you both do not understand him and do not know how to help him.

When the CYC practitioner misinterprets this behaviour as lying, he is totally misjudging the intent and moral correctness of the youth, and the youth is very aware of this lack of understanding between them, although the practitioner is not (he doesn't know what he doesn't know). Relational connections between them are weakened, and the youth's trust in the helper being able to help him is diminished.

This simple transaction occurs daily with abused and neglected youth, and our "not knowing" response prevents us from being helpful.

The use of humility, the ability to stay curious and unthreatened when confronted with attitudes and beliefs that contradict our own cherished ideas about life truths, is needed regularly if we are to be successful helpers. Using developmental awareness here will prevent relational damage, and any adult resentment based on our own life logic will not be helpful.

A skilled practitioner knows that it is not helpful to ask questions that put both the young person and himself in a no-win situation. He knows better than to ask any questions that will require the youth to incriminate himself.

Let me continue with this line of thinking about being relational and developmental with another example. I will be posing a residential program example, but be assured that the setting can be modified to a school, street corner, hospital, or family home.

I have lived in the CYC world for many years and I often see practitioners misjudge, often by overestimating, the developmental capacity of the youths and families we serve. The result is frustration on both sides and relational resistance building for everyone involved. One of the usual situations that create this relational disconnect is when a worker is using *logical consequences* (a jargon term that we have all come to accept without critical review) to teach a youth to be more sensible. Let me pose a situation:

A youth in a group home is expected to wash the dinner dishes before going out for the evening. He is given a choice by his worker to do them immediately or to have a short break before starting. All his friends are heading for the park right after dinner, and he goes with them, unable to resist the pull of his friends, leaving the dirty dishes in the sink. The worker is upset with this turn of events and ends up washing the dishes himself. When the youth returns a few hours later, the worker angrily confronts the youth and gives him a logical consequence of doing two chores the next day.

Unfortunately, this youth does not see the logic in this and storms away, to brood and grumble about how unfair this is. The worker is feeling quite justified and blames the youth for not thinking logically, perhaps even commenting on this youth's inability to grasp the obvious in his logbook entry. The worker does not reflect on how this event has damaged his relationship with the youth and may even see it as a step forward, citing realistic boundaries, and so forth.

Humility, as I have previously framed it, is the ability to stay curious and unthreatened when confronted with attitudes and beliefs that contradict your own cherished ideas about life truths. The goal is to build bridges between my logic and yours, not to force my logic onto you. The CYC practitioner, using his own belief system, sees a need for a logical consequence here and I agree with him. We only differ on what the logical consequence actually is. I would suggest that the problem here is that this worker overestimated this youth's ability to have enough self-control to resist the temptation to leave with his friends, and as a result of this the consequence is that the worker had to do the dishes, which is very logical to both of them, and the teaching value of the consequence will be useful for the worker.

A conversation between the young person and the worker can follow this incident, with the worker expressing disappointment in the youth's lack of maturity, perhaps stating that the worker has overestimated the youth's ability to make good choices. Ideally, the young person would feel the need to convince the worker otherwise.

When workers are trained to be developmental and relational, then the problem here is an overestimation of the maturity of the youth, and this is the CYC practitioner's issue as much as the youth's. Valuing a relational connection as a crucial part of the helping dynamic would stop a worker from deliberately doing anything to weaken this bond.

I can hear the groans and protests about letting the youth get away with something. I want to invoke your ability to be humble, and then think about the relational cost and physical effort required to implement the double chore logical consequence. Reflect on how it will actually make the worker less able to think developmentally, because it is an unsophisticated and self-centred response, more focused on the worker's needs than the youth's. Now I can hear the whole team, perhaps including the supervisor, commenting on how I probably never worked with difficult youth, and I can assure you that I did. New or untrained workers should not try this skill of humility until they are safe within themselves around these difficult youth, but skilled CYC practitioners can smile and see the logic in this and similar consequences that occur when we misjudge youth in our attempts to create life lessons.

## Conclusion

EFFECTIVE CYC PRACTICE is both developmental and relational. Our shift in emphasis over the past fifteen years has been to see youth and families as complex, competent people who do not require instruction and external control, but rather developmental growth and relational connection. The focus has shifted from the youth to the professional practitioner and his need to be able to join people in dark and fearful world views, then to support them to safely move toward a more satisfying destination. The concept of the reflective practitioner, open to the influence of the other person and willing to be fully present, has been developed in many different places in CYC literature.

The thinking of many different writers and thinkers such as the El Salto group has resulted in a direction for new research and CYC training that will continue to expand and develop for many more years. ●

REFERENCES

Anglin, J. (2003). *Pain, normality and the struggle for congruence.* New York, NY: Haworth Press.

Brendtro, L., Trieschman, A., & Whittaker, J. (1969). *The other 23 hours.* Chicago, IL: Aldine.

Davison, A. (1995). *Residential care: The provision of quality care in residential and educational group settings.* Hants, England: Arena.

Garfat, T. (1998). The effective child and youth care intervention: A phenomenological inquiry. *Journal of Child and Youth Care, 12,* 1-2.

Garfat, T. (2008). The inter-personal in-between: An exploration of relational child and youth care practice. In G. Bellfeuille & F. Ricks (Eds.), *Standing on the precipice: Inquiry into the creative potential of child and youth care practice.* Edmonton, AB: MacEwan Press.

Gharabaghi, K., & Phelan, J. (2011). Beyond control: Staff perceptions of accountability for children and youth in residential group care. *Residential Treatment for Children & Youth, 28,* 75–90.

Gharabaghi, K., & Stuart, C. (2013). *Right here, right now: Exploring life-space interventions for children and youth.* Toronto, ON: Pearson.

Gopnik, A. (2012, January 16). A critic at large: Inquiring minds. *The New Yorker,* 70.

Holden, M. (2009). *Children and residential experiences.* Arlington, VA: CWLA Press.

Krueger, M. (Ed.). (2004). *Themes and stories in youthwork practice.* New York, NY: Haworth Press.

Krueger, M. (2010). El Salto reflections. Retrieved from http://www.cyc-net.org/cyc-online/cyc-online-june2010-krueger.html/

Phelan, J. (2008). External controls: A child and youth care framework. *Relational Journal of Child and Youth Care Practice, 21*(1), 38–41.

Skott-Myhre, K., & Skott-Myhre, H. (2010). Parenting as/is youthwork. *Relational Child and Youth Care Practice, 23*(3), 5–13.

Skott-Myhre, K., & Skott-Myhre, H. (2011). Theorizing and applying child and youth care praxis as politics of care. *Relational Child and Youth Care Practice, 24*(1–2), 42–52.

Smith, M. (2009). *Rethinking residential child care: Positive perspectives.* Portland, OR: Policy Press.

# Chapter

## Crafting and Uncrafting Relationships in Child and Youth Care
### Human–More-Than-Human Encounters

VERONICA PACINI-KETCHABAW

*How do the differently situated human and more-than-human actors and actants encounter each other in interactions that materialize worlds in some forms rather than others?*

—Haraway, 1997, p. 130

**"Being in relationship with children"** shapes, moulds, and dominates conversations in child and youth care. Humanism flourishes in many of these discussions; the focus is on human relationships—mostly youth–adult or child–adult relationships. In my practice with children, however, I have found that being in relationship involves more than humans. Some examples that matter in the context of child and youth practice include clocks (see Pacini-Ketchabaw, 2012), doors (see Skott-Myhre, 2012), a glob of paint and a chunk of clay (Kind, 2010), and crayons (Kummen, Pacini-Ketchabaw, & Thompson, 2013). And then, as many of us who work with children and youth know well, there is technology. Being in relationship with children in our times involves being in relationship with technology: video games, computer games, social media, and on and on. It is this techno space I want to grapple with as I trace relationships outside the parameters of humanism. I attempt to inhabit the more-than-human worlds that are part of children's lives today as I challenge child and youth care to rethink its all-too-human conception of relationships. Because we live in a world in which the boundaries between categories such as humans and technology are blurring (Braidotti, 2011; Haraway, 1997), "the very genetic core of life itself" is changing fast (Braidotti, 2011, p. 56). These shifts are of paramount importance to a field that characterizes itself as caring for the relationships children and youth engage in. We need to find ways to engage with this relocation of the core of life itself.

In this chapter, then, I engage in a conversation with child and youth care about the kinds of relationships that feminist science studies scholar Donna Haraway speaks of in the introductory quote—human–more-than-human encounters. Specifically, I explore human–more-than-human relationships in the context of Minecraft, the virtual reality computer game that captivates my 13-year-old son and his friends. My intention is that, rather than merely critiquing such games, or children's engagement with them, this conversation presents an affirmative project for child and youth care that resists negative, neutralized, or reactive responses to the technological advancements of our times. I want to ask how we can "flourish together in difference without the telos of a final peace" (Haraway, 2008, p. 301). I am inspired by Donna Haraway's work as well as the work of other feminist theorists, such as Rosi Braidotti and Karen Barad, and of Indigenous scholars Marie Battiste and James Youngblood Henderson. I take seriously Haraway's question above and propose that we expand the child and youth care conception of relationships centred on humans. What might child and youth care become when we take human–more-than-human encounters seriously? My goal is not to construct a mastery project of the best and most effective of these encounters, one that is ultimately accomplished. On the contrary, my project is to work toward the impossibility of completion and engage instead with what Haraway calls grapplings, worldlings, and entanglings. My project is future oriented as opposed to closure oriented; it attempts to evoke ways of relating rather than to define or explain what relationships mean or ought to be.

The chapter is also inspired by the title of this book, *With Children*. I have given much thought to what being *with* children, working *with* children, and playing *with* children might entail in a time of ecological catastrophes, intense neocolonialism, and unprecedented technological change (see de Finney, Gharabaghi, Little, & Skott-Myhre, 2012). Child and youth care literature has taught me about being in relationship with children (Fewster, 2010; Garfat, 2003; Garabaghi, 2010), and I take this concept of relationship as both important and necessary. I want to grapple with the messiness of relationships and suggest that relationships become in the form of entanglements, and thus lack clarity (see Skott-Myhre, 2012, for a similar project). What do relationships afford in the slippery times in which we all live out our mundane day-to-day lives? Who is in relationship with whom? What kinds of subjects are created through these relationships? How messy are these relationships? How do I live in these relationships?

Haraway (1997) challenges me to engage with these questions through thinking and remaking encounters in actual, situated worlds. By *situated knowledges*, she refers to knowledges that are "reliable, partially shareable, trope-laced, worldly, accountable, noninnocent" (p. 138). Situated knowledges are about partial connections and mediated positions. This positioning "implies responsibility for our enabling practices" (Haraway, 1991, p. 193). Through the practice of situated knowledges, I join many people and things, but without claiming to be others: "The knowing self is partial in all its guises, never finished, whole, simply there and original; it is always constructed and stitched together imperfectly, and *therefore* able to join with another, to see together without claiming to be another" (p. 193). Haraway (1991) defines *objectivity* or *rational knowledge* as engaged knowledge that is always situated somewhere. She notes that it's impossible "to be from everywhere and so nowhere, to be free from interpretation, from being represented, to be fully self-contained or fully formable" (p. 196). Instead, she says that objectivity "is a process of ongoing critical interpretation among 'fields' of interpreters and decoders" (p. 196). I like when she reminds us that "rational knowledge is power-sensitive conversation" (p. 196).

In the spirit of situated knowledges, in this chapter I adopt a diffractive and interrogatory methodology in which the goal becomes to interfere and shift patterns (Haraway, 1997) in conceptualizations of relationship in child and youth care. *Diffraction*, a term from physics, forces light apart so that we see the different wavelengths—in other words, the constituent parts of light.

By forcing these apart, we can see that things are much more complex than when we take a reflective stance. Working diffractively can help to move us away from the fixity that may arise when reflection is enacted as self-expression, which tends to "hold the world at a distance" and maintain boundaries (Barad, 2007, p. 87). In this chapter I attempt to produce something different, not "a reflection of the same displaced elsewhere" (Haraway, 1997, p. 16), as I work diffractively with relationships. I want, as Haraway (1997) says, to see the action in relationships-in-the-making.

## Our "All-Too-Human" Relationships

IN HARAWAY'S MOST RECENT TEXT, *When Species Meet*, she humorously and seriously asks, "Whom and what do I touch when I touch my dog?" (2008, p. 3). Following her lead, I ask, perhaps not so humorously, Whom do I touch when I touch Minecraft? What worlds materialize in this game that intrigues my son? What humans and more-than-humans materialize in these worlds?

I find Haraway's conceptualization of relationality a productive space for thinking about relationships. When she refers to relationality, she deliberately shifts common understandings of specific entities/categories coming into a relationship: everything is intertwined and categories/entities are relational, she notes. Following physicist Karen Barad (2007), Haraway (2008) sees potential in the term *intra-acting* because it involves "the mutual constitution of entangled agencies" (p. 33). Barad (2007) distinguishes between interaction and intra-action, highlighting the productive aspects of relations: "In contrast to the usual 'interaction,' which assumes that there are separate individual agencies that precede their interaction, the notion of intra-action recognizes that distinct agencies do not precede, but rather emerge through their intra-action" in their mutual entanglement (p. 33). Thus it is through intra-action that particular material articulations of the world become meaningful.

In this conceptualization of relationality, Barad (2007) and Haraway (1997, 2008) not only suggest that subjects emerge in intra-action with others (for example, categories such as children and adults emerge in the relating),[1] but they provocatively suggest that we not limit our discussions about relationships to human partners. Here is Haraway (1997) speaking on the need to resituate our relationships with the world:

Property is the kind of relationality that poses as the thing-in-itself, the commodity, the thing outside relationship, the thing that can be exhaustively measured, mapped, owned, appropriated, disposed.... [However] I insist that social relationships include nonhumans as well as humans as *socially* (or what is the same thing for this odd congeries, sociotechnically) active partners. All that is unhuman is not un-kind, outside kinship, outside the orders of signification, excluded from trading in signs and wonders. (p. 8)

These words are important when we live in a world of constant technological advancements and contradictions. Braidotti (2006) notes that, "given the fluid, internally contradictory and cannibalistic nature of advanced capitalism, the social and cultural critic needs to make innovations in the very tools of analysis" (p. 61). These analyses, she notes, need to cut across disciplinary boundaries. Therefore, I invite child and youth care to engage in the processes of crafting relationships with disciplinary entities (and even to dismantle these entities) and, of course, to engage in thinking about relationships as political and cultural vehicles, as Braidotti suggests.

The issue of technology is an interesting one to look at as we find ourselves in constant relationship with it. Even as I write this chapter, for example, I craft relationships with the computer as I type these words. These relationships are made even more complex as we encounter messages in the media and in academia that call for us to reduce children's "screen time" or merely to "disconnect." A few weeks ago I watched, with my students, a CBC documentary that analyzed youths' brain patterns as they used their cellphones. The researchers featured in the documentary noted that the relationships youth are having with their phones may have problematic consequences for them. That same week, my son's school newsletter instructed: "Reduce children's screen time unless it's for educational purposes." Are there good and bad relationships with technology, then?

There is no doubt in my mind that new relationships and ways of relating are being shaped right in front of our eyes/I's. The calls to be suspicious of technology in children's lives are important, and ignoring them could be dangerous. However, submitting to a simplistic critique and dismissal of the evils of technology can be equally risky. Haraway (1997) suggests that we instead become "suspicious, implicated, knowing, ignorant, worried and hopeful" (p. 3). I have learned to live in the tensions she proposes: I was raised in a Catholic home in the midst of repressive Argentinean governments; I am an immigrant in multicultural Canada, which keeps its colonial histories well hidden; I trained as an early childhood educator where we learned to simplify the complex worlds through which children learn; and I later became educated in post-structural, feminist, and post-colonial theories that taught me to read and write without a truth.

In a world in which technology is more than just playing video games, we have no choice but to become implicated in it and attend to all the troubles these explosive technologies engage us in (Haraway, 1997). To make my point clearer, I quote the description of an upcoming text by Chris Melissinos, *The Art of Video Games: From Pac-Man to Mass Effect*, in which the publisher outlines the reach of these games:

> In the forty years since the first Magnavox Odyssey pixel winked on in 1972, the home video game industry has undergone a mindblowing evolution. Fueled by unprecedented advances in technology, boundless imaginations, and an insatiable addiction to fantastic new worlds of play, the video game has gone supernova, rocketing two generations of fans into an ever-expanding universe where art, culture, reality, and emotion collide. (Random House, 2012, para. 1)

With the intention of becoming implicated in my son's relationships with technology, I join him in the world of Minecraft, a space for creating and destroying worlds. A very postmodern experience, wouldn't you say? I should mention that I am not a gamer, but I am a close observer. To this space, I bring questions without straightforward answers and, at times, without answers at all.

Computer games such as Minecraft become what Haraway (1997) refers to as knowledge-making technologies. She suggests that "knowledge-making technologies, including crafting subject positions and ways of inhabiting such positions, must be made relentlessly visible and open to critical intervention" (p. 36). I take these words as my invitation to ask, "What are the collisions, entanglements, and associations that story the worlds and friendships that are carefully crafted *with* these games as nonhuman companions?" I am not interested in describing what exactly happens to the children engaged in these games, nor in outlining everything that might be going on in this game, nor in creating a project where the game is "truthfully" described.[2] Rather, I am intrigued about what might happen when we think *with* these more-than-humans as companions in relationships. I am intrigued about what these games enact and re-enact, to use Katie King's (2012) terms. What stories are told? How are they told? What kinds of relationships and modes of relating emerge through human–techno world crafting, at what costs and to whose benefit? What connections, inclusions, and exclusions are created? More importantly, what relationships are enacted and re-enacted through playing these games?

## Minecrafting

WHILE I AM WRITING THIS PAPER, I watch my son across the room playing Minecraft. For the last four months, he and his friends have been enthusiastically crafting friendships and worlds as they play and vigorously (at times, violently) discuss their related worlds in Minecraft. Survival, creations, treasures, mobs, possessions, and enchantments become entangled in the worlds they create, live, and travel. I become troubled by what is in the midst of the comfort, obsession, and joy I sense as they play and discuss this (gendered, racialized) game of conquest through nonviolent means. It is no doubt a place of discomfort, but also a place of productive undoings and redoings.

Collisions, entanglements, associations, and boundless imaginations are at the heart of crafting and recrafting worlds in Minecraft. Designed in 2009, Minecraft is "a sandbox construction game" (Minecraft, 2012, para. 1) that characterizes itself as taking an open-ended approach to computer gaming. One engages with it in the way one wants to engage; to begin, one simply creates an avatar. With no official tutorial (Moore, 2011), its wiki acts as the "ultimate source on information about Minecraft" (Minecraft, 2012, subtitle). The game involves "players creating and destroying various types of blocks in a three-dimensional environment" (para. 1). Yes, blocks—the game graphics are based on Lego blocks. Moore (2011) notes that games such as Minecraft extend the imaginations of designers, manufacturers, and players:

The process of becoming a Minecraft "player" extends well beyond the cybernetic interface of interactions with the game and the potential lusory attitude experienced while playing the game and features in the play of Minecraft ... a gamer subculture and participatory media activity that emphasizes a mobility of play as an experience of change and innovation. (p. 381)

I join my son and his friends and create an avatar.

## Avatars: Under, Above, and Inside the Skin

The default avatar is dressed as a "normal" boy. As a feminist well aware of post-structural deconstruction, I protest. "I want a different character," I tell my co-players. "You need a different skin," they quickly reply.

Of more than five hundred possible avatars in Minecraft, some of my options include the following: Cute Girl, Girl with Pink Hair, Nice Girl, and Bubble Gum Cutey. My fellow gamers easily shed their skins and inhabit other avatars. I choose to stay in my default skin and the trouble it produces for me. I am intrigued about the ways in which relationships to identities are crafted through skins. How do skins move us? How do skins come to matter in crafting relationships? How do skins permeate and transport relationships?

Skin is about both boundaries and permeability (Flanagan & Booth, 2006); thus it provides a productive space to think *with* about relating. Australian artist Melinda Rackham (2006), in an essay titled "Safety of Skin," asks questions that resonate with my ongoing discussion of modes of relating:

Where is the kernel or seed of the self when the body is composed of pixels? Are the ethereally coded soft bodies we inhabit in machine-produced data space different from the flesh bodies we inhabit offline? What is intrinsically unique about us as individuals when we are re-presented virtually? Without a hard shell, could it be possible to remain untouched and unmodified when we inhabit electronically constructed lifeworlds? (pp. 51–52)

These questions are posed to human-form avatars; in other words, Rackham interrogates the all-too-human presence in online gaming. Is there something here that we in child and youth care can learn? What kinds of avatars inhabit the field of child and youth care? How are our relationships with them crafted? How malleable are our coded skins? What skins do we touch and permeate? What kinds of worlds do we create, and how do we relate to those worlds?

The skin, Imperiale (2006) writes,

> is not a straightforward simple surface that covers our interiority. Rather, the skin is an organ, divided internally into differentiated and interpenetrating strata. The skin or the surface of the body is a surface of maximum interface and intensity, a space of flux, of oscillating conditions. The "surface" is more slippery than it might first appear. Questions regarding the surface of the body, it turns out, are not superficial but quite profound. (p. 265)

As "the ultimate site for negotiating our relationship with the world" (Flanagan & Booth, 2006, p. 3), skin acts as a habitat and house, but also as "a significant border, marking age, gender, and race" (p. 1). We cannot deny that artifacts such as computer games and computers themselves "form skins around us through screens and projections onto surfaces" (p. 2). Haraway (1991) asks, "Why should our bodies end at the skin, or include at best other beings encapsulated by skin?" (p. 178).

To this I would add, Why do relationships in child and youth care end at the boundaries of a self? Why do they so rarely account for bodies and corporeality, or for the skins that are implicated in relationships? Can we get under the skin of child and youth care? Is it the messiness of bodies, the slipperiness of skin that troubles us and halts our engagement with them?

## Crafting Worlds of Colonial Empire

The Minecraft wiki (2012) tells me that my "avatar can destroy or create blocks, forming fantastic structures, creations and artwork" (para. 1). The game can be played "across the various multiplayer servers in multiple game modes" (para. 1). The simplicity of the game is brilliant. Its complexities bring communities together to find out its boundless possibilities.

I enter what Braidotti (2006) refers to as "the ethical temperature or fibre of our era, also known as the technologically driven historical phase of advanced capitalism" in which paradoxes, however, "multiply all along the way" (pp. 1–2). I search for raw resources: iron, coal, stone, diamond, gold, leather, fire, dust, wheat, mushrooms, sugar cane, and more. Each material has certain temporal and spatial durability, and each provides a different kind of protection. I accumulate capital in the form of resources, and I can mould this precious capital into things that improve my situation through a kind of hoarding. With all of these raw resources in hand, I follow recipes to craft tools—or weapons, depending on how you see it. I need these tools and weapons to survive, to protect myself. I'm on my own in the complex web of a larger community in which everyone works individually for their own good. Working to avoid the mobs and monsters that might show up in the middle of the night, I create a house and craft my possessions to protect myself. I find many useful recipes:

| | |
|---|---|
| wooden planks | bows |
| sticks | maps |
| torches | clocks |
| cobblestone | shears |
| glowstone | arrows |
| wool | helmets |
| bookshelves | chest plates |
| clay blocks | boots |
| brick blocks | leggings |
| stairs | rails |
| shovels | mine carts |
| pickaxes | boats |
| buckets | trapdoors |
| fishing rods | levers |
| compass | pressure plates |
| swords | doors |

| | |
|---|---|
| jukeboxes | cakes |
| dispensers | fences |
| cookies | books |
| music players | beds |
| discs | signs |

And then there are multicoloured dyes and multicoloured wools, among many more recipes.

The game is clearly about acquisition. How much stuff can I accumulate? And how can I use my accumulations to tear others down (including the friends I am playing with in a closed server)? Along the way, we look not only for ways to improve our livelihoods, but also for cheap ways to get what we need (or should I say what we *want*?). An online guide to crafting Minecraft recipes reminds me that "many of the items you craft in Minecraft can be visualized ... so try not to over think things" (Minecraft Crafting, n.d., para. 5). Here is its simplicity: it is common sense. But I am also reminded that "to craft an item, resources must be placed into a crafting grid from my inventory [or crafting table for crafting more complex items] in a specific pattern to create a particular item" (para. 3). Models, grids, inventories.

Tools such as inventories, grids, models, and competencies (readers in child and youth care will know what I am referring to) function toward enclosing identities (Haraway, 1997) and eventually shaping specific relationships. They bring us clarity, reliability, purity, and freedom from bias; they allow us "to get on with the job" (Haraway, 1997, p. 136). They are about spatialization "as a never-ending, power-laced process engaged by a motley array of beings [that] can be fetishized as a series of maps whose grids nontropically locate naturally bounded bodies (land, people, resources—and genes) inside 'absolute' dimensions such as space and time" (Haraway, 1997, p. 136). Once the resources are enclosed into identities, they are ready for "further exploration, specification, sale, contract, protection, management, or whatever" (p. 136).

Living in a land that was violently taken from Indigenous peoples by European colonizers, I cannot ignore the relationships that are created through inventories, grids, and models, including the objects and subjects that are crafted through relations labelled in the name of rationality and progress. I refer to the colonial, imperial project in North America. Indigenous peoples have suffered the devastating consequences of decades of colonial and imperial practices and policies that used spatialization as their tools (Battiste & Henderson, 2000). These tools allowed the displacement of Indigenous peoples from their traditional lands, the disintegration of families, the creation of reserve systems as lands were apportioned, and, even more powerfully, the stripping from Indigenous peoples of their languages and knowledges (Battiste & Henderson, 2000). In other words, through tools such as models, inventories, and grids, we engage in processes of marginalization and dehumanization of ways of knowing, being, and doing (Battiste & Henderson, 2000). I want to learn from these terrible and very real histories of conquest. As my game moves on, I continue to gather resources to place them in my grid. I find diamonds, but first I need to deal with the lava pool.

Indigenous scholars Marie Battiste and James Youngblood Henderson (2000), working at the University of Saskatchewan, tell us about this violent way of appropriating resources within the context of education. They speak of the cognitive imperialism of education, noting that Eurocentric curricula "teach that knowers are manipulators who have no reciprocal responsibilities to the things they manipulate" (p. 88). Writing with situated knowledges, Battiste and Henderson (2000) tell us about other ways of relating that rely less on manipulation, possession, and dispossession:

> From the beginning, the forces of the ecologies in which we live have taught Indigenous peoples a proper kinship order and have taught us to have nourishing relationships with our ecosystems. The ecologies in which we live are more to us than settings or places; they are more than homelands or promised homelands. These ecologies do not surround Indigenous peoples; we are an integral part of them and we inherently belong to them. The ecologies are alive with the enduring processes of creation itself. As Indigenous peoples, we invest the ecologies with deep respect, and from them we unfold our structure of Indigenous life and thought. (p. 9)

I see these relationships as generative rather than destructive, relationships that avoid all-embracing forms of relating, that grow through complexities, and that are always historically situated. Can we learn from these ways of relating *without resorting to capturing and appropriating knowledges*? What does it mean to be in relationship with knowledges? I continue to read Battiste and Henderson's (2000) text *Protecting Indigenous Knowledge and Heritage* as a challenge to our modernist perspectives about relating to knowledges. Providing, as they note, "a limited example of the transmission of knowledge," Battiste and Henderson talk about Mi'kmaw traditions on relationship:

> The Mi'kmaw language embodies relationships. How we are kin to each other is far more important than how much material wealth we have accumulated. How we treat one another and how our lives unfold within a community are more important than the amount of education or the kinds of jobs we have. So within the philosophy of the Mi'kmaw language are the notions of how we should relate to one another and how we can retain those relationships. (p. 89)

What is our relationship to knowledges in child and youth care? Which knowledges do we privilege and which do we silence? What knowledges could we generate?

### Conquest

I come back to my avatar after two days of being away from the game and find my house destroyed. Someone has smashed the floor and walls I built with crafted resources; it was blown up and robbed. I must now rebuild a new house in unknown territory. As I attempt to understand why this happened, my fellow gamers explain to me that we have not yet set up the land claim function in the server. No land claims equals freedom to take whatever we want. Yes, this is a game of conquest!

Advanced capitalism, "the ethical temperature or fibre of our era" (Braidotti, 2006), very much dictates these kinds of relations to land. Land is there to be exploited and managed; we delineate "the boundaries of land that can be possessed and juridically administered through the institutions of property, title, and contract" (Haraway, 1997, p. 137). Battiste and Henderson (2000) tell us about a different understanding of relationship to the land in this insightful example:

A very young apprentice hunter travels the land with an experienced older hunter. Learning by observation (rather than by words) what cues to use in forecasting the seasonal and daily movements of wildlife, the hunter ensures success in the hunt when animals can be intercepted reliably and with a minimum of effort. Many factors, such as time of day, temperature, humidity, the distribution of forage plants, and the movements of other species are experienced directly under varying conditions until the pupil begins to think, unconsciously, like the prey. (p. 45)

This is a relationship of reciprocity and deep knowing (being with/in the land), where the land (including animals and plants) disciplines each toward the other. All partners matter; all partners provide for and take from each other. Land is much more than property: "Heritage is learned through a lifetime of personal experience traveling through and conducting ceremonies on the land" (pp. 253–254).

What are our relationships to more-than-human others in child and youth care? How do we claim and declaim lands? What relations to lands do we privilege? Which ones do we forget and eventually silence?

Before ending this section, I want to comment on the relationship I have crafted above as I write this chapter thinking *with* Indigenous knowledges. This is my attempt to work against relativism (another form of relationship, by the way). I am working with the practice of situated knowledges, an alternative to relativism (Haraway, 1991). Haraway (1991) says, "The alternative to relativism is partial, locatable, critical knowledges sustaining the possibility of webs of connections called solidarity in politics and shared conversations in epistemology. Relativism is a way of being nowhere while claiming to be everywhere equally" (p. 191). There are, of course, many dangers in this practice of situated knowledges. It is not innocent. Writing *with* Indigenous knowledges, as I have done above, is "neither easily learned nor unproblematic" (p. 191). In this there is "a serious danger of romanticizing and/or appropriating the vision of the less powerful while claiming to see from their positions" (p. 191). I am trying to find ways of relating that are not violent. My approach to thinking with Indigenous knowledges relies on my belief that these knowledges "seem to promise more adequate, sustained, objective, transforming accounts of the world" (p. 191) because they are located and responsible knowledge claims, not just claiming to be everywhere. This is not to say that there are not unmediated or passive ways of seeing (Haraway, 1991).

What kinds of relating are generated in child and youth care through romanticization and/or appropriation of knowledges? How does relativism creep in, and what are its consequences? How can we inhabit worlds without claiming to be the other?

### Relating: Undoings and Redoings

To end the chapter, I return to Melinda Rackham's work—specifically to her "soft-skinned e_scape" called *empyrean*, in which she puts colonial enterprises into question—to provoke new forms of relating. As Rackham (2003) describes it,

> *empyrean* is the zone of electronically constructed 3 dimensional space, a virtual geography populated by textual entities, where reality is a trace, a flicker on the screen.
>
> *empyrean* is a parrallel [*sic*] universe, an etheric arena beyond space and time—the hungry void of potentiality. it is the place of emptiness where all things are possible, the realm of the spirit, embracing the folds of the soul.
>
> *empyrean* is a world of gaps and intervals, fluidly traced by interactions with others, rather than rigidly mapped by terrritorialising agents. this soft nothingness, this zero space is transversed by intensions, relations, attractions, and transitions between energetic avatars.
>
> here we are softly embodied avatars, navigating thru a series of scapes without the regular markers of order and normalcy. there is no horizon to orient oneself. there is no up or down. here in-tensions and strange attractions make sense of otherworldly, yet oddly familiar domains. (paras. 1–4)

I see in the space Rackham describes some possibilities for a world in which boundaries are blurred and the kinds of encounters Haraway refers to in the opening quotation can materialize in interesting ways. Can such a "world of gaps and intervals, fluidly traced by interactions with others," interfere with the patterns of child and youth care? What kinds of worlds can materialize through these encounters? Can we begin to deterritorialize the mapped relationships we are familiar with in child and youth care? In my view, *empyrean* provides a productive space in which to investigate "the colonization of the virtual—confronting the re-creation of urban spaces and the pioneering metaphor that has infested the Web as users try to remake online virtual space as a poor imitation of the real" (Rackham, n.d., para. 3). This is a space that has no attachments to "reality" offline—a space "of hungry voids, of gaps and environment, which has no horizon line to anchor oneself against, and no attachment to offline hard space" (para. 3). Unlike a space of representations that already determines the kinds of relations ahead of time, in *empyrean* there are no pathways to follow; one just needs to "feel" one's way through it using one's senses. However, this is not an innocent space; it brings with it "in-tensions and strange attractions" (para. 3)

Briefly inhabiting the worlds of Minecraft and *empyrean* has allowed me to engage in relationships with technology, lands, bodies, and their discursive practices, encountering those more-than-human actors that mingle in child and youth care. Working diffractively with relationships in this chapter provided a way for me to acknowledge the multiple, complex, and troubling layers of relating that exist in our contemporary politics. Through these encounters of inhabiting, visiting, and interfering, I have also aimed at crafting and uncrafting new, yet oddly familiar, modes of relating with/for/in child and youth care. These attempts have been made in the form of inquiries and interferences, and not as a final telos. I find it necessary to refuse the need to provide practice applications. Yet, for me, practice is about asking questions (that might not have concrete answers). This, then, is my contribution to practice. I have asked,

- What might child and youth care become when we take human–more-than-human encounters seriously?

- What kinds of avatars inhabit the field of child and youth care? How are our relationships with them crafted? How malleable are our coded skins? What skins do we touch and permeate? What kinds of worlds do we create, and how do we relate to those worlds?

- Why do relationships in child and youth care end at the boundaries of a self? Why do they so rarely account for bodies and corporeality, or for the skins that are implicated in relationships? Can we get under the skin of child and youth care? Is it the messiness of bodies or the slipperiness of skin that troubles us and halts our engagement with them?

- What is our relationship to knowledges in child and youth care? Which knowledges do we privilege and which ones do we silence? What knowledges could we generate?

- What are our relationships to more-than-human others in child and youth care? How do we claim and declaim lands? What relations to lands do we privilege? Which ones do we forget and eventually silence?

- What kinds of relating are generated in child and youth care through romanticization of knowledges and/or appropriation of knowledges? How does relativism creep in, and what are its consequences? How can we inhabit worlds without claiming to be the other?

Perhaps relating is simply about being in question and always accounting for the familiar and strange companions that inhabit these relationships. More importantly, crafting relationships through these questions has called me to confront our histories, humanisms, dominant knowledges, and core identities—in other words, to face these debilitating forms of relating that are so common in our times.

In my view, confronting these truths is necessary in child and youth care as we become accountable to "the differently situated human and more-than-human actors and actants [whose interactions] materialize worlds in some forms rather than others" (Haraway, 1997, p. 130). I do not know what new forms of living might entail, but I engage with this challenge as an approach to ethics and practice that I want to experiment with. What ways of relating are emerging in front of our eyes/I's? How do we respond responsibly as we gestate in "the ethical temperature or fibre of our era"—advanced capitalism? Conquest, hostility, and mutations are crafted in my relationship with Minecraft—but not, I hope, in relations in child and youth care. ●

NOTES

1   Writing in child and youth care, Skott-Myhre (2008) brings to our attention that the boundaries of categories such as child, youth, and adult become blurry when we think of them as relational.

2   There are many interesting texts that address video and computer games. For example, see Tobin (2004), Taylor (2006), and Nardi (2010).

REFERENCES

Barad, K. M. (2007). *Meeting the universe halfway: Quantum physics and the entanglement of matter and meaning*. Durham, NC: Duke University Press.

Battiste, M., & Henderson, J. Y. (2000). *Protecting Indigenous knowledge and heritage: A global challenge*. Saskatoon, SK: Purich.

Braidotti, R. (2006). *Transpositions: On nomadic ethics*. Cambridge, England: Polity Press.

Braidotti, R. (2011). *Nomadic theory: The portable Rosi Braidotti*. New York, NY: Columbia University Press.

de Finney, S., Gharabaghi, K., Little, J. N., & Skott-Myhre, H. (2012). Conversations on "Conversing in Child and Youth Care." *International Journal of Child, Youth, and Family Studies, 3*(2/3), 128–145.

Fewster, G. (2010). *Don't let your kids grow up to be normal*. Vancouver, BC: Influence.

Flanagan, M., & Booth, A. (2006). *Re:skin*. Cambridge, MA: MIT Press.

Garabaghi, K. (2010). *Professional issues in child and youth care practice*. New York, NY: Routledge.

Garfat, T. (2003). *A child and youth care approach to working with families*. New York, NY: Routledge.

Haraway, D. (1991). *Simians, cyborgs, and women: The reinvention of nature*. New York, NY: Routledge.

Haraway, D. (1997). *Modest_witness@Second_Millennium.FemaleMan©_Meets_OncoMouse™: Feminism and technoscience*. New York, NY: Routledge.

Haraway, D. (2008). *When species meet*. Minneapolis, MN: University of Minnesota Press.

Imperiale, A. (2006). Seminal space: Getting under the digital skin. In M. Flanagan & A. Booth (Eds.), *Re:skin* (pp. 265–292). Cambridge, MA: MIT Press.

Kind, S. (2010). Art encounters: Movements in the visual arts and early childhood education. In V. Pacini-Ketchabaw (Ed.), *Flows, rhythms, and intensities of early childhood education curriculum* (pp. 113–132). New York, NY: Peter Lang.

King, K. (2012). *Networked reenactments: Stories transdisciplinary knowledges tell*. Durham, NC: Duke University Press.

Kummen, K., Pacini-Ketchabaw, V., & Thompson, D. (2013). Making developmental knowledge stutter and stumble: Continuing pedagogical explorations with collective biography. In V. Pacini-Ketchabaw & L. Prochner (Eds.), *Resituating Canadian early childhood education* (pp. 125–145). New York, NY: Peter Lang.

Minecraft. (2012). Retrieved March 24, 2012, from the Minecraft wiki: http://www.mine-craftwiki.net/wiki/Minecraft_Wiki

Minecraft Crafting. (n.d.). *A guide to all Minecraft recipes*. Retrieved from http://www.minecraftcrafting.org/

Moore, C. (2011). The magic circle and the mobility of play. *Convergence: The International Journal of Research into New Media Technologies, 17*(4), 373–387.

Nardi, B. (2010). *My life as a night elf priest: An anthropological account of* World of Warcraft. Ann Arbor, MI: University of Michigan Press.

Pacini-Ketchabaw, V. (2012). Acting with the clock: Clocking practices in early childhood. *Contemporary Issues in Early Childhood Education, 13*(2), 154–160.

Rackham, M. (n.d.). *Empyrean artist statement*. Retrieved from http://www.subtle.net/archive/nabi.html

Rackham, M. (2003). *Empyrean: soft skinned e_space*. Retrieved from http://www.subtle.net/empyrean/

Rackham, M. (2006). Safety of skin. In M. Flanagan & A. Booth (Eds.), *Re:skin* (pp. 51–80). Cambridge, MA: MIT Press.

Random House. (2012). The art of video games: From Pac-Man to mass effect. Retrieved from the Random House online catalogue: http://www.randomhouse.ca/

Skott-Myhre, H. (2008). *Youth and subculture as creative force: Creating new spaces for radical youth work*. Toronto, ON: University of Toronto Press.

Skott-Myhre, K. (2012). Nomadic youth care. *International Journal of Child, Youth, and Family Studies, 3*(2/3), 300–315.

Taylor, T. L. (2006). *Play between worlds: Exploring online game culture.* Cambridge, MA: MIT Press.

Tobin, J. (2004). *Pikachu's global adventure: The rise and fall of Pokemon.* Durham, NC: Duke University Press.

# Chapter ❼

# Post-Growth Possibilities
# for Child and Youth Care

JANET NEWBURY

**The field of child and youth care** is currently undergoing what seems to be an identity crisis. What is at stake is not the profession itself, but the ability of those who care about the well-being of children, youth, and families to meaningfully engage *with* them in supportive ways. I believe it is time for us to take our own advice, step back, and consider the development of this profession ecologically (Bronfenbrenner & Evans, 2000), that is, within the larger economic, social, and political contexts in which our practices and policy decisions take place. In doing so, I believe we may uncover opportunities to chart new and exciting paths for this work in ways that are deliberate rather than reactive.

## The Great Debate

GREAT EFFORTS HAVE BEEN MADE to establish child and youth care as a profession. This effort is a response to a number of factors affecting CYC, including "the low current status of the field and the associated difficult working conditions, low pay, limited opportunities for promotion," as well as "quality of care, more autonomy of practice, and differentiation of the child care function from other services as a distinct, potent helping modality" (Beker, 2001, p. 346). As Beker points out, not all professionalization efforts are the same,

121

and how any such process unfolds is important to consider. While there is a great deal of support behind the efforts to professionalize, he recognizes that there are those who, for a variety of reasons, do not see this as an ideal path for child and youth care.

Alsbury (2010) argues that we do indeed need to critically engage with the process of professionalization of CYC. Acknowledging the culturally contingent nature of child care practices, she suggests we might "re-conceptualize professionalization through understanding the socially constructed nature of both profession and professional identity" (p. 28). In particular, she notes the ways our educational systems and professional bodies immerse us in certain discourses about our practice, thus constraining the possibilities we entertain when it comes to our roles with children, youth, and families. Unquestioningly accepting and pursuing certain definitions of what it means to professionalize can (at best) impose limitations upon our practice and (at worst) encourage us to, even unwittingly, engage in damaging, ethnocentric practices in the name of professionalization.

Observing that our efforts toward professionalization have not (as of yet) contributed to a unified understanding of what child and youth care is (nor the rewards we seem to believe will come with professional status), Alsbury (2010) urges us to reflexively engage with our practice so that we might *open up* our conceptualizations of ourselves as professionals and, in turn, the possibilities for our supportive work with children, youth, and families. She insists that such a process requires reflexivity on both individual and collective levels. This kind of critical engagement, as suggested by Alvesson and Skoldberg (2009), encourages us to try to "break away from a frame of reference and to look at what it is *not* capable of saying" (p. 270).

## Economics and CYC

WHILE WE MAY PERCEIVE ECONOMICS to be a field of study (or an aspect of society) that is distinct from CYC practice, it is worth noting that—intentionally or not—many of our existing policies and practices have developed at least in part as responses to larger economic and social forces.

As identified by Alsbury (2010) and Charles and Garfat (2009), child care has, of course, always taken place in some form or another; the professionalization of the care of children, however, can be traced to developments that emerged alongside industrialization. Thus, CYC and economic and social developments have always been deeply connected. Beker (2001) points out that economic factors also play significant roles in the current developments within the field.

In fact, the relationship between economics and our policies and practices may run much deeper than is evident at first blush. When looking at professionalization efforts that take place in other fields of practice, we can see dimensions of the process that reflect larger economic and political trends. For instance, in the field of social work, Axelsson and Axelsson (2009) observe that in order to be recognized as a legitimate profession within the larger social context, social work participated in certain processes by which areas of "expertise" could be charted out, and particular specializations of practice could be identified. These trends reflect the individualizing processes that are described as characteristic within neo-liberal political and economic systems, by which niches need to be carved in order for growth to continue (Braidotti, 2006).

While this may sound like potentially good news for the profession, Axelsson and Axelsson (2009) caution that it may not always be good news for the families who seek support from social workers. In fact, they may be increasingly likely to face the fragmentation of services (with various professionals who have specialized skills claiming expertise over different aspects of their lives). While collaborative approaches to the work might mitigate the potentially negative consequences of specialization (indeed, government funding often requires evidence of inter-organizational collaboration), Axelsson and Axelsson (2009) note that the trend seems to be moving in the opposite direction. Barriers such as "specialized languages, attitudes and values" restrict the potential for collaboration, as does increasingly territorial behaviour among professionals. "Interorganizational collaboration may be perceived as a threat" and so professionals are, instead, likely to work in isolation from one another (p. 321).

An in-depth look at nonprofit organizations (NPOs) in Nanaimo, British Columbia, indicates that economic rationalism has made its way into the very systems by which we organize many of our services. In an article entitled "Devolution of Services to Children and Families," Burnley, Matthews, and

McKenzie (2005) note that during the eighties and nineties, the government support for grassroots community initiatives that had been enjoyed by NPOs during the previous decades began to wane. As the focus at a government level was increasingly placed on managing deficits, services previously provided by governments became the responsibility of NPOs by contract. As a result, in the ensuing years the structure of NPOs has shifted notably. For instance, (1) management practices are slowly evolving to fit a more bureaucratic structure; (2) financial shifts have led to a climate of increased competition among agencies; and (3) accountability to funders has become an increasing priority, which has in turn meant that (4) instead of focusing on the *general* development and sustenance of social capital, the emphasis is now on *specific* deliverables, changing the nature of services greatly (Burnley et al., 2005; see also Albanese, 2010, for a discussion of the shift in Canada from *universal* to *targeted* supports).

While accountability at the NPO level is indeed important, these particular shifts lead to legitimate concerns on the part of executive directors about not only the ability of their organizations to stay afloat, but also the quality of services they are able to provide (Burnley et al., 2005). Even though NPOs obtain the majority of their funding through government contracts, "funders at all levels of government are concerned about sustainability of projects and are reluctant to fund projects that will require their ongoing support" (p. 76). The short-term funding that is typical of government contracts to NPOs makes long-term planning very difficult. With short-term "measurable outcomes" required for many contracts, the nature of services is shifting from prevention in general terms to more individualized, reactive, and expert-driven approaches to service delivery.[1]

Within an economic climate of simultaneous preoccupations with growth and deficit reduction, cutbacks to social services (including income assistance and legal aid) are placing a further burden on contracting NPOs, with both the numbers and complexity of clients' struggles on the rise (Burnley et al., 2005; see also Malekoff, 2010). Furthermore, because of funders' desire for evidence of accomplished deliverables, there is an increase in administration required (with less funding going toward it), which further diminishes the ability of these organizations to provide quality support for families who need it. All of these shifts—the transition of many services from government to contracting providers, the increasingly individualized nature of services, the financial cutbacks and reorganizations, and the bureaucratization of practices—reflect shifts that are taking place within a variety of other fields of practice, including education (Newbury, 2011a; Nussbaum, 2010), mental health (Teghtsoonian, 2004), and public health (Winegard & Winegard, 2011). An ecological perspective can help us better understand how these fields of practice are not entirely distinct, and how larger social dynamics play out similarly among them.

Another example of how economic rationality is finding its way into human service practices is the recent integration of "lean thinking" into health care services (Joosten, Bongers, & Janssen, 2009), with talk of it also becoming an organizational model within British Columbia's Ministry of Children and Family Development (anonymous, personal communication, February 1, 2012). Lean thinking refers to "an integrated operational and sociotechnical approach of a value system, whose main objectives are to maximize value and thus eliminate waste, by creating cumulative capabilities" (Joosten et al., 2009, p. 343). It was initially developed by the Toyota Corporation, but has been modified for use within health care (and other) settings. Celebrated by some for its efficiency (when applied in such a way that takes into account the relational dimension of health services), lean thinking approaches have been credited with such improvements as shortened wait times, reduced waste, better organization, and even in some cases lower rates of infection (Joosten et al., 2009).

On the other hand, some have expressed concern that these findings are anecdotal and even selective, and there is reason to believe that the standardization of health care practices based on lean thinking may have some negative implications (Joosten et al., 2009). Of particular concern is the emphasis this approach places on improving operational procedures, with less detailed understanding of the sociotechnical adjustments needed to ensure not only *efficiency* of care, but also *quality* of care. Indeed, according to Joosten and colleagues (2009), "research on sociotechnical dynamics in lean organizations, especially in health care, is virtually absent" (p. 345). This is a concrete example of how economic thinking and norms have come to find their way into human service practices, directly contributing to the development of more individualized responses to the struggles service recipients may be facing, and with questionable implications. Given the fact that child and youth care embraces a relational approach to human change processes, it behooves us to exercise caution before developing practices on the basis of economic models for which "sociotechnical"[2] dynamics are secondary or even absent.

## Post-Growth Economic Developments

WHILE IN RECENT YEARS economic growth has become nearly synonymous with prosperity in popular parlance, solidarity economists like Tim Jackson (2009), with his book *Prosperity without Growth*, are exploring more sustain-
able and equitable economic models. At this point I would like to temporarily step away from my reflections on recent trends affecting CYC and related human service practices in order to take a look at some of the promising alternative economic developments that are emerging in response to the social consequences of our current system. I believe that since these developments are part of the broader context in which our practices are developing, it is worth taking them into consideration (see more about contextualizing practice in Bronfenbrenner & Evans, 2000; Newbury, 2011b; and White, 2007).

Miller (2006) describes the emerging "solidarity economy" as "innovative, bottom-up experiences of production, exchange, and consumption," which have at their foundation not growth or bottom-line capitalist logic, but an interest in meeting the basic needs of communities "while cultivating democracy and justice" (p. 1). The movement emerged initially in Latin America in response to three significant trends during the mid-1980s. As Miller (2006) describes it, first there was increasing marginalization being experienced by those who were not benefiting from free market economies. Second, there was increasing cultural dissatisfaction among some of those who did benefit economically, but sought a more gratifying counterculture. Third (and related to the former), there was increasing global communication, which enabled alliances to develop worldwide. It is important to highlight the emergent nature of these developments, as they continue to unfold in ways that are responsive to ever-changing conditions and thus are not necessarily predictable.

With the convergence of diverse groups who are resisting the deterioration of social supports, the growing gap between rich and poor, and the ecological costs of the unending pursuit of growth, fertile ground has been cultivated for greater organization as well as reliable research informing alternative economic directions (Miller, 2006). These directions, it is suggested by solidarity economists (see, for example, Cameron & Gibson-Graham, 2003), are based first on a redefinition of the space we consider to be economic. Rather than involving only individuals or firms who engage with financial matters, this "socioeconomy" comprises a space that

> embraces a plural and cultural view of the economy as a complex space of social relationship in which individuals, communities, and organizations generate livelihoods through many different means and with many different motivations and aspirations—not just the maximization of individual gain. (Miller, 2006, p. 2)

This is the approach taken, for example, by feminist economists who have long been demonstrating that "non-market transactions and unpaid household work (both by definition non-capitalist) constitute 30 to 50 percent of economic activity in both rich and poor countries" (Gibson-Graham, 2008, p. 615). Once such a conceptualization of economic activity is embraced, the possibilities for what this might look like are expanded substantially. For instance, recognizing the gendered nature of the nonmarket work referred to by the figures above might suggest that opening up conceptualizations of economic activity to include these transactions could have equalizing implications for women (see Albanese & Farr, 2012). And since the overall focus of this chapter is child and youth care, which so often falls into the category of unpaid work by women, this is a significant consideration.

While different propositions for new economic directions exist—including steady state economies (http://steadystate.org/), solidarity economies (Miller, 2006), diverse economies (Gibson-Graham, 2008), post-growth (http://postgrowth.org/), and degrowth (Kallis, 2011)—the similarities in both intention and development among them are so significant that for the purposes of this chapter I will elect not to get mired in the distinctions. What is quite interesting for my purposes, however, is Gibson-Graham's (2008) observation that although economic activity that falls within this realm is so often considered marginal, these "forms of enterprise are actually more prevalent, and account for more hours worked and/or more value produced, than the capitalist sector. Most of them are globally extensive, and potentially have more impact on social well-being than capitalism does" (p. 617).

So what *is* this movement—this "economic ontology"—that might "contribute to new economic performances" in the pursuit of more just and sustainable futures (Gibson-Graham, 2008, p. 615)?

The approach put forward by Gibson-Graham and Roelvink (2011), *diverse economies*, replaces the binary between "capitalist" and "other" economic activities with an intentional inclusion of any and all diverse practices that have economic functions. Importantly, this approach does not presume equality of value of all practices; the emphasis of a diverse economies approach is on taking different economic activities into consideration without *pre*judging them. In order to help us perceive the diversity of economic practices that may be at play, these authors offer a "diverse economy framing," which includes consideration of three categories of economic activity (transactions, labour, and enterprise) and looks at each of these from various angles (from within dominant practices, as alternatives to them, and existing outside of them). From here, deliberate questions can be posed to people within a given community in order to develop a "diverse economies inventory." It is only after the inventory has been completed that deliberation around the various practices, through reflexive conversations, will begin.

The main purpose of this approach is not to replace one dominant economic system with another, but "to facilitate ethical debates about which practices foster community wellbeing and resilience and to conduct research that supports and grows these practices" (Gibson-Graham & Roelvink, 2011, p. 29). Much like Alsbury's (2010) proposition for reconceptualizing CYC professionalization, this will likely give rise to locally driven economies that are responsive to the unique conditions in which they are situated.

## If They Can Do It, Why Can't We?

ALTHOUGH VERY PRACTICAL IN ITS IMPLICATIONS, the ontological nature of this approach is important to keep in mind. Miller (2011) offers five economic principles that can serve as tools for "re-thinking the economy" (p. 3) to facilitate the ontological shifts required for such transitions to take place. He, too, reminds readers that he is not offering an alternative, but rather a way to re-engage with reality so that multiple possibilities might emerge. I believe the transitions these principles can help foster within the economic realm are similar to the directions being pursued by many within the realm of child and youth care (see, for example, de Finney, Dean, Loiselle, & Saraceno, 2011; Gharabaghi & Krueger, 2011; Newbury, 2011b; Skott-Myhre & Skott-Myhre, 2007; White, 2007). Rather than developing our profession along the lines of economic and political systems that have proven to undermine the very people we wish to support (and potentially ourselves as professionals, as the earlier discussion indicates), I propose we take a radical systemic step and follow the lead of economic activists who share our concern for the well-being of children, youth, families, and communities, placing equity and justice at the centre of our practice.

In the following section I will outline the five principles proposed by Miller (2011) and, after briefly describing their economic implications, I will address their potential implications within the field of child and youth care.

### From "The Economy" to Diverse Livelihoods

Miller (2011) reminds us that "the economy," while real in impact, is a discursive construction, a story (p. 7). As such, it holds no more power over those entrapped in it than we give it. By intentionally telling different stories, we can open up economic realities to include more dimensions of livelihood and well-being, thus eliminating many of the constraints that we have come to take for granted within our daily lives and, indeed, within current trends in CYC practice. Miller (2011) emphasizes the fact that stories of livelihood are not "alternative" stories; they are *more complete* stories—although always partial (see also Grondlin, 2011). They can include the dimensions of life for which the economy does not provide, and which it can at times destroy. Livelihood involves, for example, emotional, relational, material, and cultural dimensions of life. Livelihood includes *all* that sustains us—including, but not limited to, finances. Such an approach can give rise to the development of new, more viable measures of prosperity that take into consideration factors beyond GDP. For instance, *Earthtrends* acknowledges the importance of factoring in ecosystems when looking at the stability of productivity over time (World Resources Institute, 2005); Paul Martin (former prime minister of Canada and former minister of finance) has recently been advocating the inclusion of "natural capital" in measures of economic development ("Paul Martin on Natural Capital," 2012); and the Royal Government of Bhutan has developed measurable indicators for gross national happiness (Centre for Bhutan Studies, 2012).

The importance of story in identity construction and change processes for individuals has long been recognized (Bruner, 2004). Much of what strength-based, relational work consists of is supporting young people to learn to tell—and live—new stories about themselves (see, for example, Garfat, 2003; Hoskins & Leseho, 1996). Indeed, child and youth care practitioners are trained to help clients seek preferred stories through the guidance of narrative and other counselling modalities (Madigan, 2011; Madsen, 2007). We are also encouraged to engage reflexively with our own practice (Fewster, 1990), but I believe we might be able to do better on this front when it comes to the stories we collectively—as practitioners, educators, and policy-makers—live by.

The story of limited resources, of expertise and specialization, and of increasingly competitive professional realities within CYC is a reflection of the larger economic story being resisted by the socio-economists cited above. By broadening our understanding of economy to include livelihood, we can recognize that, in fact, we are extremely well positioned to tap into the otherwise invisible resources that surround us. If our practices are developed based on a bottom-line logic, then regardless of how vehemently we pursue professionalization, we will continue to lag. But if our practices are developed on the logic of livelihood—a logic that takes into account the diverse assets that exist in every child, family, and community—then we might just surprise ourselves at how much becomes possible.

*Person-centred* ways of supporting people with disabilities in New South Wales, Australia, provide an example of how a collective refusal to resign ourselves to existing systemic trends can make space for practices to emerge that are more in line with the ideals that inform CYC practice already. This approach to disability services is now being embraced at a state level, with a long-term (five-year) initial commitment to infrastructure development (for more detail see Ellis, Sherwin, & van Dam, 2011). This is a step that demonstrates alternatives are indeed feasible ... if only we'd start believing different stories.

## From Economy/Nature to a Community of Life

With this principle, Miller (2011) calls into question the commonplace economic assumption that the needs of the economy (jobs, growth) are at odds with the needs of ecology (health, the natural world, lands, peoples). Rather than simply reversing the argument, Miller eliminates the binary altogether, which he illustrates, once again, is discursively constructed. As he aptly points out, having to choose between doing without either jobs or a healthy natural world is a choice between "two forms of slow death" (p. 9). This is not a choice we have to make, although the current stories we live by may convince us otherwise.

According to Miller (2011), rather than submitting to this impossible choice, we might instead elect to (1) call it into question, and consider different ways livelihood can be pursued in healthy, equitable, and sustainable ways; (2) be willing to transform "our own needs and aspirations" in such a way that we recognize the unsustainability and injustice of many of our current pursuits (p. 10); and (3) continuously invent new forms of production and distribution that can provide alternative means to the wants and needs we pursue. He acknowledges that such transitions are in their infancy, but that there is good reason to believe we can indeed open up economic possibilities along these lines.

Similarly, in fields of practice committed to the well-being of children and families, practitioners and policy-makers are experiencing this sense of impossible choices: either keep organizations afloat or provide quality care. As was discussed earlier, many organizations are finding it increasingly difficult to accomplish both (Burnley et al., 2005). In a review of child protection workers who left their jobs in British Columbia, Bennett et al. (2009) discerned that over of a quarter of the former workers surveyed reported stress and burnout to be their main reason for leaving their jobs. Largely, this stress was reported as a response not to the difficulties their clients were facing, but to the child protection system itself. Respondents noted such things as high case loads, lack of support from management, and a sense that they were unable to meaningfully support their clients. All of these conditions can be seen as closely related in complicated ways to the economic context outlined earlier. This is not to say that burnout is a new phenomenon, but rather that it can be read in part as a response to broader conditions in which practice takes place. For instance, in a 1993 study of worker burnout among CYC practitioners, Savicki notes, "The uniqueness that identifies the field may reside less in the characteristics of workers or the set of skills they practice than in the placement of workers in a multidimensional, milieu-like environment with which they struggle to wrestle therapeutic, caring order from the brink of chaos" (p. 456). He recommends that in order to better support workers and protect against experiences of burnout, a better understanding of our practice in its broader social context is necessary.

In an interview, Reynolds (2011) directly challenges the way the concept of "burnout" discursively locates the problem within individuals, when clearly—as noted by Bennett et al. (2009)—this is often largely an issue of social conditions rather than the deficits of individual workers. Reynolds (2011) acknowledges the impossible choice workers often face and, like Miller (2011), invites us to collectively seek more just and equitable conditions so that workers can successfully do their jobs *and* offer meaningful support for those who seek it (which, of course, are, or should be, one and the same). She suggests that rather than "burning out," practitioners who are working in unsupportive environments in the face of immense and legitimate stresses are "blown up." Richardson and Reynolds (2012) urge that we never forget that it is our responsibility to "promote our sustainability through contesting injustice and committing to an ethic of doing justice.... If we are not working from this ethic, we risk replicating dominance and causing harm to our clients and community members" (p. 4). Finding ourselves in positions in which the jobs we are doing are at odds with the well-being of those we serve would, I submit, be in opposition to this ethic.

But, like Miller (2011), Richardson and Reynolds (2012) offer possibilities for the pursuit of a reality in which such choices cease to be part of the story we believe about our work. They provide evidence from their own experiences and those of others of the sustaining power of (1) the refusal to submit to competitive workplace logics, (2) the intentional development of communities of support within our practices, and (3) the cultivation of interests in collective well-being over individualized fixes (which locate social problems within individuals). These possibilities and resources are achievable, and once pursued they open space for those possibilities we have not yet imagined (see also Braidotti, 2006, and Caputo, 1993). Importantly, Richardson and Reynolds (2012) also remind us that "our responses to oppressive situations will be imperfect" (p. 6), but that does not mean we are not obliged to respond. It is through collective approaches to "justice-doing" that we might better face such realities, responding imperfectly, and, ideally, edge ourselves and others toward more just conditions. Just as Miller (2011) insists that sustainable and collective well-being cannot be artificially removed from consideration within the realm of economy, Richardson and Reynolds (2012) insist that we are mistaken to believe we can proceed within fields of human service practices without placing these interconnections front and centre in our work.

## Beyond "The Market" and "The State"

A third principle offered by Miller (2011) to help us toward the ontological shift he is advocating involves allowing our imaginations to extend beyond another discursively constructed binary: the dismal choice between free market rule or state rule. He once again encourages us not to be limited prematurely, and to consider other possibilities that exist (already and potentially) beyond these two. He invites us to think contextually and consider what *else* is going on before raising our hands in despair over two unacceptable options.

Similarly, within CYC and other forms of support for children, youth, and families, there seems to be an atrophy that sets in when we consider what to do amid limited choices. However, Albanese and Farr (2012) demonstrate that, in fact, there is evidence that more contextualized and socially responsive approaches to care are already going well in Quebec and in parts of the European Union. Although many practitioners are currently at a loss as to how to address the many tensions that were outlined earlier (many of them stemming from economic conditions), by drawing from these very real alternatives we may begin to see new ways of engaging in, feeling fulfilled by, and (most importantly) effectively pursuing our work. As Albanese (2010) observes (in the context of child poverty),

> The EU framework contained objectives that Canada could learn from and model. One of the most obvious was that it promoted social cohesion, equality between men and women, interaction among policies, transparency, good governance, and the monitoring of pol-

icy. Especially effective within the EU framework was that it did not
isolate the problem of poverty but instead viewed it as connected to
larger economic, social, and political issues. (p. 103)

This example demonstrates the connection between our work and economic
realities. In doing so, it reinforces our responsibility to have a voice on a political level if we wish to support children and families in ways that move in the
direction of a more equitable society.

## From Necessity to Possibility

Miller (2011) insists that "there are no 'economic laws,' and there is nothing
necessarily inevitable about economic dynamics. We make our economies,
and therefore we can make them differently" (p. 12). When we allow ourselves
to consider that the constraints by which we have been organizing our lives,
policies, and practices are not the only possibilities in front of us, the space
is opened up to put energy into not only coping within existing conditions,
but also intentionally constructing more viable possibilities (and to recognize
that these can be rendered intelligible only if we develop contextually relevant
ways of determining what is viable).

Braidotti's (2006) writing helps me to understand this, with her distinction between two types of power: *potestas*, which is the negative power under
whose weight we often feel limited and oppressed, and *potentia*, which is a
creative power by which new realities are generated. In the realm of economics, we can actively employ *potentia* with a commitment to "begin envisioning
and creating relationships and structures that make new ways of living and
new forms of livelihood more and more viable" (p. 13).

In child and youth care, we can do the same. Recognizing that in many
ways it has been economic constraints that have led us down the road of
increased competition, workloads, and isolation, as well as diminished resources—all of which, in turn, increase experiences of burnout (or "blow
up")—then perhaps these socio-economists' observations are of great value
when considering our current professional and policy developments. By rejecting bottom-line logic with regards to relating meaningfully with children
and families—which means selecting new criteria for feasibility of services

beyond economic viability as it is currently measured—we might activate *potentia* in such a way that we can be more responsive to the unique and complex individuals we encounter through our practice.

### From "The Economy" to Economic Organizing

Miller (2011) calls for a conceptual shift away from "the economy" as a static system that can be changed only by appealing to those with power (*potestas*, that is) toward "economic organizing"—which is "something that we do" (p. 14). Similarly, White (2007) has proposed a new way of conceptualizing child and youth care practice from a more static "knowledge, skills, and self" model (by which competencies are acquired or achieved) to a "knowing, doing, and being" model, which requires *ongoing* reflexivity, responsiveness, and an understanding of the dynamic nature of the situations in which we find ourselves and simultaneously co-construct.

White's (2007) "web of praxis" model has been enthusiastically embraced within the field (see, for example, Chowdhury, 2011; Derksen, 2010; Newbury, 2011b; and Sanrud & Ranahan, 2012) and has become part of the core curriculum for undergraduate students at the University of Victoria. To me this indicates that notions of our own ongoing responsibilities within the development of CYC are resonating widely. If we acknowledge that our practice occurs within this larger context of economics, and if we embrace the approaches of Miller and White, we will recognize that not only is child and youth care influenced by how economic activity is organized, but—importantly—economic organization is also influenced by how various fields of practice develop and professionalize.

We could follow the path of many professions before us and, as pointed out by Axelsson and Axelsson (2009), develop our work by identifying what is unique about it, charting out a niche, and competing for a place of prestige and recognition on the basis of our expertise. Alternatively, we could do as Richardson and Reynolds (2012) suggest, and erase the lines we have been drawing between us and our allies, recognizing that those lines do not justly serve practitioners or those we are striving to support. Instead, Richardson and Reynolds (2012) remind us that alliances can be fluid, cultivated at various points of connection in multiple times and places. By "enacting solidarity" with professional and personal allies, we can re-vision our practice in multiple ways simultaneously—depending on the unique experiences, material conditions, cultural or political contexts, and other factors to which our eyes, ears, and hearts can thus be more receptive. This, I believe, might enable us to re-envision our practices as we have been invited to do by Alsbury (2010).

## Post-Growth Practice on the Ground

IF THIS ONTOLOGICAL APPROACH IS EMBRACED, what will we then *do* differently? How do we *enact* such conceptual shifts in our daily lives?

As is likely already clear, the locally responsive nature of the approach being advocated precludes the development of literal "how-to" lists. However, there are some strategies that can be useful when embracing such a dynamic approach to not only interpersonal relationships but also to broader social, economic, and political conditions as important components of child and youth care. What follows is not an exhaustive list, but instead some fruitful possibilities.

### Asset Mapping

A strength-based perspective is often considered to be a key component of a CYC approach to practice. The value of seeking counter-narratives that highlight strengths has been widely recognized as a hopeful way to chart new paths (Ajandi, 2011; de Finney et al., 2011; Madsen, 2007; Mitchell, 2011). Asset mapping is a practical and valuable tool for mobilizing such strengths on a *collective* level which has been embraced within the fields of community development (Kretzmann & McKnight, 1997) and economics (Cameron & Gibson, 2005). It can be useful for us to consider this as a valuable tool in maintaining our commitment to a strength-based approach.

Taking the time to map assets on an organizational or even community level can help us develop our programs, services, and organizations on the basis of capacities, not limitations. Asset mapping does not presume the absence of needs, but it is an approach that operates from the assumption that needs are more likely to be met when strengths are given the attention they require to grow (Kretzmann & McKnight, 1996). On the other hand, research indicates that paying attention primarily to needs is not an effective way to address them (Cameron & Gibson, 2005). Asset mapping can train our eyes to strengths that exist within our communities which often go unnoticed when our decision-making processes are based on economic rationalism alone. Making a point of drawing from strengths, we can further realize our capacities in ways that are generative and sustaining. This kind of asset mapping can remind us not to limit our strength-based focus to individuals, but rather to think of it in collective terms as well.

Possibilities such as (1) inviting parents to join boards of directors, (2) engaging youth as peer mentors (meaning they can be not only recipients of services but also providers), (3) developing webs of mutual support among agencies in a given community, and (4) cultivating relationships with politicians on a municipal level are all ways we can mobilize existing assets in order to strengthen not only our practices, but also informal community relations. By mapping assets regularly, we can thus foster communities of support (as recommended by Richardson & Reynolds, 2012), which will sustain us in ways that enable a decreased reliance on the growth model economy. Not only may this facilitate the development of more locally responsive services, but the development of collaborations may, in turn, contribute to more just and equitable conditions down the road. Asset mapping can likely reduce the sense of crisis and individual burdens of stress that are making their way into our profession, as noted above.

It is important to acknowledge that although such efforts are being made by individuals and organizations already, they can lead to an increased burden on their time because existing systems are designed on the basis of competition, not cooperation. This is why the approach being advocated (mapping assets at a collective, community level) requires systemic change and not just new ideas to employ within existing systems. If *community partnerships* were developed on the basis of existing community assets, then the workload is shared, and so too are the resources that sustain the work.

For example, a friend of mine works in international development. He is the co-founder of a Website that is dedicated to supporting new people in the field. Most of the work they do is text based (online), although it has been suggested they get into other forms of media to widen their reach. He recently met with the community radio station, which has a program on international aid. The program was also looking for a way to widen its reach by making its podcasts available online. Instead of each organization applying for funding in order to hire people, develop infrastructure, and so forth, a *partnership* makes it feasible for them both to reach their goals without more funding, and without detracting from their existing work in order to develop these additional platforms (W. Yeoh, personal communication, February 1, 2012). Furthermore, each organization can feel buoyed by the additional support that comes with a partnership, rather than overwhelmed by the additional work it may have taken to reach these goals in isolation. This is precisely the kind of asset-based community development Cameron and Gibson (2005) advocate, and it can be seen as a logical extension of the strength-based perspective that is already an inherent part of most CYC relational practice (see Bellefeuille & Ricks, 2008; Garfat, 2003).

### Situational Analysis

I have found value in Clarke's (2005) research methodology called "situational analysis" with regards to contextualizing child and youth care practice (see Newbury, 2011b). I see it as closely related to Bronfenbrenner's ecological model (Bronfenbrenner & Evans, 2000), but as a useful addition in that it can facilitate a perspectival shift that enables us to see situations as relationally and dynamically constituted—meaning the particular child or family seeking support is not necessarily at the "centre" of activity.

Situational analysis involves mapping all the elements in a given situation (including human, material, discursive, economic, temporal, cultural, and others), as well as charting the relationships among them. This kind of mapping—particularly if done regularly over time—can allow practitioners to recognize the relational dynamics at play, and may often shed light on dimensions of the situation that would otherwise go unnoticed. Importantly, it can also serve as a regular reminder that although a client or family may be at the centre of our concern, a situation is centreless—and factors that exist outside of our clients (including economic factors or other dynamics within their community) may be playing significant roles in the struggles being experienced.

By employing situational analysis within group meetings, for example, we might better acknowledge and respond to the *social* nature of many of the difficulties our clients might be facing. We can begin "collectively re-imagining entry points into tough situations with clients, families, and systems" (Newbury, 2011b, p. 103). In order to address the systemic barriers that often cause stress for both practitioners and families, situational analysis "allows [systemic] elements of the situation to be addressed and in turn, practices such as advocacy can be considered significant aspects of support for clients" (p. 103). It is a tool that can render different realities intelligible and, in turn, create avenues by which we can address them within our practice.

By employing situational analysis, we may recognize our work as a significant part of broader social movements (de Finney et al., 2011; Miller, 2011; Richardson & Reynolds, 2012). Situational analysis can also equip us with the resources and knowledge with which to be more effective advocates for the people with whom we work. It can fuel advocacy commitments such as (1) writing letters with (or in support of) individuals or valuable community organizations; (2) supporting local initiatives that are crucial for the well-being of all citizens and which reduce the gap between rich and poor (including resource centres, libraries, and public spaces); (3) becoming involved politically (by contributing to local publications, voting, attending public meetings, and establishing relationships with legislators and public officials); and (4) participating in an "explosion of practical experimentation" that derives from the awareness that the conditions ripe for new possibilities are constantly being cultivated (Miller, 2011, p. 19). One powerful example of advocacy-as-practice is the strategic use of group work by social work agencies in a particular community in New York to collaboratively respond to economic cutbacks in 2009. These organizations drew from their knowledge of group work processes to band together and advocate for their services. Their significant efforts included (among other things) "demystifying the issues and educating group members (staff, board, community, and consumer/clients), creating talking points and protest letter templates for communicating with legislators and public officials, and developing a story to tell that would make the issues interesting and important to people that needed to be reached" (Malekoff, 2010, p. 5). Importantly, these were not efforts made on behalf of children, youth, and families—they were efforts collaboratively *enacted with* the children, youth, and families who were directly affected by the cuts, as well as other community members. With a "dual focus on individual change and social reform," Malekoff (2010) maintains that strength-based group work as advocacy relies on the direct participation of those most affected (p. 6).

Contextualizing our practices economically and politically in these ways, we might resist the pressure to place the child or family at the centre of every intervention, and, as in the example above, refuse to be limited by the constraining choices often offered to us from within economic frameworks of feasibility.

## The Deliberate Use of Language

The deliberate use of language can be considered one of the greatest tools to which we have access in terms of cultivating different realities. Both of the strategies above—asset mapping and situational analysis—rely on it. However, Coates and Wade (2007) contend that power operates through language in such a way that it can also serve to "impede effective interventions through education, victim advocacy, reportage, law enforcement, criminal justice, child protection, and counselling"—unwittingly privileging those who have power (such as perpetrators of violence) over those who do not (such as victims) (p. 521). They remind us that written accounts of situations—such as incident reports—are not objective representations of reality but, through the language employed, can conceal or highlight certain aspects of the situation, thus making a strong case for the importance of informed and deliberate use of language.

There are a number of ways this influence of language comes into play in relation to the current discussion. For instance, psychiatric labels are increasingly employed in an effort to secure additional resources (financial or otherwise) for children in residential care or school settings (Cocksedge, 2012; Fewster, 2002; Moses, 2008). While a child's behaviour may be a legitimate response to particular environmental or social conditions (such as hunger due to poverty, a lack of sleep due to stress, energy due to sugar consumption), the use of psychiatric labelling individualizes the experience, and leads to interventions that are more likely to involve controlling or changing the child (through medication or counselling) than adjusting the conditions to which the child may be responding (Fewster, 2002; Wade, 2007). This is one example of how economic forces are directly transforming our practices, and how deliberate use of language (by resisting reliance on diagnostic categories) can be used as an act of resistance to this trend (see also Madigan, 2011).

Another example involves program development. As government dollars are increasingly allocated to short-term, measurable (with existing tools), and individualized services, organizations begin to include language that reflects these priorities in project proposals in order to secure funding to sustain their programs. In the increasingly competitive conditions described earlier, organizations that resist these practices are often left underfunded and in precarious situations (see Burnley et al., 2005; Newbury, 2009). However, perhaps if we collectively resist the use of bottom-line logic when developing our programs and instead commit to developing better vocabularies and tools by which we can advocate for programming that prioritizes well-being, we may see a reversal of the trends outlined earlier in this chapter. This is risky, but as Malekoff (2010) attests, there are great risks associated with not resisting these trends as well. By (1) being deliberate about the language employed when writing funding proposals, (2) developing and selecting evaluation tools that do not rely on individualizing or short-term fixes, and (3) infusing our professional artifacts (journals, Websites, incident reports, inter- and intra-agency communications, conferences, project proposals, and curriculum) with language that privileges "livelihood" (Miller, 2011), we might be contributing to the cultivation of a different political climate for our work.

### Prioritizing Diversity

There are two important ways we can better prioritize diversity within child and youth care. The first involves the potential that exists in diversifying notions of *what is taking place.*

For instance, Ajandi (2011) makes a point of complicating binaries (such as the "deserving" or "undeserving" mother). By looking in the spaces around dualistic notions of good and bad, or normal or abnormal approaches to motherhood, she is able to consider more dimensions of experience and legitimize more kinds of experiences. This offers a more (though never fully) complete picture from which to draw conclusions and reduces the likelihood that responses will operate prescriptively. As practitioners required to operate on the basis of evidence, or to organize our practice around measurable outcomes, we may find ourselves working in reductionist ways—teasing out complexities in order to make sense of what we encounter. But people *are* complex. If, instead, we seek the diversity that exists within a particular experience, we may find ourselves more able to meaningfully work *with* (not *for*) the children and families we encounter. Much like the "diverse economies framing" discussed earlier (Gibson-Graham, 2008), this requires different tools for assessment, different kinds of questions, and different ways of documenting what we see, but it is possible to move in the direction of diversity even within existing structural limitations (see Madsen, 2007).

The second way diversity can be prioritized involves the potential that exists in diversifying notions of *what is possible*. As discussed previously within both economics and CYC, when we refuse to be limited by the stories we are told, we can engage imaginatively with existing conditions in such a way that new realities become possible. In order to do this, we need to ensure our practices are driven not by the structures that are imposed on our practices, but by the ontology that guides our practice. It also means, as Alsbury (2010) suggests, that rather than seeking the one right direction, we need to be open to the likelihood that there are multiple right directions. As she observes, what is meaningful practice in rural, northern Canada, for instance, may differ greatly from meaningful practice in urban centres. Allowing for (and advocating for) a diversity of approaches rather than standardizing our practice may increase our ability to effectively engage with children and families. It also suggests that for the broader economic, social, and political systems to shift in such a way that a diversity of approaches might be legitimized, we need to employ a diversity of *tactics*—such as those that compose this section—in order to contribute to these cultural shifts on a collective level through our work.

## Engaging Intentionally in Uncertain Futures

I DO NOT WISH TO SUGGEST that the above strategies will—independently or taken together—create a perfect post-growth future in which all needs are met. Rather, I wish to acknowledge that the models within which we are currently embedded (economic or otherwise) are not sufficient for addressing the complex realities faced by the unique children and families with whom we engage. I believe it is our responsibility to try to better understand these imperfect conditions so that we might participate within them as deliberately as possible.

I am simultaneously excited and dismayed by various developments in both economics and child and youth care. I believe that, given the interconnections between the two fields, we might be well served to look beyond the walls of our profession and learn from the knowledge of our socio-economist allies who are also working toward the cultivation of just and equitable conditions for children, youth, and families. By mapping assets, acknowledging the complexity of situations, intentionally using language, and prioritizing diversity—and encouraging the media and our leaders to do so as well—we may contribute to the development of a society that values equity and opportunities for all, rather than seeing these as things that come with a cost. As a profession, committing to these and other reflexive practices in an *ongoing* way, we might expect to experience reduced worker burnout and a renewed commitment to our underlying values as we see them reflected around us rather than having to fight for them.

The future is necessarily uncertain. But it seems hopeful that by drawing from a wide range of human service and economic literature, we will be able to spend more time *engaging with* children and families, and less time validating our existence for funding and recognition. In short, we will have integrity as a field, and the opportunity to collectively contribute to the creation of a society that reflects values of respect, sustainability, and relational engagement. ●

NOTES

1  The results of this study reflect those of a similar U.S. study and a larger Canadian study, according to its authors.

2  This refers to "interactions between social (human behavioural) and technical elements (technologies)" (Joosten et al., 2009, p. 343).

REFERENCES

Ajandi, J. (2011). "Single mothers by choice": Disrupting dominant discourses of the family through social justice alternatives. *International Journal of Child, Youth, and Family Studies, 3/4,* 410–431.

Albanese, P. (2010). *Child poverty in Canada.* Don Mills, ON: Oxford University Press.

Albanese, P., & Farr, T. (2012). "I'm lucky" ... to have found child care: Evoking luck while managing child care needs in a changing economy. *International Journal of Child, Youth, and Family Studies, 1,* 83–111.

Alsbury, B. (2010). Considering co-constructed identities of profession and professional: Identifying a site for re-envisioning child and youth care. *Relational Child and Youth Care Practice, 23*(2), 27–38.

Alvesson, M., & Skoldberg, K. (2009). *Reflexive methodology: New vistas for qualitative research* (2nd ed.). Thousand Oaks, CA: Sage.

Axelsson, S., & Axelsson, R. (2009). From territoriality to altruism in interprofessional collaboration and leadership. *Journal of Interprofessional Care, 23*(4), 320–330.

Beker, J. (2001). Development of a professional identity for the child care worker. *Child and Youth Care Forum, 30*(6), 345–354.

Bellefeuille, G., & Ricks, F. (Eds.). (2008). *Standing on the precipice: Inquiry into the creative potential of child and youth care practice.* Edmonton, AB: MacEwan Press.

Bennett, D., Sadrehashemi, L., Smith, C., Hehewerth, M., Sienema, L., & Makolewski, J. (2009). *Hands tied: Child protection workers talks about working in, and leaving, B.C.'s child welfare system.* Vancouver, BC: Pivot Legal Society.

Braidotti, R. (2006). *Transpositions: On nomadic ethics.* Malden, MA: Polity Press.

Bronfenbrenner, U., & Evans, G. W. (2000). Developmental science in the 21st century: Emerging questions, theoretical models, research designs and empirical findings. *Social Development, 9*(1), 115–125.

Bruner, J. (2004). Life as narrative. *Social Research, 71*(3), 691–710.

Burnley, C., Matthews, C., & McKenzie, S. (2005). Devolution of services to children and families: The experience of NPOs in Nanaimo, British Columbia, Canada. *Voluntas: International Journal of Voluntary and Nonprofit Organizations, 6*(16), 69–87.

Cameron, J., & Gibson, K. (2005). Alternative pathways to community and economic development: The Latrobe Valley Community Partnering Project. *Geographical Research, 43*(3), 274–285.

Cameron, J., & Gibson-Graham, J. K. (2003). Feminising the economy: Metaphors, strategies, politics. *Gender, Place, & Culture, 10*(2), 145–157.

Caputo, J. (1993). *Against ethics: Contributions to a poetics of obligation with constant reference to deconstruction.* Indianapolis, IN: Indiana University Press.

Centre for Bhutan Studies. (2012). Results of the second nationwide 2010 survey on gross national happiness. Retrieved from http://www.grossnationalhappiness.com/

Charles, G., & Garfat, T. (2009). Child and youth care practice in North America: Historical roots and current challenges. *Relational Child and Youth Care, 22*(2), 17–18.

Chowdhury, A. (2011). Empowering at-risk families through effective parenting and family learning process. *Studies on Home and Community Science, 5*(1), 51–61.

Clarke, A. (2005). *Situational analysis: Grounded theory after the postmodern turn.* Thousand Oaks, CA: Sage.

Coates, L., & Wade, A. (2007). Language and violence: Analysis of four discursive operations. *Journal of family Violence, 22*(7), 511–522.

Cocksedge, L. (2012, February 21). A praxis-oriented approach to collective change processes for young children. *CYC-Online, 34.* Retrieved from http://www.cyc-net.org/cyc-online/feb2012/index.html#/20/

de Finney, S., Dean, M., Loiselle, E., & Saraceno, J. (2011). All children are equal, but some are more equal than others: Minoritization, structural inequities, and social justice praxis in residential care. *International Journal of Child, Youth, and Family Studies, 3/4*, 361–384.

Derksen, T. (2010). The influence of ecological theory in Child and Youth Care: A review of the literature. *International Journal of Child, Youth, and Family Studies, 1*(3–4), 326–339.

Ellis, J., Sherwin, J., & van Dam, T. (2011). *Working in person centred ways: A resource book for NSW advocacy and information services.* Sydney, New South Wales: Ageing, Disability, and Home Care, Department of Family and Community Services.

Fewster, G. (1990). *Being in Child Care: A journey into self.* Binghamton, NY: Haworth Press.

Fewster, G. (2002). The DSM IV you, but not IV me. *Child and Youth Care Forum, 31*(6), 365–380.

Garfat, T. (Ed.). (2003). *A Child and Youth Care approach to working with families.* Binghamton, NY: Haworth Press.

Gharabaghi, K., & Krueger, M. (2011). A new politic in child and youth care. *Relational Child and Youth Care Practice, 23*(3), 27–39.

Gibson-Graham, J.-K. (2008). Diverse economies: Performative practices for "other worlds." *Progress in Human Geography, 32*(5), 613–632.

Gibson-Graham, J.-K., & Roelvink, G. (2011). The nitty gritty of creating alternative economies. *Social Alternatives, 30*(1), 29–33.

Grondlin, A. (2011). Youth victims, competent agents: A second opinion on sexual victimization trauma. *International Journal of Child, Youth, and Family Studies, 3/4*, 450–472.

Hoskins, M., & Leseho, J. (1996). Changing metaphors of the self: Implications for counselling. *Journal of Counselling and Development, 74*, 243–252.

Jackson, T. (2009). *Prosperity without growth: Economics for a finite planet.* New York, NY: Earthscan.

Joosten, T., Bongers, I., & Janssen, R. (2009). Application of lean thinking to health care: Issues and observations. *International Journal for Quality in Health Care, 21*(5), 341–347.

Kallis, G. (2011). In defense of degrowth. *Ecological Economics, 70*, 873–880.

Kretzmann, J., & McKnight, J. (1997). *A community building workbook from the Asset-Based Community Development Institute for Policy Research.* Chicago, IL: ACTA Publications.

Madigan, S. (2011). *Narrative therapy.* Washington, DC: American Psychological Association.

Madsen, W. (2007). *Collaborative therapy with multi-stressed families* (2nd ed.). New York, NY: Guilford Press.

Malekoff, A. (2010). The use of group work to fight acute external threats to a community-based organization during harsh economic times. *Social Work with Groups, 33*, 4–22.

Miller, E. (2006, July/August). Other economies are possible! Organizing toward an economy of cooperation and solidarity. *Dollars and Sense: The Magazine of Economic Justice,* 1–6.

Miller, E. (2011). Occupy! Connect! Create! Imagining life beyond "the economy." Retrieved, from http://www.geo.coop/node/729

Mitchell, R. (2011). Human rights and health promotion: A Canada fit for children? *International Journal of Child, Youth, and Family Studies, 3/4*, 510–526.

Moses, T. (2008). Psychotropic medication practices for youth in systems of care. *Journal of Child and Family Studies, 17*(4), 567–581.

Newbury, J. (2009). Theory, policy, and practice entwined: Exploration through a case in point. *Relational Child and Youth Care Practice, 22*(3), 52–56.

Newbury, J. (2011a). Book review: *Not for Profit* by Martha Nussbaum: Why democracy needs the humanities. Retrieved from http://postgrowth.org/book-review-not-for-profit/

Newbury, J. (2011b). Situational analysis: Centerless systems and human service practices. *Child and Youth Services, 32*, 88–107.

Nussbaum, M. (2010). *Not for profit: Why democracy needs the humanities.* Princeton, NJ: Princeton University Press.

Paul Martin on natural capital. (2011, October 28). *The Current*. Retrieved from http://www.cbc.ca/thecurrent/episode/2011/10/28/paul-martin-on-natural-capital/

Reynolds, V. (2011). Resisting burnout in feminist activism [Podcast]. *Rabble.ca*. Retrieved from http://rabble.ca/podcasts/shows/f-word/2011/08/resisting-burnout-feminist-activism

Richardson, C., & Reynolds, V. (2012). "Here we are, amazingly alive": Holding ourselves together with an ethic of social justice in community work. *International Journal of Child, Youth, and Family Studies, 1*, 1–19.

Sanrud, H., & Ranahan, P. (2012). Pedagogical encounters of the case-based kind. *International Journal of Child, Youth, and Family Studies, 3*(2–3), 234–247.

Savicki, V. (1993). Clarification of child and youth are identity through an analysis of work environment and burnout. *Child and Youth Care Forum, 22*(6), 441–457.

Skott-Myhre, H., & Skott-Myhre, K. (2007). Radical youth work: Love and community. *Relational Child and Youth Care Practice, 20*(3), 48–57.

Teghtsoonian, K. (2004). Neoliberalism and gender analysis mainstreaming in Aotearoa/New Zealand. *Australian Journal of Political Science, 39*(2), 267–284.

Wade, A. (2007). Despair, resistance, hope: Response-based therapy with victims of violence. In C. Flaskas, I. McCarthy, & J. Sheehan (Eds.), *Hope and despair in narrative and family therapy: Adversity, forgiveness and reconciliation* (pp. 63–74). New York, NY : Routledge/Taylor & Francis Group.

White, J. (2007). Knowing, doing, and being in context: A praxis-oriented approach to Child and Youth Care. *Child and Youth Care Forum, 36*(5/6), 225–244.

Winegard, B., & Winegard, C. J. (2011). The awful revolution: Is neoliberalism a public health risk? *Opednews*. Retrieved from http://www.opednews.com/articles/3/The-Awful-Revolution-Is-N-by-Benjamin-Winegard-110415-653.html

World Resources Institute (WRI) in collaboration with United Nations Development Program, United Nations Environment Programme, and World Bank. (2005). *World Resources 2005: The wealth of the poor—managing ecosystems to fight poverty*. Washington, DC: WRI.

# Chapter 8

## Insider/Outsider
### Challenge and Opportunity in Teaching
### "The Profession That Never Was" in the United States

BEN ANDERSON-NATHE

**Like so many other child and youth care workers (CYCs),** my first exposure to the field came when I was hired by a crisis residential care facility for young people who were runaways, temporarily between foster or group care placements, or under police custody while the child protection system investigated charges of parental abuse. I loved the work. I found myself coming alive in relationship with the young people whose lives and home I got to share. And I had no idea what I was doing. When I accepted this position, during my junior year of college, I had no formal education in youth work—in fact, I had never even heard the phrase—and the on-the-job training I received in the group home was almost exclusively technical and instrumental ("do this," "don't do that," "here's how to fill out an incident report"). Still, it was the most amazing work I could imagine doing.

Although most of my peers were similarly adrift in terms of formal education to prepare us for our jobs, this facility (somewhat atypically, I later learned) prized relationships over intervention and put understanding before diagnosis. I was encouraged to build relationships with young people for the sake of the relationship itself, not for what treatment benefit or symptom relief might ensue from it. I learned reflexive practice and critical engagement with the systems and structures surrounding those young people I came to know. But I had no idea how to name my work or, for that matter, my emerging

149

professional identity. Only later, after deciding to pursue graduate education in social work and public policy, did I learn that a distinct youth work profession and academic tradition existed across Canada, the United Kingdom and other Commonwealth countries, and elsewhere around the world. Now, as a scholar and teacher of youth work in the university setting, I understand my initial confusion and inability to name my work in the context of larger cultural, professional, and institutional forces that continue to affect the identity, development, and practice of our field, specifically in the United States.

In the United States, the landscape of youth services is one in which much terrain was claimed decades ago by larger and more established professions than child and youth care. In spite of more than a hundred years of diverse approaches to meeting the needs of young people, youth work in the United States has not coalesced into a single coherent profession (Edginton, Kowalski, & Randall, 2005). Consequently, a limited number of academic programs currently exist for the education and credentialing of youth workers (Fusco, 2012), and even among those, most rest within the larger structure of a parent discipline—most commonly, social work, education, or human development and family studies. This has required most youth workers across the country to piece together their education and professional development (not to mention ongoing collegial support) wherever and however they can. As a result, workers with interests including residential care, out-of-school time, recreation and camping, juvenile corrections, and homeless youth supports (to name a few) find themselves in schools of social work and education, shouldering by themselves the burden of translating and code-switching between the practices and tenets of those disciplines and their own. Upon graduation, these youth workers often wind up working in agencies and youth-serving organizations that similarly lack an established context for or understanding of the principles underlying youth work as a distinct field. Even in light of efforts to establish shared competencies, professional associations, and credentials in our field, youth workers occupy an insider/outsider role in both education and practice; they are *in* both worlds but not fully *part of* either.

Fewster (2007) has written of child and youth care as "the profession that never was," lamenting what he addresses as the gap between CYC's transformative potential and its contemporary reality. Although the contexts in which we use it differ, I borrow Fewster's phrase for this chapter's title. It speaks to the challenges I experience as a U.S. youth worker and scholar housed within one of the disciplines that claim ownership over, fail to recognize, and sometimes contradict the existence and potential of my field. As CYCs struggle to carve out space for their practice in the field, so do youth work scholars who bear the burden of effectively preparing students while nurturing our field's theoretical and practical evolution. As members of this not-yet profession, we must find ways to sustain ourselves in the misunderstood in-between spaces of our vocational orientations and the larger institutions or disciplines that house us. In keeping with this book's aim to shine a light on current debates and contradictions in child and youth care, this chapter presents some of my challenges navigating the insider/outsider role as an early-career academic in "the profession that never was" and offers some hope for the possibilities this role can open.

## The Setting

I HAVE OFTEN DESCRIBED MYSELF AS AN ACCIDENTAL ACADEMIC. When I first began my youth work career, I had no interest even in graduate education, not to mention a life in academia. Perhaps not coincidentally, I have also been described as plagued by (blessed with?) a healthy dose of oppositional inclination; this oppositional streak drove me to graduate school and eventually into the academy. As I've already mentioned, my early direct practice with youth unfolded in environments where, sometimes in spite of institutional pressures to the contrary, colleagues and supervisors alike supported me to engage in unapologetically relational practice with young people—practice in which intervention and treatment took a deliberate back seat to the relationship itself. In diverse settings, including juvenile corrections, street outreach, community mental health, and foster care, I built relationships with young people consistent with what I now understand to be the central principles of interactive and relational youth work practice (Garfat, 2008; Krueger, 1998). Nevertheless, I routinely experienced my work with young people being effectively trumped by the graduate credentials of other service providers whose disciplines granted their perspectives and practices greater credibility than mine. My response was simple: I'd get credentials of my own, from those disciplines that would grant external legitimacy to my practice.

Over the next several years, I completed youth-related degrees in disciplines other than child and youth care (social work, public policy, and community education), each differentiated by history, values, and bodies of theory and practices. In each, I collaborated with youth work scholars and mentors to create degree options that allowed me to centre my study of young people's lives and the social conditions surrounding them, including the roles and practices of adults who choose to be present in those lives. This experience of having to carve out credibility as a youth work scholar by seeking legitimacy through a more established discipline matched that of my mentors; all had received their graduate degrees in a discipline other than child and youth work. I now see this to be common among youth work scholars in the United States; at some point in our academic preparation, we become strangers in strange lands, pursuing one field's credential for the doors it will hold open in another.

I now direct and teach in an undergraduate degree program (Child and Family Studies) preparing students for careers in the helping professions. The program is a blend of liberal education and professional preparation, highlighting interdisciplinary coursework and the completion of an integrative professional portfolio and at least three hundred hours of practicum experience in schools or social service organizations (Smith & Morgaine, 2004). Students in the major graduate with a comprehensive body of knowledge from the program's core requirements, as well as a specialization in one of eleven content areas, including (among others) early childhood education, child welfare and human services, human development, and youth work. Students receive codified knowledge (Eraut, 2000) about children and youth while also fulfilling expectations related to practice skills and competencies through the supported development of personal knowledge. In this way, the program blends features of conventional youth studies programs and youth work preparation courses (Roholt & Baizerman, 2012), and prepares students well for the complex demands of theoretically grounded practice with children and youth. That is, students graduate with demonstrated competence in both thinking about and being present with young people.

Nevertheless, even with this specialized course of study and professional preparation, the program graduates students into practice settings that often have no existing context for their degree. Degrees in the academic disciplines (psychology, women/gender studies, sociology, and comparable fields) and those from more established professions (social work or education) are well understood; blended professional and academic degrees enjoy less familiarity, despite employers' appreciation for these students' skills once they enter the field. As a result, students who approach their work with youth through interdisciplinary and holistic professional lenses bear the burden of proving their merit (and that of their liberal educations) to future employers, not to mention explaining their education and practice orientations to their colleagues from more established traditions.

Mitigating these students' experiences and preparing them to navigate the contested terrain of their field presents challenges for me as a teacher and administrator. Additional challenges come from the program's (and consequently, my own) physical and administrative location under the umbrella of a more established discipline and professional tradition. Child and Family Studies is nested within a school of social work and constitutes the only nondisciplinary academic program in the school—a common circumstance for similar youth studies programs across the United States. Consequently, students and faculty alike experience some friction between their professional identities, values, and preparation, and those of our "host" discipline. Much that can be taken for granted in a shared context presents complications for students and faculty whose fields of study and practice reflect different assumptions, orientations, and bodies of knowledge.

It is in this context that I reflect on the challenges and opportunities I have experienced as a youth work scholar on blended terrain. I share this narrative not only to provide context for the insider/outsider experiences that follow, but also because I believe mine is not a unique trajectory. In the vacuum created by so few formal programs to educate youth workers in the United States (let alone to prepare youth work scholars), many of my academic colleagues and peers have navigated these and other challenges in order to remain in the academy, similarly experiencing what Anglin (1999) has called a "dual diagnosis" of professional preparation.

# Challenges
*Lost in Translation*

AS I HAVE MENTIONED, from the start of my graduate education through the past eight years teaching at my current institution, I have been a youth worker without a disciplinary home. This is no less true for the students who graduate from our program and enter the field with a solid foundation of critical youth studies and relational practice but no roadmap for how that practice will be understood by their supervisors or peers. Most youth-serving organizations in the United States have little or no understanding of what differentiates youth work from conventional social work with young people, so our students—and we as faculty—must learn to shift quickly and effectively between the assumptions, language, and behaviours germane to our own practice orientations and those more conventionally accepted in our workplaces.

I am currently housed in a school of social work, and while it is reasonable to expect significant points of congruence and overlap between child and youth care and social work, I nevertheless routinely experience myself challenged to translate my work and the fundamental orientation of my field into terms understood by my social work colleagues. In many ways, our work is aligned; both traditions uphold a social justice mission; strive to better the conditions of children, youth, and communities; and prepare professionals to enter practice environments that often undervalue them and their work. In other ways, however, our fields miss the mark with each other, sometimes in significant ways. Lacking a large-scale public awareness of child and youth work as a distinct field of study and practice, youth workers and scholars in the United States—myself included—are left translating across language worlds as their work unfolds. Drawing from reflections on my own experiences as well as kitchen table conversations with other youth workers and scholars struggling with these same dilemmas, I present here three central tensions: (1) the centrality of relational practice in a context of intervention-based therapeutic relationships; (2) critical attention to social and historical contexts shaping the day-to-day lives of young people in tension with taken-for-granted constructs of adolescence, treatment, and more; and (3) difficulty differentiating from established disciplines.

## Relational Practice in an Intervention Climate

Even in areas where youth work is professionalized and recognized, its constituent elements are contested. Across national settings and even within some local contexts, constructions of youth work or child and youth care practice vary widely. Sercombe (2010) proposes a broad understanding of youth work according to its primary relationship (that between adult and young person) and setting (the young person's social context). Spence and Devanney (2006) articulate four points central to the practice of British youth work: voluntary involvement, association, informal relationships, and educational intentions. Anglin (1999) suggests that child and youth care practice is primarily focused on children's growth, centred around the totality of young people's functioning, oriented toward cultivating social competence, localized to the young person's environment, and concerned with the growth and maintenance of therapeutic relationships. Clearly, this is not an exhaustive list; ours is a field not lacking in critical self-examination. But what these and other traditions (e.g., relational practice in the Canadian context) have in common is a fundamental understanding that intentional and authentic relationship is primary to youth work (Krueger, 1998). Intervention, symptom alleviation, and compliance, though occasionally necessary depending upon the practice setting, take a back seat to the notion of adult and young person in relationship within the day-to-day context of the young person's whole life (Garfat, 2008).

In direct tension with this commitment to relational practice as the defining feature of child and youth care, much direct youth work in the United States unfolds in environments where the fundamental focus of the work is intervention, not relationship. This is consistent with Sercombe's (2010) assertion that American youth work functions often within discourses of child welfare and delinquency prevention or intervention, in spite of the popularity of positive youth development programming in recent years. Residential care environments are commonly funded either by child welfare or juvenile corrections and consequently reflect these systems' emphasis on intervention and outcome over relationship. School-based supports emphasize delinquency prevention and behavioural compliance. Even homeless and street-outreach programs are commonly oriented toward neo-liberal interests of market readiness (emphasizing "life skills" training that focuses almost exclusively on facilitating young people's mastery of those skills that will make them productive—and often low-wage—employees and consumers), symptom alleviation, and presumptions of criminal involvement. As much as American youth workers try to centre relational practice, emphasizing that intervention or symptom relief will unfold from there if necessary, they operate in contexts that demand the reverse; treatment plans and intervention practices precede (and often even preclude) relationship.

Certainly, many adults who work with young people encounter these frustrations; this is not unique to youth workers in the United States. It is a trend that speaks, after all, to a larger cultural allegiance to neo-liberalism and its associated emphasis on technical and instrumental knowledge and practice. What is desirable is that which is quantifiable, replicable, and efficient. Still, I argue that American youth workers may experience this tension somewhat more acutely than some of their peers trained in disciplines or professions that better prepare them for practice (such as social work or K–12 education) that is oriented more explicitly toward outcomes and intervention. Much has been said of the shift in American social work toward technical/instrumental knowledge and skills developed through increasingly competency-based curricula; critical social workers and scholars have challenged this movement as further depersonalizing the relationship between helper and helped and moving the field even further from its origins in social and structural critique (Kivel, 2007).

That said, this emphasis on intervention and instrumental skill has set the stage in which most social service (youth work, included) now unfolds. In this context—a social service network predominantly claimed by social work and its associated tradition of intervention—youth workers strive to cultivate authentic relationships in environments predicated upon diagnoses, treatment plans, and mandatory evidence-based practices. In residential care, this results in workers sacrificing moments of deliberate connection in favour of compliance with program routines and regimented treatment delivery. Rhythm and presence, so central to relational and interactive practice (Krueger, 1998) are considered ancillary to the evidence-based effective behaviour management plan structuring the group home's daily schedule. Even in informal settings like summer camp or community education, it results in the denigration of "hanging out" unless this unstructured time can be documented as *peer support* or *anger management* or *life skills training* for legitimacy and justification.

Certainly, one of the most common comments I hear from students upon entering the field—and one of my most significant challenges as a teacher of youth work—is that students' steepest learning comes in trying to translate what they believe to be true about their role (and what they know to be helpful in the lives of the young people with whom they work) into words that match with the treatment philosophies, intervention modalities, and benchmarks unquestioned in their home agencies. While this cannot be attributed solely to the lack of a formal youth work tradition in the United States, the resulting challenges are exaggerated for workers trained to privilege relationship over diagnosis and intervention who then enter organizations that presume an intervention-based model consistent with social work education.

In my role as researcher and scholar in the context of a school of social work, I often find it similarly difficult to translate my research interests into the language of social work intervention and program delivery. As I have moved through the promotion and tenure process as junior faculty, I've often had to articulate and defend my scholarly agenda with its emphasis on meaning-making, questions of lived experience, and other concerns about how young people and adults live together in the world. My interest is not, and never has been, principally oriented toward developing explanatory models, creating behavioural interventions, or evaluating program effectiveness. In my recent work investigating the biases and a priori assumptions in the discourse constituted by the popular "It Gets Better" videos (www.itgetsbetter.org), which are offered in support of lesbian, gay, bisexual, and transgender (LGBT) young people, I have sought to understand the meanings conveyed about young people, about sexuality, and about the social role of adults in responding to relational violence. I have not, however, chosen to link this investigation to a formal intervention. I am interested in thinking about how adults could benefit from critically examining their own biases, as reflected in these videos, with the belief that any resulting insight brings young person and adult closer together in authentic relationship. What is primary to me is the one-to-one relationship, not the development of programmatic intervention or curricula to transform bullying cessation programs.

As a youth worker committed to relational practice, this orientation makes sense to me. It is congruent with my training, it resonates with many others in my fields of practice, and it centres the notion of adult and young person *in relationship*, situating that relationship in the context of the young person's lived experience. Among many of my colleagues, however, my relational approach is seen as preliminary, at best. My work is assumed to be exploratory, with the intention of constructing a generalizable program to implement changed practice and eventually construct an evidence base. For my social work colleagues, an interest in this discourse and its impact on young people and their relationships with adults is compelling, but largely insofar as it can be connected to an intervention or programmatic response to static constructions of LGBT youth and bullying.

I address this tension not because I believe intervention to be unnecessary; clearly, it is an undeniable and central feature of much youth work practice. On the contrary, I suggest that focusing on relationships *first*, centring a critically informed understanding of a young person's experience as grounded in authentic youth–adult relationship, provides a more fertile ground for whatever intervention or behaviour change may ensue. Intervention is an effect, not the goal. This orientation is consistent with the blend of liberal education (youth studies) and professional training (youth work) offered through the Child and Family Studies program and many other youth work curricula across the country. It challenges students to approach interactions with young people first by cultivating authentic relationships based on an expressed interest in understanding how those youth make meaning of their own experiences, and second with the intention of intervention where appropriate, and even then, only within the context of deliberate and authentic relationship. Unfortunately for students and scholars in our field, in the absence of broader public recognition for these perspectives, we are left to adapt where we must, code-switch where we can, and hope to minimize how much meaning is lost in translation.

### Critical Epistemologies in Tension with Conventional Paradigms

The tension I and many other child and youth care workers in the United States experience between relational practice and intervention-based social service delivery speaks to larger epistemological conflicts evident among ours and other child- and youth-serving practice fields. Perhaps because of the blended tradition of youth studies and youth work in our field, child and

youth care has enjoyed a history of critical investigation of the social conditions and epistemologies framing young people (e.g., Lesko, 1996, 2001; Wyn
& White, 1997) that precedes considerations of intervention or practice skills.
This book is itself a demonstration of our field's willingness to engage critically with *thinking about* the lives of children and youth, rather than simply
attending to how professionals should/can intervene in those lives. Still, lacking a recognized context for our work in the United States, this engaged interest in the epistemologies (ways of knowing) that ground our practice is often
inconsistent with established practice in youth-serving agencies and university curricula alike.

Blended academic/professional programs rooted in the tradition of youth
studies and youth work, such as Child and Family Studies, expose students
and future child and youth care workers to critical epistemologies and socialize them to examine the a priori assumptions surrounding contemporary discourses of youth. We explicitly challenge what Lesko (1996, 2001) has named
society's "confident characterizations" of both adolescents and adolescence,
encouraging students to critique notions of development and the universality
of developmentalism. We situate adolescence within its appropriate historical,
social, and economic contexts, interrogating the construct for its contemporary relevance and searching for alternative paradigms within which to view
the lives of young people. We examine contemporary discourses surrounding the "adolescent brain," in search not of biological justifications for young
people's behaviour but rather to better understand how science functions in
service of established social conventions and a priori constructions of youth
(Males, 2009; Sercombe, 2010). Linking back to Anglin's (1999) articulation of
youth work's defining characteristics, we attend deliberately to the "totality of
a child's functioning," based on "direct, day to day work with children in their
environment" (p. 145).

But this epistemological frame is far from universal in our students' academic preparation. When students enter the field for practicum placements,
or even when they enroll in other courses across the university, they encounter
constructions of young people that directly contradict this critical epistemology. Those entering conventional social service organizations with the intention of supporting young people encounter constructions of adolescents as
decontextualized embodiments of storm and stress (Hall, 1904). Programs are

designed around a default understanding of young people as fundamentally and exclusively adolescent, with all the associated (and problematic) assumptions of risk, irresponsibility, differentiation, and defiance. Similarly, students entering formal education settings (early childhood, elementary, and secondary education) are confronted immediately with disembodied notions of age-appropriateness, which structure everything in the school environment from curriculum to behavioural intervention, but which overwhelmingly fail to address the social contexts or lived experiences of individual young people.

Perhaps this is not surprising; as fields professionalize, they must develop distinct bodies of theoretical and disciplinary knowledge. Over time, the fundamental beliefs or theoretical assumptions in these bodies of knowledge become codified, and a professional canon emerges. Once theory becomes canonical, its truths are held as self-evident for the field, and so are the frames and symbols employed to represent them. Just as people who are told, "Don't think about an elephant" cannot help but conjure up a mental picture of the animal and then hear subsequent terms like "trunk" or "ears" only in the context of the creature in their minds, professionals socialized in unquestioned adolescent theory construct sixteen-year-old bodies as fundamentally and often exclusively adolescent. In an extension of Plato's allegory of the cave, when we have no other context, we have little choice but to accept as truth the shadows dancing on the wall before us. Absent a publicly legitimized alternative epistemology to frame the contexts and lives of young people, students enter programs such as Child and Family Studies with no reason to believe the categories of "adolescent" or "age-appropriate programming" are anything other than natural and self-evident. They leave our programs with a more robust appreciation of multiple constructions of "young person" (see Roholt & Baizerman, 2012) and their associated practical implications.

Of course, this situation creates complications for teachers of youth work, as we attempt to change the default socialization messages of future child and youth care practitioners and invite them into the critical epistemologies of youth that frame so much of our work. It also introduces challenges for youth work faculty housed in schools of social work, education, or related fields, as they attempt to expand and transform some of the discourse accepted in those settings as self-evident. In my own experience, this has been true even as my School of Social Work has begun moving toward the embrace of more critical, postmodern, and post-structuralist theoretical frames. Even in this context, age remains a largely untheorized axis of identity and experience among my colleagues and across our school's broader social work curriculum. Where race and class are complicated by critical theory, adolescence is accepted as natural, universal, and—particularly in the wake of recent brain research— biologically inevitable. In our program and many others, social workers take classes about adolescence, but these courses simply reify the adolescent as a fundamental *other*. That is, much social work and educational curricula provide helpers with skills to intervene in the lives of adolescents, but not to critically examine the social constructions and contexts of those adolescents as young people in the world.

In concrete terms, this means that youth work students from Child and Family Studies leave our program critical of unquestioned adherence to the social construct of adolescence but walk into jobs in youth-serving agencies where these assumptions have never been questioned. They are put in positions where their training teaches them to critique (if not reject as oppressive and reductionist) the same point-and-level systems (e.g., VanderVen, 1995, 2000) they must enforce as part of their jobs. Acculturated by programs like ours to engage relationally with young people, *to be with youth* rather than *work on them*, they are expected to develop treatment plans and implement evidence-based practice interventions without transparency or relationships. And perhaps most frustrating of all these points is the realization students often articulate that in their U.S. context, they will remain insider/outsiders. That is, they work within the context of youth-serving institutions, but always approaching those institutions as an outsider, with a different (even if sometimes complementary) language and orientation to their work. This is no less true for youth work scholars housed in other departments or professional schools that often, due to the professional and paradigmatic dominance of American social work and education, fail to acknowledge that other approaches might be useful and even desirable.

## Challenges of Differentiation

For reasons well beyond the scope of this chapter, youth work in the United States has remained less concentrated, less highly professionalized, and less recognized as a distinct field of practice either than American social work or education, or some of our international child and youth care cousins. And although as Quinn (2012) points out, the field is experiencing more cohesion in recent years than in the past, our efforts to coalesce into an established, recognized profession in the United States are still in their infancy. Consequently, in spite of many scholars' and students' belief that child and youth care offers something unique to the youth service landscape in the United States, our larger and more defined cousins have little impetus to recognize that contribution, or even the existence of any differentiated field of youth work. And even in some circumstances where recognition for youth work's contribution does exist, it often lacks requisite institutional support (Fusco, 2012). For youth work faculty housed in other departments or professional schools, this lack of support creates significant challenges.

When I was hired into my current position in Child and Family Studies, for example, my initial contract included a clause requiring me to maintain a scholarly agenda that would result in publications to the "typical social work venues." Only after extensive conversation with the dean at the time was I able to have this clause removed, since social workers have generally not constituted the intended audience for my work. Nevertheless, in my performance review process, manuscripts submitted to journals unfamiliar to my social work peers have come under greater scrutiny than those bearing disciplinary familiarity. Publication decisions that make sense in the context of the international child and youth care field have been questioned for their validity in light of a default social work orientation. Similarly, in the promotion and tenure process in my school, it has historically been accepted as a given that external blind reviewers of a candidate's dossier must include social workers in other schools of social work. For our Child and Family Studies faculty whose research, practice, and teaching do not address social work as a discipline, this presents a structural disadvantage for which our social work colleagues have no context.

Beyond these personnel concerns, there are curricular considerations, as well. In spite of a range of efforts currently underway (through the Association for Child and Youth Care Practice, the Next Generation Coalition, and others), academic youth work programs across the country still lack a unifying accreditation or accrediting body. Consequently, faculty and administrators in these programs often face a steep challenge in leveraging funds to support curricular expansions or reforms from increasingly resource-poor public institutions. Even when political and financial will is present, curricular expansions may face other institutional barriers, such as presumptions that a course like Youth Work Theory and Practice is a duplication of content already explored in Social Work with Children and Adolescents.

In the classroom, disciplinary confusions and "turf wars" unfold as well. I teach an introductory youth work course that anchors the Child and Family Studies youth worker specialization; the course is also open to students from our school's undergraduate and graduate social work programs. The first part of the course focuses on building the epistemological and theoretical foundation for youth work practice as a distinct orientation to relationships with young people. Invariably, I encounter social work students who have been effectively socialized into the dominance of their discipline and argue that social workers already know how to work with adolescents; therefore, youth work is irrelevant. While this exchange might point toward interesting and valuable questions of what content should be included in social work and youth work curricula, and how much overlap between the two is desirable, in the most concrete terms, it speaks to the epistemological conflicts I described earlier in this chapter. In these and other ways, the disciplinary location of child and youth care in the United States—situated in complicated relationship to other established professional or academic programs—introduces complications for the current and future youth work professoriate.

## From Challenge to Opportunity

IN THIS CHAPTER, I have pointed to some of the theoretical and epistemological foundations underlying academic child and youth care programs in the United States, using my own experiences in Child and Family Studies as a starting point. I have suggested that as a youth work scholar, I struggle to locate myself—my epistemologies and practice orientations—in larger social service contexts that lack a frame of reference for these positions. And finally, I have pointed to some of the ways in which educational programs like mine may unintentionally set up students (themselves future youth workers) for difficulty when they enter practice environments that directly contradict the theoretical orientations of their education and training. In spite of these challenges, there is nowhere in higher education that I would rather be right now. With challenge and conflict comes opportunity and possibility. In the United States, in particular, ours is a field in transition. It is a profession in the making, a discipline forming, and I am excited about the invitation I have been offered to engage in its formation.

I have written elsewhere (Anderson-Nathe, Gringeri, & Wahab, 2013) that I am not a fan of binaries or dichotomous thinking; most often, I find these reductive and limiting. Having written that, I am aware that the preceding pages have laid out what I now name as an artificial and unnecessary binary (youth work on this hand, social work or education on the other). But even as I write about some of the challenges posed by youth work's contemporary location in the U.S. professional and academic context, I am reminded that ours has been a blended field from its inception. We have drawn from, been influenced by, and in turn influenced other fields in the youth-serving environment (psychology, social work, education, human development, recreation and leisure, and more). My own academic pathway has reflected this interdisciplinarity; it is no accident that the article I mentioned at the beginning of this paragraph appears in a social work journal. As our field continues to coalesce in the United States and we forge clearer links with our cousins in Canada, the United Kingdom, and across the world, we may well find the wisdom in shifting our attention away from what divides youth work from other disciplines and more toward what interesting possibility rests in the intersections.

In the preface to her exploration of culture clash experienced by a Hmong family and the American medical institution, Anne Fadiman (1997) states that

> the action most worth watching is not at the center of things but where edges meet … there are interesting frictions and incongruities in these places, and often, if you stand in the point of tangency, you can see both sides better than if you were in the middle of either one. (p. viii)

Drawing on the imagery of *la mestiza,* critical race and gender scholar Gloria Anzaldúa (2010) offers a similar perspective, calling into question the notion that owning a single identity or affiliation is a limiting rather than solely edifying position. Neither Fadiman nor Anzaldúa presents this mixing or in-between space as a neutral one, or one without pain and conflict. In fact, both suggest that being on the edges, deliberately blending rather than choosing, introduces new challenges and conflicts. They also assert, though, that it is a myth that centring within silos, being surrounded only by that which matches, brings comfort and stability. It is simply a different type of exclusion.

In the context of my challenges as a scholar and teacher of the "profession that never was," I cannot help but question whether, in some way, there might be freedom, excitement, and potential in the in-between spaces of American youth work. Situated in (albeit occasionally tense and controversial) conversation with colleagues in a school of social work, my own scholarship and ability to articulate my youth work orientation and epistemology has become richer than it might have been had I the luxury of sitting in the centre. Students who leave our program and move into contexts that do not understand them experience the pain and conflict of code-switching, yes, but they also become better positioned to function as cultural brokers, helping the young people with whom they build relationships to become multilingual as well. I believe my colleagues have benefited from my program introducing them to the notion of a denaturalized and critical understanding of adolescence, as well as alternatives to intervention-based therapeutic relationships. Likewise, my ability to prepare students to navigate the social-work-dominated social service landscape upon graduation has improved as a result of my location within those disciplinary walls.

On a structural level, as I mentioned previously, the youth-serving terrain in the United States has already largely been claimed. I suggest that part of the hardship American youth workers experience in coalescing around professional identity, association, competency, or credentialing is due to our difficulty carving out our own space. Maybe, through our critical reflection and discernment regarding increased professionalization of the field, we will learn that we don't need to designate a unique space for youth work. On the other hand, perhaps we will learn that professionalization is crucial (see also Stuart, this volume). Looking at the highly professionalized fields of social work and education, there have certainly been benefits to association and accreditation. Competencies and credentials have granted legitimacy to these fields. But at what cost? Roholt and Baizerman (2012) ask a similar question in wondering whether a separate youth work faculty is necessary in higher education. Is professional edification worth the compromise of inter- and multidisciplinarity?

I remain unsure. When I was a doctoral student at the University of Minnesota, my advisor responded to my frustration with the state of our field by saying, "Perfect cannot be the enemy of better. And better can never be good enough." Where I sit now, as a youth work scholar nested in a school of social work, I encounter challenges. I am an insider/outsider in both my field of study and the discipline that houses me. My students struggle to translate what they learn in the classroom with what they encounter in the field upon graduation. Things could be better. But in the pursuit of living at the margins rather than the centre, perhaps my "better" is to name these tensions, articulate the challenges we face as a field at the edges, and prepare our students for a life as *las mestizas*. And remembering that "better" can never be good enough, we can continue engaging with one another in conversation around what the future holds for this profession that hasn't yet been. ●

REFERENCES

Anderson-Nathe, B., Gringeri, C., & Wahab, S. (2013). Nurturing "critical hope" in feminist social work research. *Journal of Social Work Education, 49*(2), 277–291.

Anglin, J. (1999). The uniqueness of child and youth care: A personal perspective. *Child and Youth Care Forum, 28,* 143–150.

Anzaldúa, G. (2010). La conciencia de la mestiza: Toward a new consciousness. In M. Adams, W. Blumenfeld, C. Castañeda, H. Hackman, M. Peters, & X. Zúñiga (Eds.), *Readings for diversity and social justice* (2nd ed., pp. 94–98). New York, NY: Routledge.

Edginton, C., Kowalski, C., & Randall, S. (2005). *Youth work: Emerging perspectives in youth development.* Champaign, IL: Sagamore.

Eraut, M. (2000). Non-formal leaning and tacit knowledge in professional work. *British Journal of Educational Psychology, 70,* 113–136.

Fadiman, A. (1997). *The spirit catches you and you fall down.* New York, NY: Farrar, Straus and Giroux.

Fewster, G. (2007). The profession that never was. *CYC-Online, 97.* Retrieved from http://www.cyc-net.org/cyc-online/cycol-0207-fewster.html

Fusco, D. (Ed.). (2012). *Advancing youth work: Current trends, critical questions.* New York, NY: Routledge.

Garfat, T. (2008). The inter-personal in-between: An exploration of relational child and youth care practice. In G. Bellefeuille & F. Ricks (Eds.), *Standing on the precipice: Inquiry into the creative potential of child and youth care practice* (pp. 7–34). Edmonton, AB: McEwan Press.

Hall, G. S. (1904). *Adolescence*. New York, NY: Appleton.

Kivel, P. (2007). Social service or social change? In INCITE! Women of Color Against Violence (Eds.), *The revolution will not be funded: Beyond the nonprofit industrial complex* (pp. 129–149). Boston, MA: South End Press.

Krueger, M. (1998). *Interactive youth work practice*. Washington, DC: Child Welfare League of America Press.

Lesko, N. (1996). Denaturalizing adolescence: The politics of contemporary representations. *Youth & Society, 28*, 139–161.

Lesko, N. (2001). *Act your age: A cultural construction of adolescence*. New York, NY: Routledge.

Males, M. (2009). Does the adolescent brain make risk taking inevitable? A skeptical appraisal. *Journal of Adolescent Research, 24*, 3–20.

Quinn, J. (2012). Advancing youth work: Opportunities and challenges. In D. Fusco (Ed.), *Advancing youth work: Current trends, critical questions* (pp. 207–215). New York, NY: Routledge.

Roholt, R. V., & Baizerman, M. (2012). Preparing the next generation of professoriate in youth studies: Mapping the contested spaces. In D. Fusco (Ed.), *Advancing youth work: Current trends, critical questions* (pp. 127–140). New York, NY: Routledge.

Sercombe, H. (2010). The gift and the trap: Working the "teen brain" into our concept of youth. *Journal of Adolescent Research, 25*, 31–47.

Smith, C., & Morgaine, C. (2004). Liberal studies and professional preparation: The evolution of the Child and Family Studies Program at Portland State University. *Child and Youth Care Forum, 33*, 257–274.

Spence, J., & Devanney, C. (2006). *Youth work: Voices of practice*. Leicester, England: National Youth Agency.

VanderVen, K. (1995). "Point and level systems": Another way to fail children and youth. *Child and Youth Care Forum, 24*, 346–367.

VanderVen, K. (2000). Cultural aspects of point and level systems. *Reclaiming Children and Youth, 9*, 53–59.

Wyn, J., & White, R. (1997). *Rethinking youth*. London, England: Sage.

# 3

**We end** *With Children* with a philosophical reflection by Mark Krueger, one of the co-editors of this book, and a rip-roaring chapter by Gerry Fewster, who for the past forty years or so has been the voice of critical reflection and un-abashed critique in the field of child and youth care. Mark Krueger's chapter provides us with an opportunity to "see the mind at work" as he reflects on his readings of *The First Man* and interphases his own reflections on youth, self, and context. Fewster's work has covered just about any topic imaginable, and he has repeatedly been at the centre of controversy and often-contentious debate within the field. Fewster's message has, however, been quite consistent over all these years: "Not so fast!" he yells out whenever the field appears to be straying too far from what he believes to be its core. For Fewster, child and youth care is fundamentally about *care*, and as is apparent in this closing chapter of *With Children*, there is much to be said about care, and not always in caring ways. ●

# Chapter 9

# Reading Camus's *The First Man*

MARK KRUEGER

**Albert Camus's semi-autobiographical novel** *The First Man* was published in 1995, thirty-five years after his death in a car crash in 1960. He was forty-six. The unfinished manuscript was found in the wreckage. Recently, while browsing, I found a used copy in an independent bookstore in Milwaukee. One of the reviews on the back cover read, "The result is a moving journey through the lost landscapes of youth that also discloses the wellspring of Camus' aesthetic powers and moral vision."

I sat down and paged through the book. I was eager to learn more about how Camus's youth shaped him as a thinker, activist, and writer. Like Vaclav Havel, another writer/playwright/activist I admired, Camus saw the absurdities and injustices in the world and continued to speak out on behalf of humanity and peace. In arguing against nihilism, he believed in the power of the human desire to make meaning by choice and interpretation. This was and is inspiring to me. In my own life, I try to remind myself of the power of human beings to make better choices.

As a professor of youth work, I was also interested in his childhood. From what I knew, he had grown up in poverty in Algeria, raised by a stern Spanish grandmother and a near-deaf mute mother. His father had been killed in World War I when he was an infant. The community where he lived was diverse with Arab, Christian, Italian, French, and Spanish youth. This book would tell me more.

I was first introduced to Camus when I read *The Stranger*. The simple way he wrote, juxtaposed contradictory sentences, and presented moral dilemmas and questions impressed me. In his review of *The Stranger*, Sartre (1946/2007, p. 76) wrote: "The choice the great novelists like Camus make is to rely on images rather than arguments because of their belief in the futility of all explanatory principals. Instead they rely on the power of words that appeal to the senses." I keep this on a notecard to inform my reflective writing in youth work.

In more recent years, I read Camus's short stories in *Exile and the Kingdom*; his articles in *Combat*, the newspaper he edited for the French Resistance organization he was part of by the same name; and passages from his recently published 1951–1959 notebooks, which include notes taken while he was writing *The First Man*.

The editor's note in *The First Man* was written by his daughter, Catherine. She explained that the work had been kept from the public eye for several years by her mother, Francine, who was afraid it would not be well received. Just before his death, Camus had alienated French intellectuals, including his friend Sartre, who favoured a French communist regime and an independent Algeria under Arab rule. Catherine wrote that he "had condemned the Gulag, Stalin's trials, and totalitarianism in the belief that ideology must serve humanity not the contrary, and that the ends did not justify the means" (p. iv).

Camus also favoured a federated, multicultural Algeria in which Arabs and Europeans would live side by side and be equally represented. Thus, during the period before and after he received 1957 Nobel Prize for Literature and was working on this book, he was unpopular among many of the intellectuals in France. He had antagonized both the Left and the Right.

After Francine's death in 1979, voices emerged in France that suggested Camus had not been so wrong. Convinced that an autobiographical account of their father's life would be of interest to his fans and historians, Catherine and her twin brother, Jean, decided to share the book with the public. And, once she learned how to "deal with a work of literature," it was finally published in 1995.

According to his daughter and several reviewers, *The First Man* was his most personal novel. Instead of the carefully crafted sentences and passages he was noted for, the unfinished manuscript was handwritten in long, lyrical sentences and paragraphs (I could not help but think of Kerouac). Even though they knew their father would not approve, the children decided to leave the material "in raw form" with only minor edits, because this would allow readers to hear their father's voice. The book was well received in France and elsewhere.

## Reading the Novel

I BOUGHT THE BOOK AND TOOK IT HOME. Over the next several months I read and reread parts, and made mental and written notes. Many of his scenes reminded me of scenes from my youth that I had written about. I wove these experiences into my written review. I also referred back to Camus's notebooks and a biography by Lottman (1980), which was close in detail and character to *The First Man*.

While formulating his ideas for the book, Camus offered this explanation in his notebook: "The first man repeats the entire journey in order to discover this secret: he is not the first. Every man is the first man, nobody is. This is why he throws himself at his mother's feet" (Camus, 2008, p. 125). Whether Camus or his father was the first man is a subject of speculation. The truth is probably both.

The story was based on Camus's mid-life reflections on his childhood in North Africa after his father was killed in the Battle of Marne, told through the story of his lead character, Jacques Cormery. *New York Times* reviewer Victor Bombert titled his 1995 review "Boyhood's Dark Fire." The interplay between quiet tension and excitement, good and bad, death and life, and dark and light was a constant theme in the narrative.

Written in the third person, the action and dialogue moved quickly back and forth in time and place, from his mid-life to childhood, and France to North Africa. Almost like watching a film, images flashed back and forth across the page. It was as if Camus were following filmmaker Wim Wenders's suggestion that images are more truthful when seen through the eyes of a child (Wenders, 2001). Camus seemed to be searching for both the innocence of youth and the movement of his reflections in nonlinear time. I was reminded of Hemingway's "Big Two-Hearted River," Virginia Woolf's *The Waves*, Turgenev's *Fathers and Sons*, and Norman Maclean's *A River Runs Through It*, in which youth unfolded as the character moved across the landscape with a longing and searching for something more, as I did for most of my youth.

Like these authors, Camus worked with a sense of detachment to paint landscapes that drew the reader into the lives of his characters. Drawing on his experience as a climatologist, he used weather to convey mood in many scenes. For example, similar to Turgenev's story "Bezhin Lea" about a horseman's encounter with peasant boys, *The First Man* opened with a description of the movement of clouds into the countryside. The lead character, Jacques Cormery, was about to be born:

> Above the wagon along a stony road, big thick clouds were hurrying to the East through the dusk. Three days ago they had inflated over the Atlantic, had waited for a wind from the West, had set out, slowly at first then faster and faster, had flown over the phosphorescent autumn waters, straight to the continent. (p. 1)

Having grown up next to Lake Michigan in Milwaukee, where the clouds and wind had a daily impact on my mood, I immediately felt part of the story, and began to juxtapose some of the sketches I had written from my reflections on my youth with Camus's sketches, first in my mind then later on paper. In this scene, he described how middle-aged Jacques reflected on his childhood on a ship crossing from France to North Africa after he had visited his father's grave:

> But he had escaped, he could breath, on the giant back of the sea. He was breathing in waves, rocked by the great sun, at last he could sleep and he could come back to the childhood from which he had never recovered, to the secret of light, of the warm poverty that had enabled him to survive and overcome everything. The fragmented reflection on that copper of the porthole, now almost motionless, came from the sun that pressed with all its weight on the shutters of the dark room where the grandmother was sleeping and plunged a

very slender sword into the darkness through the one opening that a
sprung knot had left in the button strap of the shutters. The flies were
missing. (p. 41)

In a scene from my youth when I couldn't sleep and took my father's car
late at night to the shore of Lake Michigan, I had written in my sketchbook:

> I park next to the rocks where the waves can crash over the top, wash
> down the sides, and cocoon me inside. One wave after another is fol-
> lowed by a quiet, womblike moment. Then as if coming up for air my
> lungs filled with a new energy, the lights from the night ships shine
> through the watery windshield like diamonds on the horizon.

Camus defined Jacques's quest in mid-life:

> No one had known him [his father] but his mother and she had for-
> gotten him. Of that he was sure. And he had died unknown on earth
> where he had fleetingly passed, like a stranger. No doubt it was up
> to him to ask, to inform himself. But for someone like him, who has
> nothing and wants the world entire, all his energy is not enough to
> create himself and to conquer or understand that world. After all it
> was not too late; he could still search, he could learn who this man
> had been who now seemed closer to him than any other being on
> earth. He could ... (p. 28)

In middle age I too wanted to know about my father and grandfather. Of
Jacques's return back home to see his mother after visiting his father's grave,
Camus wrote:

> When he arrived at the doorstep, his mother opened the door and
> threw herself in his arms. And there, as she did every time they were
> reunited, she kissed him two or three times, holding him against her
> with all her strength; and in his arms he felt her ribs, the hard jut-
> ting bones of her shoulders, trembling a bit, while he breathed the
> soft smell of her skin, that made him remember the spot, under her

larynx, between the two jugular tendons, that he no longer dared to kiss, but that as a child he loved to nuzzle and fondle on those infrequent occasions when she took him on her knees and pretended to sleep, his nose in that little hollow that to him had the scent of tenderness all too rare in his young life. (p. 55)

In my sketchbook I had written:

(*Milwaukee, 1957*) I can hear them talking.

"How did you feel when our father died?" my uncle asks my father.

"I'm not sure. Scared I guess. We were young, perhaps a little sad and relieved, like the boy in James Joyce's story about the dead priest."

"That's a good way to describe it. It was different when Mother died, wasn't it?"

"Yes, she was such a gem."

"Yes, a real gem," my mother sighs to my aunt.

They, my aunt, uncle, father, and mother, are in the kitchen of our second-story flat on Milwaukee's Northwest Side, drinking cocktails. I'm in my room, reading and waiting—14 going on 15. It's about 10:00 p.m.

After the company is gone and the house is dark, I go in the kitchen for a drink of water. Something moves. My father is dancing again in the moonlight. He is still dressed in the shirt, tie, and vest he wore to the life convention he attended at the life insurance company with his brother who is in town from New York where he runs a branch office. Both men have worked all their adult lives for the company. With his hands in his pockets and his pants legs pulled up, my father shuffles his feet to the music in his head. When he turns toward the window you can see his face. He's smiling, but his eyes are distant.

I grab the car keys off the kitchen table, tiptoe down the back stairs, take a deep breath of late August air, back the Dodge out of the garage, and creep between the rows of clapboard duplexes—the houses and people in them less and less familiar and appealing now.

At the end of the alley, I turn east. Burleigh Street is bathed in the humid, warm glow of lights. A sole pigeon disappears beneath the front of the car and reappears above the hood before flying off. The playground where I play basketball with my friends and the cemetery where my brother taught me to drive pass on the left.

Once I reach Lake Michigan, I park next to the pavilion, which sits on the bluffs like a balcony above nature's great symphony, and get out. No one else is here. I repeat the word *pavilion* over and over again until it loses meaning, then drive down to the shore.

Camus reflected on the mystery surrounding Jacques's grandfather's death, which had left him to grow up without father or grandfather.

He died prematurely, worn out by sun and labor and perhaps, by his marriage, without Jacques ever being able to discover what disease he died of. Left alone the grandmother disposed of the little farm and went to live in Algiers with her younger children, the others having been sent out as soon as they were young enough to be apprenticed. (p. 84)

That night as I sat in the car by the shore of Lake Michigan, I imagined, as I often did, the events that led to my grandfather's death, also a mystery:

*(Milwaukee, 1917)* The train pulls slowly from the station toward the yards. From the step of the caboose, my grandfather, a conductor for the Milwaukee Road, watches the last of the passengers leave the platform, their silhouettes intermittently reappearing in the steam and between the passing steel girders. Near the end of the platform, he jumps off, goes to in the washroom, and looks in the mirror. The face he sees does not look like his; his body has arrived but not the rest of him.

After he cleans up he takes the trolley to his house on the South Side. Small and packed together, the houses and shops pass like images in the moving pictures. By the time he gets off, the wind has shifted away from the lake, and the temperature has risen about 10

degrees. Mist halos the street lights. He lives with his wife and sons
in a bungalow on the corner of Bow and Arrow Streets. My grandmother, a thin stern-looking but loving German woman with spectacles and premature grey hair tied in a bun, greets him at the door.
He looks handsome in his conductor uniform.

"Welcome home, husband."

He kisses her on the cheek and takes off his jacket, which she
hangs up for him. As usual, dinner is ready. Their sons, my father,
Will, 10, and my uncle, Charles, 12, have been fed and gone out to
play. She sits across from him at the dining room table and listens as
he paints vivid pictures of the wide Missouri and the rolling hills on
his trip to South Dakota. She listens intently, then, when she feels the
time is right, says, "The roof is leaking."

"I'll take a look at it tomorrow," he says and puts a spoonful of
mashed potatoes in his mouth.

After dinner, still restless from his travels, he goes to the neighborhood pub and drinks a few beers with his German friends. They
talk quietly about the war—once the primary language in schools,
German is no longer spoken in public. Even though they oppose the
war, they have become unpopular. President Wilson has stirred up a
furor against the Huns, here and overseas.

When he gets home, my grandfather, a pacifist, reads Nietzsche ...
"all philosophers have the failing of thinking man is now," and falls
asleep with the book in his lap.

In the morning, after breakfast, he climbs on the roof to fix the
leak. It's a nice spring day. He works at a steady pace; time passes
unnoticed. In the distance, he can see the ships in the harbor and
the cream brick buildings downtown that give the city its nickname,
Cream City. My grandmother knits beneath him at the kitchen table.
As the sun sinks below the barren elm branches, he feels a slight
chill....

In a conversation with his uncle after World War II about the "Huns," Camus said they weren't all bad people. My German father told me about how he
was beat up by other boys after President Wilson stirred up hatred for the Ger-

mans. Like Camus, he lived in a poor neighbourhood with ethnic violence. I grew up after World War II in a neighbourhood of German, Jewish, Italian, and Greek families. By then we had, for the most part, become Americanized and learned to live together almost as if we did not have differences other than religious. Like Camus, I longed for a sense of culture and place.

In passages such as the ones below, Camus showed how the rules of the game, the importance of public and private space, the inventiveness and creativity of youth, motion, and play shaped his philosophy and helped him escape the moods created by the weather and life that surrounded him:

> Then, still running, through the heat and the dust that covered their feet and their sandals with a single gray layer, they dashed on to the gray field. It was a vacant lot behind a cooperage, where among rusted hoops and old rotten barrel bottoms bunches of anemic grass sprouted between patches of chalky tuff. There amidst loud cries they would draw a circle in the tuff. One of them would take up a position in the circle, racquet in hand, and others would take turns hurling the wooden cigar into the circle. If the cigar landed in the circle the thrower took the racquet, and then he defended the circle. The more skillful of them would hit the cigar on a fly and drive it far away. In that case he had the right to go where it had landed, make the cigar jump by hitting its edge with the edge of the racquet, then drive it still farther.... This poor man's tennis, which had a few more complex rules, would take up most of the afternoon....
>
> When either the weather or their mood did not lend itself to running around the streets and the vacant lots, they would first gather in the hall of Jacques's house. From there they went out the back door and down into a small yard enclosed on three sides by the walls of houses. On the fourth side a big orange tree stretched its branches over a garden wall; when it was in flower, its scent rose above the wretched houses, drifting through the hall or down a small stone stairs to the yard.... It was there, in one of those the cellars that the children would gather. Jean and Joseph, the two sons of the Spanish barber, where in the habit of playing there. Since it was at the door to their hovel, the cellar was their own territory. (pp. 44–45)

I saw myself as a boy playing kick the can in the alley, running bored around the house and neighbourhood, and later playing four-square with the troubled boys I worked with. It reminded me of this scene into which I had woven a reference to Milan Kundera, another writer I admire for his ability to question the "foolish certainties" in life, and French philosopher Foucault's use of motion, which seemed relevant to my attempts to escape the existential hum, something I had also seen throughout Camus's work.

(*1954*) I sit in my father's chair in the living room of our second-story flat on Milwaukee's northwest. For at least four reasons I was eager to read Camus's last book. First, I wanted to see how his childhood had shaped him as the writer, thinker, and activist I admired. I had read some of his other work, but not this one. Second, I knew reading his youth would inform my own youth. I would "read" my youth as I read his. And third, his resilience during a difficult childhood would provide insight for understanding troubled youth. Like many youth I worked with, he grew up without a father. He was raised by a near-deaf, mute mother, and stern grandmother in poor neighborhood of Arab, Spanish, and French youth. Lastly, Camus was about the same age as my father, and this might provide something about the times of his youth. Slide and stare at my feet, imagining my foot bones the way they appeared in the x-ray machine at the shoe store. Dust floats in the winter sunlight that flows through the barren elm branches that cathedral the narrow street outside. I'm 12. I just filled the water canisters above the heat vents from the coal furnace in the basement. Rocky the cat is asleep on the floor in front of me.

My mother is in the kitchen checking the items in the grocery bags against the receipt. My older brother is out with his friends. My father is in the bathroom, the smell of his aftershave wafting over the classical music he plays on Saturday afternoons. He turns off the music and leaves on the backstairs to get a haircut. My mother sets a can of soup on the sink next to the drawer with the can opener.

"'Like a golden ring falling into a silver basin.' After first acknowledging that the small acoustical detail could be inconsequential I think Thomas

Mann sounded that faint, clear, metallic tone to create silence. He needed that silence to make death/beauty audible" (Kundera, 1999, p. 143). I read Milan Kundera's thoughts in *The Book of Laughter and Forgetting* about how the innocence of death/beauty in childhood and youth is slowly drowned out in the noise and clutter of life. And Camus wrote in his notes, "It's not the melancholy of ruined things that breaks the heart, but the desperate love of what lasts eternally in eternal youth: love of the future" (2008, p. 129).

Thinking it's a can of tuna perhaps, the cat strolls into the kitchen. I look at the photographs on the mantel: The four of us on my uncle's second story porch, one of my father in a bar, looking dapper in vest and tie with a dart cocked in front of his right eye, one of my mother taken before she met my father smiling coquettishly from beneath the brim of her flapper hat (my favorite), and one of me in a swim suit, bent sideways, ribs protruding with arms stretched up the shaft of an oar and my brother in a row boat behind me, both of us waiting for my mother to shoot the photo so we can row around the raft on our two-week vacation "up north."

"He's such a Jekyll and Hyde," my mother says about my father on the phone to my aunt.

To pass the time, I shoot "buckets" in the alley on the basketball hoop and backboard my brother and I put on the garage roof.

One by one, I chase down rebounds from jump and hook shots until the sun gets low in the sky, and the melted snow freezes and makes it too slippery to play.

My mother cooks bologna, beans, and fried potatoes for dinner. Afterwards she knits while I read about horses and my older brother makes a model airplane, cutting and gluing pieces of balsa wood to a tissue-paper pattern. Later he will bake the paper skin tight around the frame in the oven. And in spring he will go into the attic, start them on fire, and throw them out the window for me to douse on the ground with the garden hose.

Before I go to bed, I do a flying bird nest on the gymnastic rings my brother and I hung from the rafters in the attic. Back and forth I swing inverted with my hands and feet behind me in the rings like a bird over the old Victrola phonograph, appliances, photographs, and clothes in boxes.…

And after his periods of stasis, Foucault usually succeeded in achieving dramatic accelerations in his thinking and action. Thinking was action, and action was motion—and as a thinker and as a person Foucault chose to be in motion. . . . To detach oneself from oneself— such a distance enables motion, and in turn, motion enables a recurrent activity of self detachment. (Rabinow & Rose, 1994, p. xxii)

Camus gave a glimpse of the Arab, Spanish, Italian, and French diversity in his community in this scene in *The First Man* as Jacques makes his way to the movie theatre with his Spanish grandmother:

The neighborhood movie house was just down the street from their building and bore the name of a Romantic poet, as did the street alongside it. Before going in, you had to pass an obstacle course of Arab peddlers' stands bearing helter-skelter displays of peanuts, dried salted chick peas, lupine seeds, and sugar coated barley in loud colors, and sticky sourballs. . . . A swarm of flies and children, both attracted by the same sweets, buzzed and shouted as they chased each other.… Jacques would escort his grandmother who had sleeked back her white hair for the occasion and fastened her eternal black dress with a silver brooch. She would sedately part the howling kids who blocked the entrance and present herself at the one ticket window. (p. 93)

The scene moved into the movie house and described how Jacques sat next to his Spanish grandmother, trying to read for her the words below the silent movie above the noise of the music, wishing his mother, who never went to the movies, might be with him. In this scene in which his near-deaf, mute mother had dressed to go on the street, much to the chagrin of his stern grandmother, Camus shows his wish for a better life for her:

"You went to the hairdresser," Jacques said. She smiled with the look of a little girl caught in some misdeed. "Yes, you know, you were coming." She had always been coquettish in her almost invisible way. And as plainly as she dressed, Jacques did not remember her ever wearing anything ugly. (p. 121)

Both my parents were raised by stern, widowed mothers who also wore black dresses, worn shiny over the years. My mother used to dress up in different outfits and ask my opinion. I was her little man. I often wished she would get dressed up again in her flapper hat and escape from the world in which she found herself trapped.

(*1954, Milwaukee*) The tires crunch ahead on the frozen snow. I reach in the trunk and grab an armful of newspapers, heavy with Sunday inserts, and peddle house to house. When I get cold I sit inside next to my father, the smell of his Old Spice mixed with the lingering smell of booze.

Eventually, the sun rises and falls on my face like a warm wash cloth. I let Rocky out last night. He shows up for a few minutes then goes back on the prowl. Mostly Jewish, German, and Italian families live in the clapboard and brick duplexes and bungalows on my route. "You have to live through the depression and war to understand," says my mother when I ask her why we stay here. "Besides, your father would never pick up and leave. I would, but not him."

"You ought to," I tell her.

Jacques grew up amid these extremes in "mothering," passive and aggressive men, men who died violent deaths, and mean priests. He incorporated parts of these characters throughout the story into his own ever-changing and developing identity as a soccer player, philosopher, and writer influenced by the school and teachers who fed his hunger for discovery.

In Mr. Germain's class, they felt for the first time that they existed and that they were objects of highest regard: they were judged worthy to discover the world. And even their teacher did not devote himself just to what he was paid to teach them; he welcomed them with simplicity into his personal life, he lived that life with them, told them about his childhood and the lives of children he had known, shared with them his philosophy but not his opinions, for though he was for example anti-clerical, like many of his colleagues, he never said a word against religion in class, nor anything that could be the object of a choice or a belief, but he would condemn with all the more vigor those evils over which there could be no argument—theft, betrayal, rudeness, dirtiness. (p. 146)

A letter Camus wrote to Mr. Germain after he received the Nobel Prize was published in the back of the book. Camus spoke of what he had learned from his teacher. He had made himself visible, as I was trying to do.

Passages and notes such as these—combined with passages of the boy winning a playground fist fight (eerily similar to a fight I was in at the same age), experiencing hard work in the cooperage, developing an appreciation for artisans, living with a grandmother who was stern, even mean, but loving in the way impoverished grandmothers might have been in those days, concerned that their children had the discipline and simple values needed to escape to a better life—take us deep into the world of dualities, absurdities, and imagery that shaped Camus as the young thinker; a world where a quest to be and know self merges with the outer world of conflicts, confusion, paradox, and epiphany; a world in which as a young man I too found myself.

(1954) After all the papers are peddled we drive to my grandmother's asphalt-sided bungalow, which is heated with a small coal stove in the kitchen. She's a heavyset woman whose legs seem to go straight into her shoes without ankles. With her eyes hidden behind her puffy cheeks and spectacles I never know if she is glad to see me or not, but the coffee cake is always ready. Every Sunday she makes coffee cake, and sometimes pigs in blankets (sausages cooked in bread), but no pigs today, just the coffee cake. While my father talks to her, I go into the unheated parlor where she keeps the Christmas tree until Easter. It's dark, except for a small sliver of light that shines through the bottom of the sliding door.

In the notes and sketches in the appendix, Camus wrote about Jacques:

> Cultivated, athletic, debauched, a loner and the best of friends, spiteful, unfailingly dependable, etc., etc.
>
> He doesn't like anyone, "No one could be more noble in spirit," "cold and distant," "warm and passionate," everyone thinks he's an energizer except he himself, always lying down.
>
> Thus expand the personality.
>
> When he speaks: "I begin to believe in my innocence...." (p. 294)

*(1954)* Voices muffled, they talk for a while then my father stands by the door and says, "It's time to go, son." On the way home I sit next to him with the coffee cake in my lap. Church bells ring in the background. "Mind over matter," I repeat a line to myself that I learned when I used to go to Christian Science Sunday school before I started playing touch football in the park with the Jewish boys who went to temple on Saturday. He reaches over and pinches my leg, "Everything copacetic son?" I don't know how to respond. I just pick at the crumbs, the crusty edges of my own life not yet formed.

When we get home, my father goes back to bed. I sit in his chair again. My mother and brother are still sleeping. The house is quiet. My mother must have let the cat in. He jumps up in my lap. Another church bell rings.

Of his mother's faith, Camus recalled:

As for Catherine Cormery [his mother], only she with her gentleness might have suggested faith, but in fact her gentleness was that faith. She never dissented nor agreed, laughed a little at her brother's jokes, but would call the priests she met "Monsieur Curé." She never spoke of God. In fact that was a word Jacques never heard spoken throughout his childhood, nor did he trouble himself about it. Life, so vivid and mysterious, was enough to occupy his entire being. (p. 165)

And I wrote in my sketchbook:

The clock ticks. I pet the cat, and repeat the word *copasetic* over and over again until it loses meaning. Then I look again at the pictures on the mantel.

The dart is cocked.

Near the end of the book, in summary of his reflections, Camus wrote:

From the darkness within sprang that famished ardor, that mad passion for living, which had always been part of him and even today was still unchanged, making still more bitter—in the midst of the family he had rediscovered and facing the images of his childhood—the sudden terrible feeling that the time of his youth was slipping away, like the woman he had loved, oh yes he had loved her with great love, with all his heart and his body too … he told her youth was passing … perhaps because she was so intelligent and outstanding she rejected the world as it was. (p. 283)

*(Milwaukee, Spring, 1968)* "See the cardinal?" Suzanne says a few days after we meet and walk along the bluffs in the park.

"Where?"

"In the tree. It's bright red."

"I'm partially color blind."

She smiles, puts her hands on my head, and gently turns it toward a branch in a tree. "See there?"

"Yes," I pretend.

We sit under a tree. "Do you ever think there are no words for feelings?" I ask.

"Yes, that's why I paint."

"But images, like words, are symbols. Do you ever think images aren't enough?"

"I don't think much when I paint."

In the evening she gives me a drawing of a naked man crouched in a beam of light. He's bald with long, lean muscles and sunken eyes, and does not cast a shadow. I hang it at the head of my bed. In the morning her gentle breaths fall in steady beats on my chest.

Camus wrote, "Then her blood on fire she wanted to flee, flee to a country where no one would grow old ... where life would always be wild and radiant ... and he too perhaps more than she, since he had been in a land without forefathers and without memory" (p. 284).

Camus the philosopher/writer was evident in these notes at the end of the book about the development of Jacques as a character:

> Learning justice and morality means to decide whether an emotion is good or bad according to its consequences. J. I can give in to women, but if they take all this time ...
>
> I've lived too long, and acted and felt, to say this one is right and that one is wrong. I've had enough of living according to an image others show me of myself. I'm resolved on autonomy, I demand independence and interdependence.

## Summary

READING AND SEEING CAMUS'S CHILDHOOD in a mosaic of his and my experiences reinforced the importance of place, play, work, relationships, and creativity in development. The contexts in which they shaped a man who overcame many obstacles in his life to become a powerful thinker, writer, and activist provided new insight. I was drawn into the story with curiosity and a renewed desire to understand.

Like the stories of many young people, Camus's life was full of risks that he had to overcome. He was able to cope and learn from his experiences, and to see a world in which others could live a moral life of choice and interpretation. He survived abuses, racism, and violence, and insisted later that his life as a poor child in Algeria was relatively happy, as quoted in Lottman (1980):

> Poverty, first of all, was never a misfortune to me.... To correct a natural indifference I was placed halfway between misery and the sun.

Misery prevented me from thinking all is well under the sun; and in history, the sun taught me history is not everything. (p. 21)

An argument can be made that Camus understood and loved his youth, and therefore he was against killing youth in wars. Early on he also began to see the dualities that were present in life. This made him the moral thinker he became an adult. I am going to talk about him in my classes and make his book recommended reading. Perhaps some of the students will identify with Camus and juxtapose their experiences with his, along with those of the more contemporary thinkers, artists, and poets of their generation who have an influence in helping them understand themselves and the worlds in which they and youth live. This will make them better youth workers and advocates for youth. ●

REFERENCES

Brombert, V. (1995, August 27). Boyhood's dark fire [Review of *The First Man* by Albert Camus]. *New York Times*. Retrieved from http://www.nytimes.com/books/97/12/14/home/camus-firstman.html

Camus, A. (1995). *The first man* (D. Hapgood, Trans.). New York, NY: Vintage.

Camus, A. (2008). *Notebooks, 1951–1959* (R. Bloom, Trans.). Chicago, IL: Ivan R. Dee.

Kundera, M. (1999). *The book of laughter and forgetting* (trans. Aaron Asher). New York, NY: Harper Perennial.

Lottman, H. (1980). *Albert Camus: A biography*. New York, NY: Doubleday & Company.

Rabinow, P., & Rose, N. (Eds.). (1994). *The essential Foucault: Selections from the essential works of Foucault, 1954–1984*. New York, NY: New Press.

Sartre, J.-P. (2007). *Existentialism is a humanism*. New Haven, CT: Yale University Press. (Original work published 1946)

Wenders, W. (2001). *On film (essays and conversations)*. London, England: Faber and Faber.

# Chapter

## Be Gone, Dull Care

GERRY FEWSTER, WITH CEDRICK OF TOXTETH

## A Preparatory Word

**Child and youth care** is not a tightly knit profession governed by rigid prescriptions and exclusive practices. Is this a deficit to be remedied or an intrinsic quality of our discipline that should be embraced, nurtured, and explored?

In support of the latter, the authors of this chapter argue that our relative
freedom from the traditional mould makes it possible for us to become who
we are, think for ourselves, share our experience, and savour the opportunity
to remain open and responsive to the needs of kids, whoever they are and
wherever they may be.

In taking an unfettered look at the concept of "caring," this chapter celebrates that freedom. In the first section, a former columnist with the journal
*Relational Child and Youth Care Practice* takes a predictably irreverent jester's
swipe at the topic. Riding roughshod over the personal and professional motives,
meanings, and methodologies commonly associated with the verb "to care," he
argues that even the title "child and youth care" is a pretentious oxymoron. It's
pretty devilish stuff but *wise words in the mouths of fools do oft themselves belie.*

In the second segment, a former editor of the aforementioned journal
responds with a more reasonable, respectful, and responsible perspective.
Acknowledging the hidden wisdom of his former columnist, he argues that

caring about others is actually a deeply rooted human quality that can be defined and incorporated into "professional" practice. This is an option that requires considerable understanding and discipline, but the challenge is far more exciting and worthwhile than pursuing the well-trodden pathway toward some protected stall in the professional marketplace.

# 1

## It's Time to Get Rid of the "Care" Package

CEDRICK OF TOXTETH

> *Begone, dull care*
> *I prithee begone from me*
> *Begone, dull care,*
> *From me and CYC*
> *I care for him, I care for her*
> *I care most care-fully*
> *But since I care, it's only fair*
> *That they should care for me.*

—traditional ditty desecrated by Cedrick

**When will you CYC toadies** wake up and realize you'll be hanging around the bargain basements of the labour markets for as long as you keep etching the word *care* into your grotty little shingle? Used as a noun, child and youth *care* is on a par with car *care*, home *care*, lawn *care*, and that good old tender loving *care* (even the nurses tossed this one into the incinerator). Make it a verb and you become a bunch of *care*givers, looking after kids nobody else wants to deal with (and for good reason). If you want to make it an adjective, go ahead and sell yourselves as *caring* do-righters who would just love to make the world a better place by caring about everything and everybody. Well, dippity-do-to-dah-to-ya.

If I'm correct about this, which I am, hanging on to this mushy word means you'll never be up there eating prawn sandwiches and sipping martinis with the real professionals. I'm talking about the folks with specialized knowledge and expertise like pediatricians, psychiatrists, psychologists, lawyers, educators, and those greasy guys in dark suits who manage your expansive financial portfolio (oh, don't you wish?). Most of these high flyers don't even claim to care. In fact, the less they care, the more their services are respected, sought after, and (weep over this one) generously remunerated. You see, real professionals realize that hard-working folks don't hand over good money for "caring" unless it's to the Salvation Army. They understand their clients want somebody to solve their problems and take away their pain (real or imagined). They want objective, duly certified experts who can deliver the goods (read "positive outcomes"). Sorry folks, but you won't catch real professionals hanging around street corners looking for clients, supervising trainee psychopaths, or dragging some screeching brat to a time-out room. Why should they? There are peons, who are only too eager to do that for minimum wage—simply because they "care." And they call *me* a fool....

Of course, if you're dumb enough to believe that the kids are your "clients," then you can continue to care until all those little moo-cows come home; just don't moan about not being respected or paid as a professional. The truth is that the kids don't hire you. Be honest, in many cases they don't even want you around. You won't get any money from them (unless you run a Fagin program or something equally creative), and there's no point in looking to them for the respect and gratitude you so humbly deserve.

So who wants you? Who hires you? Who pays for your services? Who evaluates your performance? Well, I'll leave you to come up with the answers. But, for me, the more important questions are, What do they want from you? Are you able (or willing) to deliver the goods? Are you prepared to accept the conditions established by a self-serving, power-seeking Association that tells you what you must do and how you should practise as a certified child and youth care worker? And the biggest question of them all, Who, or what, do you really care about?

When it comes to the C-word, what really gets under my motley are those bleating boneheads with their pathetic Mother Teresa syndrome. I'm talking about the self-righteous bores who sacrifice themselves in the service of others. Oh, give me a pig in a poke, these folks are not only a pain past the perineum; their lack of awareness and honesty renders them toxic—if not evil. I agree with that ancient Hebrew jester the Hasidic Rabbi of Lublin, who said:

> I love the wicked man who knows he is wicked more than the righteous man who knows he is righteous. But concerning the wicked who consider themselves righteous, it is said: "They do not turn even on the threshold of Hell." For they think they are being sent to Hell to redeem the souls of others.

I'm not saying CYC folks are wicked (apart from Claudia Boffit, who is definitely evil). In my little book of truth, there's only one group of sinners more dangerous than those who use the C-word without knowing what their real motives are, and those are the ones who use it as a cover-up for motives they *do* know about. Either way, take a peek behind this noble and deceptive facade and you'll find yourself staring at a whole bunch of less-than-noble intentions. Oh go ahead, this isn't about you—it's about all those other sinners.

You won't have to dig very deep to uncover the caregiver's most valued reward—power and plenty of it. All tyrants, dictators, saints, cops, and those who hang out the "I Care" shingle (including Claudia B., who hovers about when I'm hungover) have a pathological need to call the shots. They all rely upon some form of power differential to make their wretched "targets" conform. Religions, politics, cultures, social institutions (families included), physical strength, punishment, specialized knowledge, and expertise are all used to keep the peons in their places. If we tell our governments where to stuff their caring, they simply make new laws, hire more cops, and build more prisons so they can care for us more. But if you want to see the power motive in full swing, just pop into any classroom in any school and there it is—blatant power imposed in the name of caring. And if that's not enough, take a look at how most parents care for their kids in that vicious little arrangement called "the family"—a power-based system if ever I saw one.

Professionals who work with kids have their own caring power plays. As you'd expect, shrinks have the best deal; they can designate, medicate, incarcerate, and, above all, obfuscate in the name of psychiatric care without challenge—such humble caring people they all are. Then we drop through the ranks of the caring fraternity until we find ourselves in the CYC bargain basement where the power of caring has a very different flavour. For whatever reasons—humility, timidity, or stupidity—you folks have chosen to give deference to the "experts," even though you are the only ones who understand what's really happening for kids (a pox on you for this). So you mince around using whatever you can to create that critical power differential in your own lowly domain. I could spend hours on this topic, but I could never say it as clearly and profoundly as Mick McMahon, who lived at Toxteth House for Rotten Kids: "What you plonkers call caring, I call fucking manipulation. It's all about what you want, not what I want." Sadly, Mickey-boy will never be given a medal for his brilliant insight.

If you can bring yourself to delve beyond the sentimental slosh of interpersonal caring (your own included), chances are you'll be peering into the abyss of eternal fear rather than gazing into the crystal waters of love and universal relatedness. Step into the darkness and you'll quickly discover the rejection, aloneness, abandonment, and isolation that lurk in the grisly shadows of your tortured psyche. With Mommy and Daddy no longer around to hold your hand, you'll scramble around in search of some other lonely wanderer, the special one who would walk at your side, caring for you as you would care for him or her. Oh, to hear the words "I need you"; to whisper softly, "You belong to me"; to finally affirm the bond that will keep you cared for and safe till death you do part. What a prospect. What a romance. What a crock!

Well, if this is what you want you may as well become a professional caregiver. This way you have endless options and get modestly paid for your troubles. At first blush, kids may seem like the best targets. They're easier to control than grown-ups and, if you can help them turn their lives around, they'll have every reason to be grateful, acknowledge you, care about you, and follow you around like fuzzy chicks in a farmyard. And when that doesn't come to pass—as it won't—there are still those fleeting moments to keep your hopes alive. That brief smile after doing chores together, the tentative hug after a "counselling" session, and the unexpected handmade Christmas gift are all precious illusions of a caring that never was. Then there are the achievements—that first star in arithmetic, the drama prize, high school graduation, the job at Wal-Mart—none of which would have happened without you and your selfless caring. Of course you don't expect anything in return, although some small token from somebody sometime would be nice. But worry not, there are other kids who need you, any one of them will fit the bill, and someday you'll get everything that's coming to you. Meanwhile, don't fasten your seatbelts and forget about the sunscreen. For me, I'll take the carefree life anytime.

# 2

## I Care to Differ

GERRY FEWSTER

**Well, true to form,** my irrepressible friend Cedrick has used his fool's privilege to turn the divine into the demonic. Calling for the removal of the word *care* from our professional title, he goes to some length to propose that this term is no more than a convenient euphemism used to cover up multiple forms of manipulation and trickery. In the helping professions, it's an excuse for meddling in other people's lives for personal gain, not only in the pursuit of power but also in a misdirected attempt to assuage the practitioner's own pain.

As you might expect, I fundamentally disagree—and it would be a pretty boring chapter if I didn't. Begrudgingly, I do think he makes a few valid points, some of which I'll attempt to address. To begin with, I don't think the C-word would be at all contentious if we could share a common understanding of what it actually stands for. Cedrick's cynical definitions aside, I believe this term can be used to represent our most sacrosanct commitment to the well-being of kids. I don't want to get involved in a semantic slugging match with a professional fool (except to say that my co-author doesn't seem to know what a noun is), but I would like to begin by making a distinction between caring *for* and caring *about*. In my view, both are integrated aspects of child and youth care and should serve to guide our professional activities—please bear with me.

## Caring For or Caring About? Take Your Pick

CARING *about* is a cognitive construct that, unless specified otherwise, has no intrinsic empathic qualities. I can care about the poverty-stricken people of Baronia simply because I want them to buy my new line of spandex loincloths. By the same token, caring *for* denotes some form of action, without necessarily implying any heartfelt involvement or connection. Anybody who tried caring for my crumbling aunt Edwina through her last eighty years would know exactly what I mean. So, I begin with the premise that, in child and youth care, caring *about* or *for* is based upon some level of understanding and empathy on the part of the practitioner.

As any brief review of CYC literature will reveal, caring *for* kids is the overwhelming concern, while caring *about* them runs a very distant second, third, or even fourth. Fair enough, you don't get paid for caring about something, and "advocacy" is often considered to be a threat by those who run the show and hold the purse strings. Yet, for me, a reluctance to link and integrate these two aspects of caring is not merely a careless omission, it's glaring neglect. There can be no doubt that across our troubled planet, kids are facing an unpredictable and scary future. All we have come to know about healthy growth and development suggests they are at risk on a scale never before imagined. Is it possible that much of what you see and respond to in the daily lives of youngsters in your care is actually symptomatic of these broader concerns? Take a moment, or a couple of days, to step back and examine this proposition—you might be surprised. If this doesn't make sense, keep stepping back until it does.

I'm convinced that no profession is better able to understand and express the global plight of young people. Specific labels aside, folks engaged in child and youth care work are to be found in all regions of the world, and if their collective voice could ever be orchestrated it would reverberate in all directions. These are not the philosophers, academics, journalists, or bleeding hearts trotting out clichés like "our children are our future." These are the people who know and understand what's happening for kids from the inside out. The good news is that through structures like regional associations and the CYC-Net, we've been generating a compelling dialogue for many years. Now it's time to move beyond our obsession with professional development and let the world know that we are all responsible for whatever future is in store for kids everywhere, and, as things stand, that future ain't looking so good.

In the caring *for* department, I still hear CYC folks complaining that their caring amounts to little more than glorified babysitting. Well, if this is so, I could also argue that the care a neurosurgeon provides for his or her patients amounts to little more than a medical pat on the head. Like Cedrick, these misguided souls have bought into the shallow belief that precision and pragmatism define professional practice. While the skills of a surgeon are highly specific and exact, those of us who work in the hazy domain of human relationships require skills that must be constantly adjusted in response to the most subtle shifts and variations. Caring for others interpersonally is a multi-faceted enterprise involving emotions and actions that call for the highest levels of commitment, understanding, and expertise. Those who refer to this as "babysitting" are either blind to the opportunity or unwilling to face up to the challenge. Either way, they should be looking for vacancies at McDonald's. Those who are aware realize that the foundational requirements for effective relational practice—being fully present, accessing intuition, reflecting the experiences of another person—are skills that can take as many years to master as those of the oft-cited head technician. If this isn't professional caring, then show me the way to the nearest dog pound. And does all this suggest that CYC professionals should be more respected and better paid? Well, of course, but it will never happen as long as they refer to themselves as "babysitters" and behave accordingly.

## Caring as a Developmental Aspect of the Self

CARING IS A NATURAL HUMAN STATE that requires constant nurturance and development. We come into this world with an inherent ability to attune our feelings to the experiences of others (e.g., Stern, 1985). Newborns in intensive care units persistently respond to one another's distress, and many a mom will tell you how her baby "instinctively" understands and responds to how she is feeling, and vice versa (see Chamberlain, 1999). These are the earliest reflections of personal "empathy" and interpersonal "attunement" that precede the development of the mind and lay the foundations for mindful caring. If nurtured through childhood, these basic qualities can evolve into the deepest forms of human connection, compassion, and love (see Fewster, 2010).

When babies turn into toddlers, it may appear that natural empathy and attunement have been completely overridden in an all-out attempt to dominate the world and everybody in it (e.g., Rosenberg, Rand, & Assay, 1985). During this phase, often referred to as the "terrible twos," the child's behaviour is more likely to appear psychopathic than empathic. Demands for instant gratification and complete disregard for the feelings of others, parents and siblings included, cannot be moderated by rational appeals based upon morality or fairness, and the usual methods of discipline serve only to intensify the power trip. Parents who understand this to be an essential developmental task, a time when the fledgling self needs to know that it can have some impact on the world, will not suppress this quest with overly harsh discipline and punishment. Parents who were never given an opportunity to express their own healthy narcissism during their early years have a particularly tough time during this phase.

What needs to be understood is that, on the inside, the youngster's world does not consist of interesting people with complex feelings, thoughts, and sensitivities. As the child's developing cognitive structures begin to create complex new images of other beings who are both separate and connected, natural empathy is gradually incorporated into the mix. Until that happens, the child still lives in a world of objects (including Mommy, Daddy, and Teddy) that must be controlled or manipulated to bring about pleasure and avoid pain. Difficult as it might be for parents to believe, natural empathy has not been lost, but only placed in storage while the developmental tasks are attended to. Yet, interestingly enough, even kids in the throes of this intensive narcissistic adventure will usually stop dead in their tracks if someone close is genuinely distressed. In other words, that natural state of empathy and attunement will then override the developmental task.

Caring for and about others becomes possible when the self has learned that it can be effective in the world and cognitive development enables the child to see others as separate beings with their own thoughts, feelings, and experiences. This is what object relations theorists refer to as "object constancy"—a fundamental step toward individuation in which the natural state of empathy can be reclaimed and assimilated into the equation. This is a process that integrates essential human qualities into complex, ever-changing cognitive concepts and structures, but so what? What matters is that an effective and empathic self is ready to continue its journey in the company of other selves. Developmental theorists often refer to this reconnection as *rapprochement* (e.g., Cashdan, 1988).

## Developmental Interruptions

WHILE I'VE ARGUED that caring is an inherent human trait, I've also suggested that its development and expression can be interrupted and inhibited. This raises the question as to whether those interruptions can be addressed later in life, and I believe they can. This is important for CYC folks to understand on two counts. If the C-word is to be retained as a professional commitment, then it behooves us all to be aware of, and attend to, any aspect of our own experience that might stand in the way of our ability to care. It's also reasonable to assume that the interruptions in our personal development can be found in the histories of the kids we are paid to care for and about. After all, how many of our young "clients" have selves oozing in empathy and minds that care deeply for the well-being of others and the world in general?

As with most developmental interruptions, the first three years of life are critical. If, like me, your perfectly healthy childhood narcissism was suppressed, and the quality of your reconnection (*rapprochement*) was correspondingly weak, your sense of separation and individuation may remain questionable. My life as a "helper" began at a very early age when I was assigned the task of keeping my family happy. I was well into my twenties before I realized that my caring for others had undisclosed strings attached. The secret formula was: if I care about others, they will care about me. As an ambitious young professional, it was hard for me to accept that in caring for my "clients" I was actually trying to care for myself, and even harder to acknowledge that I was confused about the distinction between my life and theirs. I struggled to resolve this early interruption but always found myself wandering alone down the endless alleyways of self-deception.

Working with a therapist, I discovered that my early narcissistic adventures were effectively suppressed by the most powerful of all sanctions. In the tried-and-true traditions of behaviour modification, my parents chose to ignore my outbursts. This may have curbed the behaviour to some degree, but, on the inside, the constant flow of rejections stirred a little boy's deepest fears of rejection and abandonment. Rather than risk separating from those I needed most, I learned to please and look after them, casting my individuation to the wind. While I learned grown-up ways of disguising my incomplete individuation, my compulsive caring for others was a strategy that found its way into all my relationships, personal and professional. For me, the key was to learn how to stay inside my own personal "boundary" and complete my own individuation without invading others through my strategic caring. In this way, it became possible for me to experience empathy and caring without the entangled strings attached. Even though I can still fall into the old habit from time to time, I now understand the difference.

This is just one example of how empathic caring might be inhibited by developmental interruptions and how these missing pieces can be incorporated into the equation later in life. I find this to be a useful proposition both in my own life and my professional practice. Blindly pursuing the missing pieces is by far the most common factor in strategic caring—whether trying to please and fix people or striving to gain power and control over them. While these two strategies may look very different on the surface, they are actually two sides of the same coin. We might prefer the compulsive helper to the control freak, but, traced back to the nest, they are birds of a feather.

Some people still have difficulty understanding the paradox of how individuation (separation) is the key to connection (relationships). The simple statement is that the more I understand my self, the more I can understand the other as a separate being. And the more I understand what separates us, the more I can come to understand and cherish those things that connect us. This is the foundation of empathic caring that makes compassion and love for all beings possible.

## The Social and Cultural Suppression of Caring

FOR THOSE OF US who have enjoyed the many material benefits of Western cultures, our inherent capacity for empathy and caring is more likely to be triggered by memory, or vicariously through a movie or a book, than in the flow of everyday life. We have bought into a pervasive belief that our basic nature is competitive and that happiness is to be found through social status and material wealth. With this in mind, we have come to regard caring as a means to an end—an effective way to help someone achieve a desired objective such as crossing a busy road, overcoming an illness, getting a university degree, or ensuring a place in heaven, rather than as an end unto itself. Thus we have created a social world in which expressions of caring are seen as helping behaviours that deserve recognition and rewards—a medal or a citation. Cut off from the core of our humanity, such acts are more likely to be motivated by guilt and power than by empathy and caring—token gestures that make up the skimmed milk of human kindness.

Nowhere is this repressive socialization more apparent than in our educational systems. At the age of five, a critical time in the emergence of self, our children are thrust into a rule-based, regimented world in which little or no attention is given to personal feelings, subjective experiences, or individual needs and choices. From the get-go they are taught how to perform, conform, and compete with one another for the cherished prizes of academic success— from the gold stars of kindergarten to the Ph.D.s of Harvard. Those who have established a solid developmental foundation may develop the resilience to hang on to their inner sense of being, but the ever-growing numbers who have stumbled along the way don't stand a chance. They struggle to find a place in an alienated world in which dropping out, acting out, drugging up, bullying, and gang warfare are preferable to failure and isolation. These are the kids who come into the CYC networks, and they keep coming at us ad infinitum.

## Strategic Professional Care

SOME TIME AGO I was involved in a research project examining patterns of interaction among members of interdisciplinary teams in child and adolescent mental health services. One of the most disturbing findings was that concern for the client ranked seventh in the list of professional priorities. The major "undisclosed" concerns were (1) preserving professional status and role, (2) defining presenting problems (diagnoses), (3) determining actions to be taken, (4) establishing lines of authority and accountability, (5) evaluating outcomes, and (6) conducting follow-up meetings. Of particular interest was the observation that, in general, the front-line workers (most with CYC status and training) were (1) the most acquainted with the client, (2) the most involved in treatment intervention, (3) the least influential in decision making, and (4) the lowest paid. I doubt this picture has changed over the last twenty years.

For the most part, professional services are not designed to care for, or care about, kids. Their assigned mandate is to "fix" them and slot them back into the senseless stream in the least time with the least cost. Those who present the greatest threat are drugged or incarcerated, or both. Those who haven't strayed too far are given remedial interventions designed to draw them back into line with threats of deprivation and punishment for noncompliance or failure. For those who fail to take advantage of this opportunity, there's a well-established procedure. First, parents, teachers, and sundry experts collude to ensure that the problem is clearly identified to be within the child. Then comes the "diagnosis," proclaimed by a duly qualified expert, and the youngster is tagged with a label deemed to both classify and explain the identified disorder. The adults breathe a sigh of relief. Not only is everybody off the hook, but the label also opens the door to the remedial system—sorry, no label, no service. Caring agencies classify themselves in terms of the labels they will accept and bill the parents or the funding authorities accordingly. In this way, kids, the serviceable objects, are slotted into the system with their access labels held up for all to see. Oh, such empathy, such compassion … such caring.

If you think I'm dramatizing, or otherwise distorting, this picture, take a close look at the number of kids in your area or domain who have been tagged with, and medicated for, these trumped-up disorders (if anyone is prepared to let you have the figures). And this is precisely why I believe our unsophisticated, undefined, and unorganized profession should keep the C-word etched deeply into its humble shingle. As good old Cedrick has already pointed out, we have already drifted too far into the "fixing" mentality, deferring to the "experts" and blindly following the remedial prescriptions of those who are being paid to preserve the status quo. We administer the daily "treatment" protocols for phony diseases. We impose punishments to enforce compliance to arbitrary "normative" rules. We dish out rewards to enhance "desired" performance. We use relationships to manipulate emotions. We are urged to help kids to succeed without questioning the prescribed criteria for "success." And we churn out unmitigated garbage to identify and measure irrelevant "outcomes" for whoever seems to have authority and power.

In a world cut off from the heart and soul of its own humanity, "nonstrategic empathic caring" is a radical notion that shakes the agents and systems of repression to their core. Any suggestion of caring that involves feeling, connection, and love is perceived as a challenge to their professional way of being, a threat to their worldly ambitions. Their inclination is to dismiss such expressions as wishy-washy claptrap regurgitated by well-meaning do-gooders. But I want to push it back in their faces over and over again. I want them to understand that we have reached the brink and that the time has come for us to reclaim our lost humanity and pass it on to our children before it's too late. Sorry, but caring isn't always about being nice.

## Caring as Professional Practice

IN CHILD AND YOUTH CARE, *nonstrategic empathic caring* is not so much a professional stance as a methodology waiting to be defined. Beginning with the proposition that our work is essentially relational, I want to conclude by identifying some of the ingredients that might be incorporated into such a definition. These are not abstract ideas cobbled together for this chapter; rather, they are principles I've been using in my own practice and teaching for many years. It won't be possible for me to spell out these approaches in detail, but I hope you'll get the drift of my case and be in a position to come to your own conclusions and create your own methods. If you're interested in learning more, I want you to know that I've been saying these things for a long time in many different locations and publications. If you're not familiar with my work, you may wish to take a look at a series of articles I recently penned for *CYC-Online* titled "The Ten (New) Commandments for Child & Youth Care" (2011–2012).

## Toward a Working and Workable Definition

1. **Care enough** to enhance your capacity for caring. Sounds simple enough but, as I've already indicated, developing and expressing accurate empathy is both a quality and a highly sophisticated skill. Empathy, caring, and compassion are elements along a developmental continuum that rarely evolves without interruption. In order to embrace the C-word, you must know and understand your

own developmental history, identify the interruptions (missing pieces), and be prepared do your own remedial personal work.

2. **Care enough** to establish your own sense of "boundary." In relational work, it's essential to know where you end and your "client" begins. This means taking ownership of your own experience and judgments, saying your real yes's and no's while recognizing the kids as unique and separate beings who have the inner resources to take charge of their own lives in their own way (nothing to fix).

3. **Care enough** to create a safe, accepting, and responsive space in which youngsters can be seen and heard for who they really are—free from the judgments and aspirations of others. Within this space, you must be able to suspend your own stuff and learn to experience the world from the place of an other. This perspective-taking ability is an essential skill for the caring practitioner to develop and refine from his or her boundary (e.g., Selman, 1980). It is one of the essential elements in creating a place in which the youngsters learn how to establish their own personal boundaries and assume responsibility for their own experiences and actions. Forget about behavioural outcomes—this is what an effective working relationship is all about.

4. **Care enough** to learn how to empathically and accurately mirror the experience of an other. This isn't the same as "reflective listening" in the tradition of Carl Rogers, although it might appear that way on the surface. Caring practitioners come from their hearts as well as their heads, and their reflections are more about feelings than words. Their intention is not only to reiterate thoughts, but also to reflect inner experience in a way that enables the other person to feel seen and heard on the inside. This type of mirroring requires considerable understanding and practice, but, in my opinion, it is the most valuable and effective CYC skill of all.

5.   **Care enough** to show up. It goes without saying that caring prac-
     titioners must know how to be fully present in their relational
     work. This can be difficult in child and youth care settings where
     so much is going on and so many expectations are hanging over-
     head. The skill is to know how to "bracket off" all the extraneous
     stuff and bring the self solidly to the contact boundary. Alterna-
     tively, if you don't show up, if you're not fully there, nothing of
     value is going to happen. It might sound "motherhood," but in
     my experience becoming present requires commitment and ef-
     fort. Learning to breathe is always a good start.

6.   **Care enough** to learn about a young person's developmental and
     family history from his or her perspective. This is important in
     identifying the interruptions and missing pieces, but it also has
     a more powerful and pervasive value. Finding a place of empathy
     for kids whose behaviour and attitudes are offensive can some-
     times be a stretch, but once their relational story has been shared
     and understood the negative judgments tend to dissipate. This
     doesn't mean letting the kid off the hook. Understanding how he
     or she got to this point is valuable information in assisting the
     youngster in making different choices in the future.

## A Final Word for the Caring Ear

THESE ARE ONLY A FEW of the ingredients that might contribute to some
clear understanding of what caring child and youth care practice is all about.
If you still think this stuff is less than professional, inferior to prescribing
medication or administering archaic diagnostic tests, there's nothing more for
me to say. Should you consider my stance to be just another piece of neo-New
Age, touchy-feely, huggy-duggy, lovey-dovey, anti-scientific sentimentalism,
let me remind you of a classic piece written four centuries ago, in 1624:

No man is an island, entire of itself; every man is a piece of the conti-
nent, a part of the main. If a clod be washed away by the sea, Europe
is the less, as well as if a promontory were, as well as if a manor of
thy friend's or of thine own were: any man's death diminishes me,
because I am involved in mankind, and therefore never send to know
for whom the bell tolls; it tolls for thee.

—John Donne, from *Devotions Upon*
*Emergent Occasions*, "Meditation xvii"

And if you have no time for ancient thinkers, I'll leave you with a quotation
from one of our most celebrated contemporary philosophers:

Remember, I'm rootin' for yer ... we're all in this thing together.

—Red Green

REFERENCES

Cashdan, S. (1988). *Object relations therapy: Using the relationship.* New York, NY:
W.W. Norton & Co.

Chamberlain, D. (1999). Selected works by David Chamberlain [Special millennium issue].
*Journal of Prenatal and Perinatal Psychology and Health, 14*(1–2).

Fewster, G. (2010). *Don't let your kids be normal.* Vancouver, BC: Influence Publishing.

Fewster, G. (2011–2012). The ten (new) commandments for child & youth care. *CYC-Online,*
*148–159.* Retrieved from www.cyc-net.org

Rosenberg, J., Rand, M., & Assay, D. (1985). *Body, self & soul: Sustaining integration.* Atlanta,
GA: Harmonics.

Selman, R. L. (1980). *The growth of interpersonal understanding.* New York, NY: Academic
Press.

Stern, D. (1985). *The interpersonal world of the infant.* New York, NY: Basic Books.

# Contributors

**Ben Anderson-Nathe** received master's degrees in social work and public policy, both focusing on young people and youth-serving systems. He holds a doctorate in education, with an emphasis in youth studies and community education. Ben's practice and teaching emphasize relational engagement with youth in multiple service systems, including residential care, homeless and runaway youth services, juvenile corrections, informal education and recreation, sexual health, and religious settings. His most recent research centres around professional development of youth workers, gender and sexuality, and analysis of social discourses surrounding queer youth and other young people. Ben is currently associate professor and program director of the Child and Family Studies Program at Portland State University, and he co-edits (with Kiaras Gharabaghi) *Child and Youth Services*, a Taylor and Francis journal.

**Gerry Fewster** has been caring for and about kids for over fifty years. During that time he has worn many professional disguises and manipulated many roles to suit his purposes. Throughout it all, child and youth care has been his saving grace—an expansive profession that grants the freedom to explore direct experience of being with kids beyond the old worn-out prescriptions. Where else would his relationship with his co-author, Cedrick, be tolerated?

**Kiaras Gharabaghi** is associate professor and director of the School of Child and Youth Care at Ryerson University. He is co-editor of *Child and Youth Services*, an international peer-reviewed journal about children and youth services around the world. Following over twenty years in practice, Kiaras has been doing research in the areas of residential care (in Canada and internationally), education and social pedagogy, policy and regulatory frameworks for youth services, and system collaboration and organizational change. His recent books include *Professional Issues in Child and Youth Care Practice* (London: Routledge, 2008), *Being with Edgy Youth* (New York: Nova Science Publishers, 2012), and with Carol Stuart, *Right Here, Right Now: Life-Space Intervention with Children and Youth* (Toronto: Pearson, 2013). Kiaras can be contacted at k.gharabaghi@ryerson.ca.

**Mark Krueger** is a pioneer in child and youth care training and education and one of the most loved and respected scholars, commentators, and philosophers of the field. He is a researcher, a conceptual wizard, an innovator, and a novelist. Mark lives in Wisconsin some of the time, and in New Mexico the rest of the time.

**Doug Magnuson** is associate professor, School of Child and Youth Care, at the University of Victoria, B.C. He has a B.A. in philosophy, an M.A. in outdoor education, and a Ph.D, in educational psychology. His youth work career included outdoor education, a group home, and community centre work. He is the former editor of *Child and Youth Care Forum* and *Child and Youth Services*. An abridged c.v. can be seen at www.web.uvic.ca/~dougm.

**Janet Newbury** lives in Powell River, B.C., where she is the president of the Powell River Diversity Initiative Society and the vice president of the Sunshine Music Festival board, as well as being involved in a number of other exciting community-based initiatives. She is also an instructor in the School of Child and Youth Care at the University of Victoria (where she recently completed a Ph.D.), a founding member of the Post Growth Institute, and an associate with the Taos Institute. Janet has written extensively for both academic and popular publications, and is deeply committed to collaborative approaches to social change.

**Veronica Pacini-Ketchabaw** is a professor and coordinator of the Early Years Specialization in the School of Child and Youth Care at the University of Victoria. Dr. Pacini-Ketchabaw has written extensively on the history of child care in Canada; the experiences of young children and early childhood educators in early childhood spaces; and post-humanist, post-structural, post-colonial and anti-racist feminist perspectives in early childhood studies. She is co-editor of the journal *Canadian Children*.

**Jack Phelan** is a certified CYC practitioner who teaches in the BCYC faculty at MacEwan University in Edmonton, Alberta. He has been an advocate for CYC professional associations and improving the quality of CYC practice, especially in residential care facilities. Jack has explored CYC practice in many countries and supports the international CYC community. Post-secondary CYC education and the quality of CYC educational programs around the world have been his focus for many years. He mostly enjoys talking with practitioners, and attends as many CYC conferences as possible, as well as offering workshops. Jack can be reached at phelanj@macewan.ca.

**Hans A. Skott-Myhre** is an associate professor in the Child and Youth Studies Department at Brock University. He is cross-appointed to the graduate program in Popular Culture, as well as being core faculty for the Interdisciplinary Ph.D. in Humanities and adjunct faculty in the Child and Youth Care program at the University of Victoria. Dr. Skott-Myhre spent twenty-five years as a youth worker and family therapist working primarily with runaway and homeless youth before retiring into academia. He is the author of *Youth Subcultures as Creative Force: Creating New Spaces for Radical Youth Work* (University of Toronto Press, 2009) and co-author with Chris Richardson of the forthcoming book *Habitus of the Hood*.

**Carol Stuart**'s career began in residential care in Ontario, and she has thirty-five years of experience in the child and youth care field across Canada. She has worked in residential and community-based organizations and been a faculty member at the Schools of Child and Youth Care with Grant MacEwan Community College (now University), the University of Victoria, and Ryerson University. She is currently the dean of Health and Human Services at Vancouver Island University. She is the author of *Foundations of Child and Youth Care* (Dubuque, IA: Kendall Hunt, 2009), the co-author of *Right Here, Right Now: Life-Space Intervention for Children and Youth* (Toronto: Pearson, 2013), and the managing editor for the *Relational Child and Youth Care Practice* journal. Carol has had a major role in developing the competencies and certification exams for child and youth care and is a certified CYC in Alberta, Ontario, and internationally with the Child and Youth Care Certification Board (CYCCB), Inc.

# Index

**Books in the Studies in Childhood and Family in Canada Series Published by Wilfrid Laurier University Press**

*Making Do: Women, Family, and Home in Montreal during the Great Depression* by Denyse Baillargeon, translated by Yvonne Klein • 1999 / xii + 232 pp. / ISBN 0-88920-326-1 / ISBN-13: 978-0-88920-326-6

*Children in English-Canadian Society: Framing the Twentieth-Century Consensus* by Neil Sutherland with a new foreword by Cynthia Comacchio • 2000 / xxiv + 336 pp. / illus. / ISBN 0-88920-351-2 / ISBN-13: 978-0-88920-351-8

*Love Strong as Death: Lucy Peel's Canadian Journal, 1833–1836* edited by J.I. Little • 2001 / x + 229 pp. / illus. / ISBN 0-88920-389-x / ISBN-13: 978-0-88920-389-230-x

*The Challenge of Children's Rights for Canada* by Katherine Covell and R. Brian Howe • 2001 / viii + 244 pp. / ISBN 0-88920-380-6 / ISBN-13: 978-0-88920-380-8

*NFB Kids: Portrayals of Children by the National Film Board of Canada, 1939–1989* by Brian J. Low • 2002 / vi + 288 pp. / illus. / ISBN 0-88920-386-5 / ISBN-13: 978-0-88920-386-0

*Something to Cry About: An Argument against Corporal Punishment of Children in Canada* by Susan M. Turner • 2002 / xx + 317 pp. / ISBN 0-88920-382-2 / ISBN-13: 978-0-88920-382-2

*Freedom to Play: We Made Our Own Fun* edited by Norah L. Lewis • 2002 / xiv + 210 pp. / ISBN 0-88920-406-3 / ISBN-13: 978-0-88920-406-5

*The Dominion of Youth: Adolescence and the Making of Modern Canada, 1920–1950* by Cynthia Comacchio • 2006 / x + 302 pp. / illus. / ISBN 0-88920-488-8 / ISBN-13: 978-0-88920-488-1

*Evangelical Balance Sheet: Character, Family, and Business in Mid-Victorian Nova Scotia* by B. Anne Wood • 2006 / xxx + 198 pp. / illus. / ISBN 0-88920-500-0 / ISBN-13: 978-0-88920-500-0

*A Question of Commitment: Children's Rights in Canada* edited by R. Brian Howe and Katherine Covell • 2007 / xiv + 442 pp. / ISBN 978-1-55458-003-3

*Taking Responsibility for Children* edited by Samantha Brennan and Robert Noggle • 2007 / xxii + 188 pp. / ISBN 978-1-55458-015-6

*Home Words: Discourses of Children's Literature in Canada* edited by Mavis Reimer • 2008 / xx + 280 pp. / illus. / ISBN 978-1-55458-016-3

*Depicting Canada's Children* edited by Loren Lerner • 2009 / xxvi + 442 pp. / illus. / ISBN 978-1-55458-050-7

*Babies for the Nation: The Medicalization of Motherhood in Quebec, 1910–1970* by Denyse Baillargeon, translated by W. Donald Wilson • 2009 / xiv + 328 pp. / illus. / ISBN 978-1-5548-058-3

*The One Best Way? Breastfeeding History, Politics, and Policy in Canada* by Tasnim Nathoo and Aleck Ostry • 2009 / xvi + 262 pp. / illus. / ISBN 978-1-55458-147-4

*Fostering Nation? Canada Confronts Its History of Childhood Disadvantage* by Veronica Strong-Boag • 2011 / x + 302 pp. / ISBN 978-1-55458-337-9

*Cold War Comforts: Maternalism, Child Safety, and Global Insecurity, 1945–1975* by Tarah Brookfield • 2012 / xiv + 292 pp. / illus. / ISBN 978-1-55458-623-3

*Ontario Boys: Masculinity and the Idea of Boyhood in Postwar Ontario, 1945–1960* by Christopher Greig • 2014 / xxviii + 184 pp. / ISBN 978-1-55458-900-5

*A Brief History of Women in Quebec* by Denyse Baillargeon, translated by W. Donald Wilson • 2014 / xii + 272 pp. / ISBN 978-1-55458-950-0

*With Children and Youth: Emerging Theories and Practices in Child and Youth Care Work* edited by Kiaras Gharabaghi, Hans A. Skott-Myhre, and Mark Krueger • 2014 / xiv + 222 pp. / ISBN 978-1-55458-966-1

*Abuse or Punishment? Violence Towards Children in Quebec Families, 1850–1969,* translated by W. Donald Wilson • forthcoming 2014 / ISBN 978-1-77712-063-0